Bird Families
of North America

Bird Families
of North America

PETE DUNNE
and KEVIN T. KARLSON

HOUGHTON MIFFLIN HARCOURT
BOSTON · NEW YORK · 2021

For information about permission to reproduce selections from this book,
write to trade.permissions@hmhco.com or to Permissions,
Houghton Mifflin Harcourt Publishing Company,
3 Park Avenue, 19th Floor, New York, New York 10016.

hmhbooks.com

Library of Congress Cataloging-in-Publication Data

Names: Dunne, Pete, 1951– author. | Karlson, Kevin, author.
Title: Bird families of North America / Pete Dunne and Kevin T. Karlson.
Description: Boston : Houghton Mifflin Harcourt, 2021. |
Includes bibliographical references and index.
Identifiers: LCCN 2020051084 (print) | LCCN 2020051085 (ebook) |
ISBN 9780358164074 (hardcover) | ISBN 9780358164043 (ebook)
Subjects: LCSH: Birds—North America—Identification.
Classification: LCC QL681 .D878 2021 (print) | LCC QL681 (ebook) |
DDC 598.097—dc23
LC record available at https://lccn.loc.gov/2020051084
LC ebook record available at https://lccn.loc.gov/2020051085

ISBN 978-0-358-16407-4

Book design by Eugenie S. Delaney

Printed in China

IMO 10 9 8 7 6 5 4 3 2 1

*This book is dedicated to our dear friend Pete Bacinski (1949–2019),
who devoted much of his life to the study and appreciation of birds and nature,
and who shared his knowledge and passion with countless others.*

Contents

Note to Reader

This book intends to impart to readers a fundamental understanding of the 81 bird families in the United States and Canada as defined by the American Ornithological Society. The families are arranged in accordance with the seventh edition of the AOS Checklist, current to the 59th supplement. Two exceptions to the checklist are as follows: gulls and terns are listed as separate families and the northern and southern storm-petrels as a single unit. While the birds of Mexico are considered part of North America by a number of world ornithological groups, including the AOS, if we refer to North America as a bird occurrence location in the text, it includes only the United States and Canada.

This book is a tribute to the birds that have enriched our lives since childhood, and to all who pursue them for fun and enjoyment.

To the best of our abilities, as of 12:01 A.M., March 31, 2020, the families shown here are correct (with exceptions noted). However, science is relentless in its pursuit of order and deeper understanding, so it is likely that additional changes will have been made to the taxonomic order between the time this manuscript was submitted and its publication date.

We recommend you consult the latest supplements to the AOS Checklist of North American Birds to be sure.

Introduction

"Well, we don't know her, or her family," intoned Laura Lee in the saccharin-sweet syllables that betrayed her southern society roots. The "her" was a birder newly arrived in East Texas.

Southerners put great stock in family, recognizing that even without firsthand familiarity with an individual, much can be surmised about a person's character by regarding their heritage and family ties. The same goes for bird families. While it's not correct to say "If you've seen one vireo, you've seen them all," it is accurate to assert that if you are familiar with one of these small, hook-billed, foliage-gleaning members of this strictly New World family, you can ascribe similar properties to other members of the group.

It is also fair to assert that an understanding of bird families is fundamental to any appreciation of birds, because it is what unites and distinguishes them. Determinations made at the species level are always subject to reevaluation and change. A good example is Baltimore Oriole, once considered a distinct species, then lumped with the western Bullock's Oriole to create Northern Oriole, only to be re-split decades later, assuming full species status once again, a distinction both Baltimore and Bullock's Oriole enjoy today.

Bird family groups have traditionally been more systematically stable, shifting at times in the taxonomic ranking but generally secure in their unifying complement of traits and species array. Some bird families trace their formulation all the way back to Carl Linnaeus, a Swedish botanist whose search for order among living organisms was the foundation of the science of taxonomy. He organized and classified living things according to their shared and differentiating traits. Later, Alexander Wilson and John James Audubon relied upon their understanding of bird families when engaged in their pioneering efforts to understand North America's birds.

Sadly, the current emphasis on plumage-based field marks, coupled with our societal urge to cut to the chase and simply pin the name to the bird, has prompted many new birders to regard the identification of individual species as the end-all and be-all of bird study—an end in itself rather than a means to greater understanding. Such a species-by-species approach makes it difficult to appreciate birds for what they are: members of well-organized groupings united by common traits—a determination that is, as Audubon and Wilson understood, fundamental to bird study. There are birders out there who can tell the difference between a White-eyed and a Bell's Vireo, but cannot begin to describe a vireo and what distinguishes members of this family from warblers or flycatchers. This book strives to put the horse in front of the cart and regard North America's birds from the standpoint of families—a focus that will enhance an understanding of birds and make the differentiation of species more meaningful. It is, in essence, a guide to *understanding* North American birds instead of merely *identifying* them. A secondary objective is to clarify recent changes made in taxonomy at the family level. The current emphasis of using

Flickers are large, vocal woodpeckers whose chisel-like bills excavate nesting cavities that are used by a number of bird species in subsequent seasons. This Yellow-shafted Flicker male is with the chicks.

DNA as the foundation of family groupings has led to a reshuffling of some families formerly united on the basis of structure and behavior. While not all families have been affected, many among the passerines, or perching birds, have been reconstituted. These changes are reflected here.

Bird Families
of North America

Anatidae: Ducks, Geese, and Swans

Arguably, this is the most recognized bird group on the planet, an assertion underscored by the well-known aphorism "If it looks like a duck, swims like a duck, and quacks like a duck, then it probably *is* a duck." Distributed widely across the planet, waterfowl are found almost anywhere there is open water. Pete once flushed an incubating Northern Pintail from her nest next to a cattle-watering tank in the arid Pawnee Grasslands of Colorado.

Waterfowl are medium to large mostly aquatic birds. While their fully webbed feet are admirably suited for swimming, no bird group is so accomplished on land, air, and open water. Some ducks are nimble enough to perch on branches, even corn stalks, and some rank among the planet's swiftest of fliers, though several waterfowl species are flightless. All navigate well on the surface of water, and many are accomplished divers. For example, Spectacled Eider can dive over 200 feet to the bottom of the Bering Sea to forage on mollusks.

Most waterfowl have longish to very long necks; flattened, blunt-tipped bills; and webbed feet with an elevated hind toe. Many (mostly males) are colorfully arrayed with a supremely waterproof outer layer of feathers that cover an inner lining of dense, insulating down.

In the Northern Hemisphere, the male pairs with a female on the wintering grounds and in spring follows her to the breeding grounds. Most pairs have large egg clutches, and egg dumping by a female into another's nest sometimes occurs.

Dramatic declines in waterfowl populations at the beginning of the twentieth century gave rise to the conservation movement, which was responsible for the formation of our National Wildlife Refuge System (NWRS). Funded primarily by hunters, the NWRS also serves a multitude of other avocational interests, including birdwatching and photography. These and other conservation movements were, and continue to be, responsible for the slowing and reversal of waterfowl declines.

BLACK-BELLIED WHISTLING-DUCK
Dendrocygna autumnalis

Orange billed and almost garish looking, Black-bellied is a resident of tropical and subtropical regions in the New World. Nimble footed, this bird of coastal lagoons and shallow ponds with adjacent trees forages mostly on seeds and grain in shallow water and agricultural land. Black-bellied Whistling-Duck shows a pervasive pattern of vagrancy north of its range. The bird's orange bill on a gray face renders it unmistakable.

In the United States, it occurs as a breeder or permanent resident in far southern states, especially Texas, Arizona, Louisiana, and Florida. It occurs locally as a resident from Mexico south through Central America to Argentina.

FULVOUS WHISTLING-DUCK
Dendrocygna bicolor

This gangly duck of well-vegetated marshes, lagoons, and wet (often cultivated) fields has a cosmopolitan distribution, but in the United States it is a sometimes nomadic resident of the southern U.S. from coastal Texas to Florida and south to the West Indies. Feeding day and night on seeds and fruits, it forages mostly in tall grasses, with a dedicated partiality for rice fields. Whistling-ducks explode into flight from a resting position when alarmed.

EMPEROR GOOSE *Anser canagicus*

Short necked and petite billed, this goose spends most of its life within the tidal zone, a feathered Prince of Tides. It breeds in coastal lagoons in western Alaska and Siberia and winters coastally along reefs and rocky

Geese are large waterfowl that are celebrated for their flocking tendencies and (mostly) wedge-shaped flock configurations in flight. Clockwise from upper left: Snow (left) and Ross's Geese, dark-plumaged Lesser Snow Geese, Cackling (left) and Canada Geese, Lesser Snow (left) and Ross's Geese in flight, Eastern Brant, Greater White-fronted Goose.

beaches from the Aleutians to northern California. These white-headed, gray-cloaked birds are essentially vegetarians, feeding on leaves and berries in summer and seaweeds and algae in winter. In flight, note the white tail, dark underwings, and contrasting dark rump.

SNOW GOOSE *Anser caerulescens*

Immortalized by Paul Gallico's novel about love, war, and a disfigured painter's search for purpose, this common to abundant goose occurs in both light and dark plumage. Mostly a New World species, it breeds across Arctic Canada and Alaska south to Hudson Bay and winters widely across North America. The majority of birds are white with black wingtips. Dark morphs have dusky bodies with white heads. Highly gregarious, Snow Geese typically feed in flocks numbering from hundreds to many thousands. Consuming roots, leaves, grasses, and grain, they may cause damage to soil and root systems in places where large numbers of birds forage, creating "eat-outs," or areas bereft of vegetated cover.

ROSS'S GOOSE *Anser rossii*

This small wedge-billed goose is typically found feeding among winter flocks of Snow Geese, which it closely resembles. Breeding in Arctic Canada from northern Nunavut Province south to the western side of Hudson Bay, Ross's Geese winter primarily in central California, New Mexico, and the Texas coast, where birds forage on plants, sedges, and grains, especially barley and rice. The rare dark morph has less white on the head than dark morph Snow Goose, and has a white belly. According to the organization Ducks Unlimited, Ross's population numbers have increased dramatically, from about 250,000 birds in 1990 to well over 2 million today. Hybrids with Snow Geese are occasionally found thanks to recent overlaps in breeding territories.

GREATER WHITE-FRONTED GOOSE
Anser albifrons

Common and tawny brown, this goose is a favorite of hunters, who fondly call them "specklebellies," although birds in their first year lack markings on the belly. They breed globally across much of the Arctic, and winter from southern British Columbia south to the Mexican Plateau, with concentrations in the Sacramento Valley, the Salton Sea, coastal Texas, and Louisiana. They are rare along the Atlantic Coast, where vagrant birds are usually from the Greenland race. The birds'

bright orange legs make them conspicuous when they mix freely with other geese.

BRANT *Branta bernicla*

Small and dark bibbed, this marine goose breeds in estuarine habitats across Arctic regions of the Northern Hemisphere, including Alaska, Canada, and Greenland. It winters coastally, usually in single-species flocks, along tidal estuaries and bays from Washington State to Baja, and from New England to the Carolinas, where it forages mostly on sea lettuce and eelgrass. On the breeding grounds, it consumes grasses, moss, and lichen as well as aquatic plants. Flying flocks are usually disorganized, seemingly incapable of holding a V-configuration. Their call sounds like a cross between a honk and a purr. Two subspecies occur: Black Brant on the West Coast and Eastern Brant on the Atlantic Coast. Black Brant has a dark belly, while Eastern Brant has a whitish one.

CACKLING GOOSE *Branta hutchinsii*

This miniature Arctic-breeding Canada-type goose may in fact be four separate species, or simply a small race of Canada Goose. Distinguished from Canada Goose by its smaller size, shorter neck, petite wedge-shaped bill, and dark breast (most subspecies), this mostly western goose winters from Washington to central California, the southern prairies and Texas coast, and from New England to the mid-Atlantic region. Uncommon elsewhere, these "toy" Canadas mix with Canada flocks, where their smaller size easily distinguishes them.

CANADA GOOSE *Branta canadensis*

Common and widespread, this iconic goose is found everywhere in North America at some time of the year, except southern Florida. While it's the emblematic bird of the U.S. Fish and Wildlife Service, this species is regarded as a pest in some places thanks to large numbers occurring year-round in temperate areas. This is because of the availability of open water at places such as golf courses and corporate centers. In the first half of the twentieth century, they were uncommon to rare along the East Coast, now a wintering stronghold. Mostly vegetarian, Canada Geese are found wherever water, short grass, and/or agricultural land combine.

MUTE SWAN *Cygnus olor*

Perhaps no bird found in North America enjoys such divided regard. On one side of the argument are game management engineers and biologists who consider this Old World transplant an insatiable interloper that competes with native waterfowl for food and crucial aquatic nesting habitat. On the other side of the divide are a near-militant assemblage of swan lovers who are won over by the species' beauty and the appeal that prompted wealthy landowners to import the birds into their Victorian garden arrangements. Now feral, these descendants of those imports have colonized portions of the mid-Atlantic, southern New England, southern Ontario, and the Great Lakes, far from their ancestral home in central and northern Europe. Immortalized in Hans Christian Anderson's "The Ugly Duckling," these now permanent residents of shallow, richly vegetated, freshwater lakes and wetlands perform a valuable function in winter by keeping northern waters partially free of ice so that smaller waterfowl can forage on the freshwater plants overlooked by this voracious feeder with a boardinghouse reach. Highly territorial, the birds aggressively drive rival waterfowl out of their breeding territories, but outside the breeding season may gather in loose flocks of 50 or more birds in fresh, salt, and brackish water.

TRUMPETER SWAN *Cygnus buccinator*

Once common and widespread across much of North America, our largest native swan was nearly hunted to extinction. By 1918, when the international Migratory Bird Treaty Act outlawed the hunting of all swans,

Swans are exceptionally large, long-necked birds whose boardinghouse reach allows them to access aquatic plants beyond the capacity of lesser fowl. The orange-billed Mute Swan (left) was introduced to the New World, while Tundra Swan (center) and Trumpeter Swan (right) are native species.

the survival of these magnificent birds was in doubt. In 1933, only 66 Trumpeter Swans occurred south of Canada. Protection and decades of concerted reintroduction have gradually increased their numbers, and now hardly a sizable forested freshwater lake or marshy pond in Alaska and western Canada can be found that does not host a pair.

This species was named by English naturalist John Lawson (1674–1711) for the "trompeting" sounds they made in the wintering flocks found in tidewater South Carolina. Continued reintroduction in the West and the Great Lakes region has resulted in these totems of America's wilderness turning up in various parts of the eastern United States from New Jersey to, perhaps once again, South Carolina.

TUNDRA SWAN *Cygnus columbianus*

As the name suggests, this northernmost North American swan breeds on open tundra ponds, often near coasts, from Alaska to Baffin Island and the shores of Hudson Bay. With a shorter, straighter, and more slender neck than Trumpeter Swan and the curvaceously necked Mute Swan, these smallest of North American swans (14–19 pounds compared to Trumpeter's 21–32 pounds) spend the winter in family groups or large flocks mainly from New Jersey to South Carolina, and from British Columbia to California. They forage on agricultural lands by day and retreat to open water by night. Tundra Swans

also winter in the intermountain West from British Columbia south to Nevada.

MUSCOVY DUCK *Cairina moschata*

This large (6–8 pounds) duck of tropical and subtropical portions of the Americas is mostly blackish with a greenish gloss. It is distinguished by its large size, long tail, knobbed or crested head, warty face, and clawed feet on short, sturdy legs. These sturdy legs and claws facilitate perching in trees, in whose large cavities females deposit their eggs. Found naturally in tree-lined rivers from the Rio Grande south to South America, this somewhat sinister-looking duck was domesticated in pre-Columbian times and taken to Europe, where it became a popular domestic fowl because of its size and meaty breast.

Returned to the New World by colonists, a portion of these captive birds escaped and became part of what is now a widespread feral population, whose white or piebald progenies are fixtures on farm ponds, urban lakes, and irrigation ditches across much of the United States, especially Florida. Only in the Rio Grande Valley of Texas do wild Muscovy Ducks exist north of Mexico.

WOOD DUCK *Aix sponsa*

As beautiful as Muscovy is not, this small, compact bird of freshwater swamps, rivers, and sheltered ponds is built somewhat like a Spanish galleon, with a cropped stern,

raised tail, and ornate bow (head). The male, with his crested head and multicolored face pattern, seems dressed for Mardi Gras. The female is stylishly gray but also has a distinctive, goggled face. She is perhaps best known for her high, goosebump-raising squeal call, *OoEEK,* often uttered as birds flush. Nesting in tree cavities and specially constructed boxes throughout North America, Wood Ducks breed across all of southern Canada and much of the United States but reach their highest breeding and wintering densities in the southeastern U.S. In winter, some birds retreat into northern Mexico. Despite having broods of up to 15 chicks, the birds were once feared heading for extinction owing to excessive hunting and habitat loss. Responding well to concerted management, these forest beauties represent one of the enduring successes of the conservation movement.

BLUE-WINGED TEAL *Spatula discors*

Small and widespread, this somewhat spatula-billed dabbling duck is found in shallow freshwater ponds and mudflats, often in small flocks. The white crescent on the face of males confers instant recognition.

These early fall migrants leave their extensive North American breeding range as early as August en route to wintering grounds in the southern United States, the West Indies, Mexico, and Central America.

CINNAMON TEAL *Spatula cyanoptera*

This colorful western dabbler closely resembles Blue-winged Teal in habits and habitat but is restricted as a breeder to the western United States and Canada, particularly the marshes of the intermountain West, where it nests near Blue-winged Teal, and where hybridization infrequently occurs. Wintering from northern California east to the Florida panhandle, and south through Central America to northern Ecuador, this species is also a resident in South America.

NORTHERN SHOVELER
Spatula clypeata

Widespread and somewhat iconic, these dabbling ducks occur in Europe, Asia, and North America. Easily identified by their outsized, spatula-shaped, food-straining bill, Shovelers frequent shallow, freshwater environments. They usually group in tight single-species flocks and feed with necks

Dabbling ducks (a.k.a. "puddle ducks") are surface feeders that forage on vegetation below the waterline. In most species, males (drakes) are strikingly plumaged, while females (hens) wear more conservative garb. Clockwise from upper left: drake Wood Duck, drake Northern Shoveler, drake Northern Pintail, Black-bellied Whistling-Duck, hen Mottled Duck, drake Green-winged Teal.

Five species of dabbling ducks, including one female Blue-winged Teal, whose cryptic plumage differs from the more boldly colored males. Clockwise from upper left, all males unless noted: Cinnamon Teal; American Wigeon; Blue-winged Teal; Blue-winged Teal female; Gadwall; Mallard.

stretched forward and bills submerged in a quest for small marine invertebrates and aquatic plants. Shovelers breed across much of Canada and the western United States and winter mostly south of the breeding range across the southern U.S. south to the West Indies, Mexico, Central America, and Colombia.

GADWALL *Mareca strepera*

This dapper New and Old World duck of freshwater marshes, flooded fields, and shallow ponds breeds widely across Canada and the northern United States, north to Alaska. The male with his tastefully gray attire has a wink of white on the folded wing, reminiscent of a handkerchief in a gentleman's dinner jacket. The female resembles a female Mallard except for the squarish head, more petite bill, and white speculum in the wing.

Gadwall winters in mixed or monotypic flocks coast to coast across the United States, and south to Baja, the Yucatán, Cuba, and Jamaica. This species has proliferated under management practices championed by the National Wildlife Refuge System; its vegetation-rimmed shallow impoundments are ideal for this freshwater dabbler whose diet is primarily freshwater plants.

AMERICAN WIGEON *Mareca americana*

Compact and round headed, this altogether amiable dabbling duck with rufous flanks and gray head is a common and widespread northern breeder from Alaska to the Maritimes, south to the Prairie Pothole regions and marshes of the intermountain West. Known for its comical, two-note whistled call, it winters in small freshwater marshes and ponds with vegetated edges across the southern United States into Central America and the West Indies. In mixed-species flocks in winter, it often outnumbers all other species. Birds feed by grazing on grasses and dabbling for aquatic vegetation.

EURASIAN WIGEON *Mareca penelope*

A striking Eurasian breeder of tundra and taiga regions, Eurasian Wigeon ranges from Iceland to Siberia and winters sparingly from the mid-Atlantic Coast to Florida in North America, but more commonly in Pacific Coastal areas from British Columbia to southern California. It is rare elsewhere. Eurasian typically mixes with similarly sized and shaped American Wigeon, from which they may be distinguished by the male Eurasian's rusty head and descending single squeal note.

MALLARD *Anas platyrhynchos*

This quintessential duck is widespread across both the New and Old Worlds. The emblematic bird of Ducks Unlimited, the male's day-glow green head and curlicue tail render it instantly recognizable. In many locations, it is the most commonly seen duck and is frequently seen grazing on short-cut grass. Highly promiscuous, males mate with a number of other waterfowl species, giving rise to offspring with an array of hybrid traits.

AMERICAN BLACK DUCK *Anas rubripes*

This sooty-bodied duck of eastern North America resembles a dark, olive-billed female Mallard. The hardiest of dabbling ducks, Black Ducks winter farther north than any other dabbler and breed in a variety of aquatic habitats, including tidal marsh. They occur generally east of the prairies in the United States and Canada. Vacating much of their northern breeding range by autumn, Black Ducks winter widely across the eastern United States and Canada, feeding in fresh, brackish, or tidal waters. In addition to aquatic plants, they consume many invertebrate species, including mollusks. Where ranges overlap, Black Ducks often hybridize with Mallards.

MOTTLED DUCK *Anas fulvigula*

Mottled Duck is a local southern species that resembles Black Duck, but differs with a buff wash to the head and neck and with buff fringes to the upperparts. It occurs in mostly freshwater habitats along the Gulf Coast and southeastern Atlantic states, and all of Florida. Mottled somewhat resembles a female Mallard or American Black Duck but with a bright yellow bill in males. It hybridizes regularly with Mallard but very infrequently with Black Duck, since their normal breeding ranges don't overlap.

NORTHERN PINTAIL *Anas acuta*

Dapper and slender necked, this dabbler of the Old and New Worlds brandishes a rakishly plumed tail (males), but the buffy brown female shares only the species' slender, gooselike lines and pointy tail. A common breeder across northern North America, it winters across the southern United States south to northern South America. Pintails often occur in large single-species flocks in shallow freshwater marshes and ponds. When numerically subordinate in large mixed flocks, this widespread duck mixes with other puddle ducks, most notably Mallard and Gadwall.

GREEN-WINGED TEAL *Anas crecca*

Common and widespread, this duck of fresh and tidal marshes breeds in northern and central North America. The closely related Eurasian Green-winged Teal occurs throughout Asia and northern and central Europe. It generally winters south of northern breeding areas, where it gathers in large, mostly single-species flocks in shallow marshes and mudflats. The winter range encompasses most of the United States and southern Canada south to the West Indies, Mexico, and northern Central America. The piping call notes of large wintering flocks may approach the level of a din. A metallic green speculum on the wing is obvious in flight, which is rapid and wheeling.

CANVASBACK *Aythya valisineria*

Among Chesapeake Bay waterfowlers, the "Can" holds a place of pride over all other waterfowl and is celebrated for the succulence of its wild celery–fed flesh. Able to attain speeds in excess of 50 miles per hour, this greyhound among ducks uses its wedge-shaped head and scimitar-like wings to cleave a path through November gales that ground lesser fowl.

Large and chestnut headed, this North American diving duck breeds in the Prairie Pothole region of Canada and northern plains states. It winters in large, tightly packed flocks in deep freshwater lakes, rivers, bays, and estuaries across the southern and

coastal United States south to southern Mexico. The tightly packed flocks of pale-backed birds resemble a large sheet of sailcloth spread on the water. This species experienced a marked population decline in the latter half of the twentieth century, which caused it to be removed from the ranks of game birds. In Audubon's time, the duck was so numerous that even a fair shot was expected to kill 50 to 100 birds in a day. This could be one of the reasons for its greatly reduced numbers today.

REDHEAD *Aythya americana*

Redhead is darker backed than Canvasback, with which it commonly associates in the Prairie Pothole marshes where the two chestnut-headed divers breed, and in the deeper fresh- and saltwater bays, lakes, and estuaries where they winter. It is known for its large broods and practice of dumping eggs in the nests of surrogate females; broods in excess of 20 eggs have been recorded (but 10 to 15 is typical). Despite the bird's high productivity, Redhead numbers fell during the twentieth century, and for many years it was not hunted, despite large wintering populations in the Gulf of Mexico. The winter range extends from the Great Lakes to Guatemala.

RING-NECKED DUCK *Aythya collaris*

It was a cold, snowy day in March, and Pete, a boy of seven or eight, crouched in the lee side of a sheltering cove in Whippany, New Jersey, hoping for magic that soon appeared in the form of five fast-flying ducks, whose unfamiliar shapes disappeared behind a veil of snow. Breathlessly, he listened to the sound of the flock hitting the water and was soon transfixed by the sight of five shadowy bodies As he peered at them through his 6-power binoculars, the birds' boldly patterned bills assured him these were ducks he'd never seen before. But it was only when the birds approached to within 10 feet that he saw the narrow copper-colored ring on the neck of the males, the first and only time

he has seen this hardy diver's namesake trait.

Wintering as far north as these freshwater obligates can find open water, these birds of forest bogs breed across much of Canada and the northern states. They winter across the southern United States, the Greater Antilles, and Mexico to Central America, and are often the first of northbound migrants to appear on frozen inland lakes in the spring. Rarely found in salt water, these peak-headed ducks consume large numbers of freshwater invertebrates and are particularly fond of dragonfly larvae. Winter flocks may number over 500 birds where food is plentiful.

GREATER SCAUP *Aythya marila*

Known to the market gunners of coastal New Jersey as the "Bluebill," this hardy widespread taiga and tundra pond breeder relocates in winter to large inland lakes, coastal bays, and estuaries along both coasts. Today the bird's hand-carved effigies garner top dollar in antique stores and hark to those days when men like Captain Jesse Birdsall of Barnegat, New Jersey, trained the barrels of his famed double-barreled eights upon the tight-packed rafts of wintering birds. What they lacked in epicurean esteem, these mostly mollusk-eating divers made up for in numbers. Breeding across northern Europe, Asia, and North America, the birds gather during winter in flocks that may number in the thousands, making them irresistible targets.

LESSER SCAUP *Aythya affinis*

While closely resembling Greater Scaup, this slightly smaller species with a smaller bill, peaked rear crown, and thinner neck is restricted to North America, breeding from Alaska to Hudson Bay, but is widespread in winter across most of the United States, southern Canada, Mexico, and the West Indies. While found in bays and estuaries, it greatly favors bodies of fresh water, except in northern coastal locations. Thus, it is the most likely scaup species in interior locations in winter.

Six species of beautiful male diving ducks. Clockwise from upper left: Redhead, Hooded Merganser, Surf Scoter, Lesser Scaup, Ring-necked Duck, Canvasback. Canvasback is the only one of these ducks whose population numbers have declined dramatically in recent years.

More varied in its diet than Greater Scaup, Lesser Scaup forages on seeds, roots, and other vegetative matter along with aquatic invertebrates.

STELLER'S EIDER *Polysticta stelleri*

This smallest of the four eider species has the most restricted range. Breeding on freshwater coastal ponds in Alaska and Siberia, it retreats in winter to rocky coasts of southern Alaska and the southern Bering Sea. Many observers go their lives without encountering this rare and localized stunning northern denizen, named after its discoverer George Wilhelm Steller.

SPECTACLED EIDER *Somateria fischeri*

For many years, this goggle-eyed breeder of Arctic Alaska and Siberian tundra lakes and bogs kept the location of its wintering grounds secret. Then in 1995, the signals from a radio-tagged eider prompted biologists to make an exploratory aerial reconnaissance over the frozen Bering Sea. There they found massed concentrations of Spectacled Eiders, whose combined body heat was keeping the water open in several polynyas (areas of open water within a frozen water body).

This allowed the birds to dive to depths in excess of 200 feet to feast on the bounty of mollusks on the sea floor. In light of our new insight, the world population of this rare sea duck grew from 32,000 to over 120,000 birds. Even with this increased number, it is still federally listed as an endangered species.

KING EIDER *Somateria spectabilis*

This circumpolar breeder spends most of its life in the waters adjacent to the seasonal polar ice cap, where it dives in search of mollusks, crabs, shrimp, and sea urchins. In winter, some birds wander south to the rocky coasts of southern Alaska and the Pacific Northwest, as well as New England and the upper mid-Atlantic region. In northern areas, winter flocks may number in the hundreds, but farther south smaller numbers often join flocks of Common Eider. One June, Pete spent several days camped at the edge of the seasonal ice sheet as thousands of hormonally fueled King Eider waited impatiently for tundra ponds to thaw. The Arctic air vibrated with the croaking and owl-like cooing of impatient adults, but the ice remained firm.

When females incubate their eggs, they

don't leave the nest to feed, and go over 20 days without food.

COMMON EIDER *Somateria mollissima*

Common to abundant, this sea duck is our southernmost and most widespread breeding eider, with populations in Europe, Asia, Greenland, and North America. They breed primarily on islands along rocky coasts, where many birds also winter. A portion of the population withdraws south in winter, seeking out natural or manmade rocky environments. Here they dive for mollusks, crabs, urchins, and other marine invertebrates, which they masticate in their industrial-strength stomachs.

Eiders have been celebrated for centuries for the insulating quality of their down feathers, whose density and warmth surpasses all other waterfowl. Eider down is commercially harvested by gathering some portion of the feathers that female eiders pluck from their bodies to line their nests. Harvest begins near the end of the hatching cycle to ensure reproductive success and maintain a lucrative market. An eider down comforter may cost in excess of $10,000.

HARLEQUIN DUCK
Histrionicus histrionicus

Breeding near fast-flowing mountain streams in northern forested terrain, this small rough-and-tumble diving duck winters where rough surf meets rocky shores. Bobbing like feathered corks in the winter chop, the boldly patterned males are unaccountably cryptic, and much darker and harder to see than their harlequin-colored pattern suggests. Dusky brown females resemble miniature female Surf Scoters.

While they are sometimes found among eiders or scoters, Harlequins' partiality to rough, fast-moving water discourages companionship. They feed on mollusks and crustaceans in winter; in summer they consume prodigious numbers of aquatic insects and larvae that they glean from the bottoms of swift-flowing freshwater streams. Widespread and common across their circumpolar breeding range, Harlequins winter from Newfoundland and Labrador to Virginia in the East, where they favor rock jetties. In the West, they winter from the Bering Sea to southeastern Alaska south to Washington State. Small groups of 3 to 12 birds are typical. Harlequins frequently sit on rocks when resting or sleeping.

SURF SCOTER *Melanitta perspicillata*

Known to market gunners as the "skunk head," which refers to the male's white-capped head, this large, coastal-wintering sea duck dives for mollusks and crustaceans, often just beyond the breakers, and occasionally concentrates in rafts over mussel beds. Migrating and wintering in large flocks, whose tightly packed skeins skim just above the water, these hardy sea ducks winter along the Atlantic and Gulf Coasts, and from the Aleutians to Mexico in the West. Breeding from subarctic to forested lake habitats in the western United States, Surf Scoters are limited to North America. They are the least common of the three scoters, but they may be the most abundant scoter species in some locations in winter, especially in southern coastal locations.

WHITE-WINGED SCOTER
Melanitta deglandi

Nearly eider-sized, this largest of scoters breeds near freshwater tundra and taiga ponds across northern North America from western Alaska to Hudson Bay, typically farther inland than Surf or Black Scoters. Since it winters farther north than Black and Surf Scoters, White-winged is the default scoter off the upper New England coast in winter. On the West Coast, it winters from southern Alaska to California. In all plumages, the large white patch on the inner wing, which is obvious in flight, easily identifies White-winged Scoter. More than other scoters, White-winged turns up on inland lakes

during migration and winter, most notably the Great Lakes.

BLACK SCOTER *Melanitta americana*

Our smallest scoter, plump and all dark with an orange-knobbed bill, breeds on small tundra and subarctic lakes and streams in Canada and Alaska. In winter, it prefers shallow waters off both the Atlantic and Pacific Coasts south to northern Florida and central California. Like other scoters, the birds' dietary focus on mollusks makes it not particularly prized by hunters or diners due to the strong fishy taste and smell. This species is vocal, even in winter, with males giving a quavering, keening whistle and females a low growl.

LONG-TAILED DUCK *Clangula hyemalis*

This Arctic breeder is known to the Inuit people of northern Canada as the "aggia-juk," and to the old water fowlers of South Jersey as the "south southerly," both colloquial names that are phonetic renderings of the male Long-tailed Duck's yodeled call. So incessant was the sound of lovestruck birds, emanating from seemingly every suitable tundra pond, that early northern explorers dubbed it the "oldsquaw," allowing that the constant clamor recalled the gabble of old "squaws." (This term has recently been deemed offensive to Native Americans, and we only use it here with no disrespect to explain the historic origin of its original name, Oldsquaw, which the bird was called for many decades.) Even the scientific name of this most abundant of Arctic ducks, *Clangula*, or "noisy winter duck," attests to its vocal proclivities.

The smart-looking black-and-white drake is a favorite of birders everywhere. Feeding primarily on mollusks, birds augment their diets with insect larvae and plant material in summer. In winter, birds range coastally in shallow bays and inlets from Canada to the Carolinas and Alaska to Oregon.

BUFFLEHEAD *Bucephala albeola*

Small, compact, and energetic, these diving ducks burst from the water when flushed. Breeding in abandoned Northern Flicker holes in lakeside aspens across boreal Canada

Diving ducks are exceptional swimmers, but less adept on land because their feet are located near the rear of their bodies. They can forage beneath the surface at depths beyond the upended reach of dabbling ducks. Clockwise from upper left (all males): Ruddy Duck, King Eider, Common Goldeneye, Long-tailed Duck, Harlequin Duck, Bufflehead.

west to Alaska, the birds feast on seasonally abundant aquatic insects and their larvae in summer. In winter, when they gather in small, loose flocks on inland lakes, back bays, and seacoasts, their diet switches to small fish, shrimp, and mussels. White-crowned males are readily identified, while mostly grayish brown females have a peanut-shaped white patch on the cheek. Buffleheads frequently mix with other ducks, including dabblers.

COMMON GOLDENEYE
Bucephala clangula

Named for their bright yellow eyes, these hardy and wary divers breed in tree cavities adjacent to freshwater lakes in the forests of northern Europe, Russia, Asia, and North America. In winter, they retreat to coastal locations or swift interior rivers as far north as open water provides, where they pursue aquatic invertebrates by diving into onrushing waters, allowing the current to ferry them downstream for another dive. Males are distinguished by the white oval patch on the face; females by their yellow-tipped gray bills and overall brownish plumage.

BARROW'S GOLDENEYE
Bucephala islandica

Named after Sir John Barrow, a founder of the Royal Geographical Society, this northern, mostly New World species has two divided breeding populations; one ranges from Newfoundland and Labrador to Iceland, the other in western mountains from California and northern New Mexico to Alaska. Over much of their range, the birds breed in tree cavities adjacent to freshwater lakes. In tree-impoverished Iceland, birds tuck their nests into rocky crevices. In winter, crescent-faced males and mostly yellow-billed females retreat to nearby coastal locations and larger unfrozen lakes and rivers, south to central California, Colorado, and Massachusetts. There they feed on mollusks and crustaceans and frequently join flocks of Common Goldeneye.

HOODED MERGANSER
Lophodytes cucullatus

The smallest member of this tribe of fish-eating divers, or "sawbills" (so named for the fish-grabbing serrations lining the bill), is limited to North America, where it breeds widely but locally in hollow trees and unused Wood Duck nest boxes near forested lakes and streams across much of northeastern and northwestern United States and Canada. It winters mostly along the coast from New England to Texas, and from southern Alaska to Baja. White-hooded, black-trimmed males can be confused only with the more compact Buffleheads. The female's puffy head has a pale buffy trim. In winter these birds form small to large loose single-species flocks in sluggish tidal creeks or ponds, or they may be solitary.

COMMON MERGANSER
Mergus merganser

This large, heavy-bodied sawbill is distinguished by its thin, bright orange bill and black-and-white plumage. It breeds near freshwater lakes, ponds, rivers, and side streams in forest habitats, where it finds hollow logs and tree cavities large enough to accommodate its size. Breeding across northern Europe, Asia, and northern North America, it retreats in winter to fast-moving rivers north to the freeze line, less commonly in brackish, coastal waterways where it dives in pursuit of small fish.

RED-BREASTED MERGANSER
Mergus serrator

Breeding primarily on northern lakes, ponds, and rivers in Arctic and temperate forests of northern Europe, Asia, and North America, this shaggy-crested sawbill winters primarily along seacoasts, where it dives in pursuit of fish. In winter, it is found along all coasts from New England and southern Alaska south to Baja and the Gulf of Mexico. Unlike Common Merganser, Red-breasted may gather in small flocks in winter and fish

cooperatively, often in shallow water just beyond the breakers.

RUDDY DUCK *Oxyura jamaicensis*

A small, North American "stiff tail," Ruddy Duck resembles the quintessential bathtub duck, complete with flattened, outsized bill; cocked tail; and compact, no-necked proportions. Breeding widely in the Prairie Pothole regions of the United States and Canada, Ruddy Duck is famous for its disproportionately large eggs (a 1-pound female may produce a clutch of 6 to 10 eggs three times her weight). Wintering primarily on large inland bodies of water or brackish lagoons and bays, often in the company of American Coots, these small divers feed mostly on aquatic vegetation and aquatic invertebrates. Reluctant fliers, Ruddy Ducks become airborne only after an effortful foot-pattering takeoff.

Masked Duck, another stiff-tailed duck of Mexico and Central and South America, is an infrequent visitor to Florida and south Texas.

Cracidae: Chachalacas, Curassows, and Guans

This group of large, long-legged, forest birds of tropical and subtropical regions is part of an ancient order of fowl-like birds, the Galliformes. Comprising 50 species in 11 genera, the members of Cracidae are widespread across Central and South America, but only five species are found in Mexico, and only one, Plain Chachalaca, ranges far enough north to occur (barely) in the United States. Members of this turkeylike clan have long necks, small heads, chickenlike bills, blunt wings, long broad tails, and four toes. Their gizzards are muscular and well developed, which helps with digestion of their diet of berries, buds, and leaves. Long, strong legs enable the birds to move about freely on the forest floor.

Plain Chachalaca is the United States' sole representative of this New World family of nimble jungle fowl. It is a common resident in woodlands along the Rio Grande in Texas.

Most members of this family are cryptically patterned in black, gray, and brown, with many also having white or rufous bellies. Clutches are typically small, and young are highly precocial (mostly self-sufficient soon after hatching).

PLAIN CHACALACA *Ortalis vetula*

Stalking through the dense, dry mesquite thorn scrub forest bordering the Rio Grande, these smoke-colored, long-tailed skulkers might easily go unnoticed but for their loud, raucous, namesake call, typically given by birds at dawn or when alarmed. While Plain Chachalaca are largely terrestrial, their four-toed feet are admirably designed

for perching and roosting. They forage among tree limbs, from which they may hang upside down to reach fruit. They are usually found in small to large groups, and the raucous cacophony of calling birds approaches the level of a din. Ranging from extreme south Texas to northern Honduras, the birds are locally common despite being hunted across much of their range. In the United States, Plain Chacalaca is limited to the Lower Rio Grande Valley, with the greatest density found in the Santa Ana National Wildlife Refuge.

Odontophoridae: New World Quails

This family comprises 32 species distributed across South, Central, and North America. They are chunky, small to medium-sized terrestrial game birds with short, powerful legs.

In North America, they are found mostly in dry habitats. The legs are unfeathered, and their bills are small and slightly decurved, well suited to a diet of mostly seeds. While filling much the same ecological niche as Old World quails, the two families are not closely related. New World quails are highly social and typically found in flocks. They prefer to run when disturbed, and take flight only when danger is imminent. When pressed, flocks explode into flight on rapid whirring wings, with birds going in all directions to confuse predators. Clutch sizes range from 2 to 6 chicks for some South American species, and from 10 to 15 for Bobwhite and other North American species. The large clutch size compensates for a typically high mortality rate.

While some quail species are cryptically plumaged, others are ornate, and many have crests or brandish rakish plumes. Several species, most notably Northern Bobwhite and California Quail, are avidly hunted.

Formerly known as Harlequin Quail, which seems to fit this unusual plumage better, Montezuma Quail occurs in foothills and mountains of the southwestern United States. It is highly sought after by birders and often freezes in place when danger approaches, making it very difficult to see.

This family of chunky, ground-hugging game birds features several species that frequent desert habitats, including Scaled Quail (upper right), which is exclusive to these locations. Clockwise from upper left: Gambel's Quail, Scaled Quail, Northern Bobwhite, California Quail.

MOUNTAIN QUAIL *Oreortyx pictus*

These large, handsome, spike-plumed birds of brushy chaparral and dry evergreen-forested slopes are typically the only quail species found within their array of higher altitude habitats and range, which extends from southwestern British Columbia to Baja, California, and east to western Nevada. Secretive in their typical heavily vegetated habitats, the birds can be damnably hard to find except during breeding season, when almost every sizable boulder and Joshua tree in the northern Mojave seems to support a displaying male.

NORTHERN BOBWHITE
Colinus virginianus

Known reverentially to hunters across the South as "birds," this widespread species' namesake call is heard over a large area from southern New England to Florida, and from the eastern plains states and Texas south into Mexico. They're overall ruddy brown, and males have a pronounced head pattern. Coveys of 8 to 12 birds rove in an array of habitats, from pinewoods to agricultural fields, but the birds are especially partial to pastures and fallow fields adjacent to woodlands. Hunted extensively, this species has experienced a dramatic decline throughout its range owing in part to habitat loss and changes in agriculture, and it is an increasingly high priority for conservation. Stocking captive-raised Bobwhites for hunting on private lands has infused the wild gene pool with unwary birds, which contributes to their decline when these birds mate with wild ones.

SCALED QUAIL *Callipepla squamata*

The desert air is heavy with the wholesome reek of creosote bush as the rain stops, and

mother "Cottontop" leads her brood of tiny puffballs across the desert floor in search of insects and pooled water. While adult Scaled Quail satisfy much of their moisture needs from the seeds, insects, and green herbage they consume, chicks need water, which is why the breeding season of this hardy desert quail coincides with the July and August monsoon season. At home in desert scrub and grasslands from northern Mexico to northern New Mexico, and from western Oklahoma to southeastern Colorado, males and females with their scaly blue underparts and white tufted crest are almost identical. Usually found in coveys of 30 to 40, the birds move like creeping shadows between stands of protective cover. Scaled Quail generally prefer more sparsely vegetated terrain than Bobwhite and avoid uninterrupted grasslands.

CALIFORNIA QUAIL
Callipepla californica

While this is for the most part the only quail found within its mostly California range, California Quail is common, confiding, and often seen crossing dry streambeds or foraging through well-vegetated suburban areas. Flocks of 25 to 50 birds are typical, but flocks approaching 1,000 birds have been reported. The bird's three-note contact call, *put way do,* is sometimes an inadvertent backdrop to Hollywood movie soundtracks. This species occupies diverse habitats, and Pete has pursued it in the coastal range with Band-tailed Pigeon flying overhead, and in central coast wine country with Roadrunners crossing dry streambeds and Phainopeplas calling from adjacent oaks.

GAMBEL'S QUAIL *Callipepla gambelii*

While mostly similar in appearance and habits to California Quail, Gambel's is overall paler, grayer and less patterned below, and the range of this southwestern desert species (southern Utah to Mexico) barely abuts that of California Quail. Gambel's often occurs in the same desert habitat as Scaled Quail, but also inhabits agricultural land, and takes most of its water from succulent plants when available.

MONTEZUMA QUAIL
Cyrtonyx montezumae

Known to avid hunters as "Mearns" Quail, these harlequin-patterned birds of dry pine-oak forests and oak grasslands are locally common in desert foothills (3,000 to 10,000 feet) of southern Texas, New Mexico, Arizona, and northern Mexico. The birds use their strong legs to dig for tubers and bulbs and apparently don't require drinking water. Montezuma Quail often sit motionless for long periods, and flush reluctantly after sensing danger, so coveys of 7 or 8 birds are usually difficult to find. The male's shrill, trembling whistle resembles the sound of an aerial bomb dropping.

Phasianidae: Partridge, Grouse, Pheasants, and Old World Quail

This widespread family group is represented in North America by both native and introduced species, a tribute to our enduring epicurean fascination with meaty fowl. Ranging in size from quail to turkey, the birds of this family are mostly ground dwelling, moving about on short sturdy legs and often in flocks. Many have spurs on their lower legs, and grouse have feathered legs and sometimes feathered toes. Many are cryptically colored, but males and some female pheasants have brightly colored, sometimes iridescent feathers and elongated upper tail feathers that are used in display. Members of this family typically produce large clutches, and young are highly precocial (mostly self-sufficient soon after hatching). Some can fly before becoming fully feathered. Most of the family's 177 species are found in the Old

World, but the largest member of the family, Wild Turkey, heralds from the New World, and several grouse species have a circumpolar distribution. Flight is explosive and effortful on short rounded wings and usually of short duration.

CHUKAR *Alectoris chukar*

This hardy, compact, medium-large, Old World native of arid Asian habitats was first introduced to North America in 1893. Subsequent releases of this prized game bird have led to its permanent status throughout much of the Great Basin.

While boldly marked, stationary birds seem to melt into rocky semiarid landscapes, and their deliberate movements might easily be dismissed as heat wave distortion. Foraging in small flocks mostly on the ground for shoots, leaves, insects, and seeds (particularly cheatgrass seeds), they tend to feed uphill in the early morning hours, scratching for bulbs and rhizomes. While preferring to run from danger, flushed birds are strong, fast fliers and are often seen perched on large boulders.

HIMALAYAN SNOWCOCK
Tetraogallus himalayensis

This large Asian native was introduced into some of Nevada's high alpine meadow slopes to fill what game management engineers perceived as a game bird vacuum. The release of 19 birds into the Ruby Mountains of northeastern Nevada and subsequent releases led to the birds being established by the 1980s, marking the last successful introduction of any game bird species into the United States. At 6 pounds, it is considerably larger than any other grouse in its North American habitat and range.

The mostly gray-brown birds with boldly patterned necks flash white primaries in flight. Ground foragers, birds glide to lower elevations in the morning, then walk uphill during the day, foraging on vegetation (primarily cheatgrass) along the way. Though

Of these three popular game birds, only Wild Turkey (bottom) is native to the New World. Ring-necked Pheasant (top) and Chukar (center) are native to Asia.

nonmigratory, birds at higher elevations (6,000 to 10,000 feet) descend to snow line in winter. The U.S. population is not believed to exceed 1,000 birds.

GRAY PARTRIDGE *Perdix perdix*

One of our more successful introduction efforts, this chunky, medium-sized European grassland species has established itself in several disparate parts of North America. It is primarily found in the northern Great Plains of the United States and Canada, where it thrives in disturbed (typically short) grassland and agricultural landscapes. These rusty-faced, mostly gray birds gather in coveys of up to 15 birds and, when disturbed, flush in unison, making a scratchy cackling call.

RING-NECKED PHEASANT
Phasianus colchicus

Many people are surprised to learn that this large, widespread, plume-tailed game bird is a native of Asia. First imported to the eastern United States as early as 1790, the bird did not fare well in the mostly forested habitat. Later, in the 1880s, several dozen birds from Chinese stock were released into the Willamette Valley of Oregon, where they flourished in this agricultural hotbed. Most North American pheasants resemble those northern Chinese birds.

Today this species is resident in most northern states and southern Canada, with pockets found in some more southern states. While declining in some areas, populations appear stable in their core North American strongholds, where they favor corn- and grainfields adjacent to thick, weedy cover and cattail marshes. The flashy, copper-colored males and sandy brown females segregate into single-sex flocks during the winter. Rapid but short-distance fliers, pheasants often run from danger, and rugged birds have been known to absorb a load of birdshot and still run a quarter mile to cover.

RUFFED GROUSE *Bonasa umbellus*

This large, ruddy brown to grayish brown forest grouse is native to North America and found in a variety of forest types, from Pacific Coastal rain forest to mixed deciduous and coniferous northeastern woodlands. Showing a preference for early successional woodlands rather than mature forest, Ruffed Grouse is partial to forest supporting aspen buds and wild grape tangles.

Usually solitary, in winter birds may gather in sheltered areas in groups of up to six individuals. Known as "partridge" in New England and "pheasant" in the southern Appalachians, the well-camouflaged birds flush from nearly underfoot and rocket away before the leaves settle. It is a skilled marksman who drops one of these wily yet honest gamebirds. While largely unaffected by hunting pressure, populations are cyclical, with wet summers and cold winters taking a toll, and the species has declined dramatically in some areas.

GREATER SAGE-GROUSE
Centrocercus urophasianus

Pointy tailed and near turkey-sized, this grouse could serve as a poster child for the sagebrush plains that dominate much of the Western grasslands biome. Found almost exclusively where sagebrush thrives, this western endemic's digestive system is specialized to digest the leaves of this aromatic woody plant. It is known for its courtship displays involving multiple males, only one of which wins copulation rights. Displaying males fluff their white ruffs and spread their spiky tail feathers in fanlike array. Once accounted numerous, the bird's population has declined by as much as 90 percent in the face of changing land-use practices and natural-gas production. In winter, they gather in flocks of up to 100 birds. While some retraction has occurred at the periphery, Sage Grouse continues to occupy much of its historic range, where it remains uncommon and local.

Plump bodies, chicken-like bills, and short sturdy legs are all hallmarks of grouse and ptarmigan. Clockwise from upper left: Rock Ptarmigan, Willow Ptarmigan, White-tailed Ptarmigan, female Spruce Grouse, Ruffed Grouse, Blue Grouse.

GUNNISON SAGE-GROUSE
Centrocercus minimus

This smaller version of Greater Sage-Grouse is isolated to the Gunnison Basin of Colorado and is now considered a distinct species. Habits are similar, but the plumage is slightly different.

SPRUCE GROUSE *Falcipennis canadensis*

This dark forest grouse is resident in dense spruce forests across much of subarctic Canada and Alaska, and in boreal forest habitat in the lower 48 states south to southeastern Idaho and northern New York. Foraging on the ground or among tree limbs, the birds consume mostly spruce needles in winter, but augment their diet with leaves, berries, and flowers in warmer months. Fairly common and widely distributed, they are generally tame and easily approached, earning the nickname "Foolhen." Flushed birds often perch on the nearest tree limbs. Males are boldly patterned with gray and black, while females are cryptically patterned gray or brown.

WILLOW PTARMIGAN *Lagopus lagopus*

Plump and feather footed, this Arctic grouse is found throughout Arctic regions of the Old and New Worlds. The largest and most numerous of the ptarmigan species, in the moorlands of the British Isles it is known as the Red Grouse, where it retains its rusty brown plumage year-round. Other races become almost wholly white, except for their black tails in winter. Preferring low, moist, willow-strewn tundra habitat, the birds forage in flocks for mostly buds and twigs of heather, willow, and birch. In winter they may gravitate to open vegetated habitats, most notably broken spruce and birch forest. While mostly nonmigratory, North American birds sometimes reach northern Minnesota and southern Ontario. Willow Ptarmigan is the only grouse species in which both parents attend young.

ROCK PTARMIGAN *Lagopus muta*

Smaller and smaller billed than Willow Ptarmigan, this Holarctic grouse prefers rocky terrain with sparse vegetation, mak-

ing it ideally suited for high Arctic conditions, where it thrives on buds and catkins of ground-hugging dwarf birch. The male's brown summer plumage lacks the warm reddish tones of Willow Ptarmigan, but females are very similar in appearance. In winter, plumage is white, with the male sporting a black eye-stripe.

WHITE-TAILED PTARMIGAN
Lagopus leucura

This mountain ptarmigan is the only member of this genus that sports a white-sided tail in summer and winter. Unlike other ptarmigan, White-tailed is limited to North America, where it is found in sparse, low alpine tundra from Alaska to Washington State as well as in separated populations along the Rockies from Colorado to northern New Mexico. Mostly a permanent resident, it shows limited altitudinal movement in winter, when it occurs in flocks.

DUSKY GROUSE *Dendragapus obscurus*

This large dark "Blue Grouse" of western interior mountains is found in open, mixed (aspen-conifer) forests from the Yukon to Arizona and New Mexico. It also occurs on dry slopes with sparse trees. Males frequently display on rocks or logs, whereas Sooty Grouse prefers trees. In winter, birds retreat to denser Lodgepole Pine and Douglas-fir forests and a diet of needles.

SOOTY GROUSE
Dendragapus fuliginosus

Large and dark plumaged, this grouse of open coniferous forest ranges from southeastern Alaska to central California. In summer, birds forage at higher altitudes, where they feast on berries ripening in alpine meadows. In autumn, birds descend to stands of firs on lower slopes and a dependable supply of needles. Sooty and Dusky Grouse were formerly grouped together as one species called "Blue Grouse," and their plumages are quite similar.

SHARP-TAILED GROUSE
Tympanuchus phasianellus

Hardy and adaptable, this northern grouse is as much at home in the sagebrush deserts of Wyoming as at the broken edge of the boreal forest on the south slope of the Brooks Range in Alaska. In summer, birds feed on grains, herbaceous plants, berries, and insects; in winter, they favor buds and catkins of assorted deciduous tree species. Smaller than Ring-necked Pheasant and usually found in small flocks, they flush sequentially, not en masse, showing white-sided pointed tails.

GREATER PRAIRIE-CHICKEN
Tympanuchus cupido

When Audubon painted his rendering of two "Pinnated Grouse" cocks vying for the

Prairie-chickens were once a common component of the prairie ecosystem. Now there are few places where observers can enjoy the sight and sounds of lekking Lesser Prairie-Chickens. Note the inflated air sacs of the males, which are covered by rust feathers on the sides of their necks.

attention of a female, the species was already mostly extirpated from the East. The last of the oak-scrub–adapted "Heath Hens," as they were called, were killed in a fire on Martha's Vineyard in 1932. Today this totem to America's declining wilderness is found in a handful of eastern prairie states, where tall native prairie grasses mix with low shrubs and weeds. A Texas coastal subspecies, Attwater's Prairie-Chicken, is extremely endangered, while the balance of the North American population is threatened.

LESSER PRAIRIE-CHICKEN
Tympanuchus pallidicinctus

Very similar to Greater Prairie-Chicken, this slightly smaller, more western chicken was once common to abundant in the arid short- and midgrass prairies of North America. It is now locally common in dry grasslands and shin oak habitats in Colorado, Kansas, Oklahoma, and along the New Mexico–Texas border. In summer, this bird feeds more on insects than does Greater Prairie-Chicken, but shin oak constitutes an important food resource throughout the year.

WILD TURKEY *Meleagris gallopavo*

This large, stately, bronze-colored forest fowl is a New World native and as iconic as the bison. Common and increasing, it is found in every state except Alaska, as well as in Mexico and Central America. When early colonists arrived, they found an abundance of "bustards," a meaty bird weighing as much as 16 pounds, and worthy of a discharge of powder and shot. Declining in measure with the felling of the eastern forests, the birds have staged a remarkable comeback in the twentieth century, due to reforestation and in no small part to active management and reintroduction. Having adapted to suburban and even urban environments, this fowl of deciduous woodlands (especially oak) and adjacent open habitats is now a fixture on suburban streets. The birds have even been seen in Central Park, New York.

Phoenicopteridae: Flamingos

These tall, statuesque wading birds are almost caricatures of themselves. All five pink-bodied species are set on almost impossibly long legs. When the serpentine neck and boomerang bill are added, the birds may stand five feet tall. Their emblematic likeness is incorporated into the business signage of half the tourist enterprises in Florida, and their effigy is the centerpiece of half the yard art displayed in America.

Found as a resident species in tropical regions, flamingos flourish in shallow lagoons, saline lakes, and mudflats. Populations of Greater Flamingo occur in Africa,

Flamingos are long-legged wading birds that use an unusual scooplike bill to siphon food from the water.

Flamingos are typically seen in small to very large flocks, and they breed in colonial fashion.

India, South America, Mexico, Spain, Portugal, and southern France. In the Americas, Greater Flamingo is resident on the north coast of the Yucatán Peninsula, Cuba, the Greater Antilles, and southern Bahamas. Audubon found the birds in the Florida Keys in 1832, but that U.S. population was nearly or completely wiped out by plume hunters in the late 1800s, including a viable breeding population in northern Florida Bay. In recent times, a flock of up to 100 flamingos of questionable lineage has flirted with the heat haze overlying Florida Bay.

Flamingos feed by sweeping their bill through the water and trapping algae and aquatic invertebrates behind the ridges in the bill. The pink coloration of flamingos derives from its diet of tiny shrimp. Highly social, the birds rest, nest, and breed in flocks that may number, for some species in biologically rich habitats, in the tens of thousands. Highly vocal, sounds range from a grunt to a growl to a gooselike honk.

(AMERICAN) GREATER FLAMINGO
Phoenicopterus ruber

Larger and pinker than several flamingo species, this species is partially migratory in the New World, perhaps accounting for what are presumed to be wild birds among the flamingo flock in the Everglades that may be escapees from Florida theme parks.

Prior to 1900, the American subspecies of Greater Flamingo was found in the Florida Keys, and it has recently been advanced that some native birds may have survived the millinery slaughter to become the foundation of the flock in Florida Bay, their numbers augmented over time by feral stock and wandering wild birds from the Yucatán, Bahamas, or Cuba.

Podicipedidae: Grebes

This family of small- to medium-sized, lobe-toed diving birds enjoys a worldwide distribution, with all members of the family clad in thick, silky, furlike feathers. Grebes range in size from the diminutive 4- to 6.3-ounce Least Grebe to the Great Grebe of South America, weighing in at about 4 pounds.

Once prized and killed by the millinery trade for their furlike plumage, the birds are now protected. Preferring to swim from danger, grebes can dive so quickly that gunners engaged in the millinery trade swore that grebes could react to the muzzle flash and be submerged by the time the shot pattern dimpled the water—hence their name for Pied-billed Grebe, "the hell diver." They are also capable of controlling their depth and submerging slowly by trapping water beneath their feathers. Clad for much of the year in gray or brownish feathers, some species don reddish hues and rakish plumes

The tiny, tropical Least Grebe is the smallest member of this family in North America, and it occurs only in south Texas and the West Indies, including the Bahamas, in small ponds with emergent vegetation.

when breeding. While the plumages of the sexes are similar in most species, the feathers of some young appear striped. Some species engage in spirited water-splashing court-ship displays that involve diving and paired aquatic dances.

The most aquatic of all bird groups, grebes swim, dive, dance, forage, even nest on the water (on floating vegetative nests). With legs set well back on their bodies, these denizens of marshes, lakes, and ponds are ideally designed for swimming and diving. Similar to loons, grebes require a labored wing-flapping, foot-pattering start to get air-borne and are awkward on land. In flight, the trailing feet serve as rudders on these nearly tailless birds. Grebes carry their chicks on their backs and tuck them under their feath-ers when danger is near.

Most species have pointy bills suited to catching fish, their primary prey, but Pied-billed Grebes have a thickish, bullet-shaped bill that allows them to ingest crustaceans like crabs and crayfish as well as small fish. Except for Least Grebe of south Texas, all seven North American grebe species are migratory, and several winter in coastal marine environs.

Peculiar to grebes is their habit of ingest-ing feathers, which adults also feed to young birds. While the function of these ingested feathers is unknown, it evidently plays some role in digestion.

LEAST GREBE *Tachybaptus dominicus*

Our smallest grebe, Least resembles the dark, drab chicks of some larger species. Found in well-vegetated lakes, ponds, and ephemeral bodies of water from Texas south into Cen-tral America, Least Grebes use their nut-pick-shaped bills to pluck insects from the surface, or dive to consume aquatic insects and small fish. Within their tropical and sub-tropical range, Least Grebes are able to breed throughout the year, with additional clutches sometimes laid before earlier clutches fledge. Their high-pitched, droning calls are an unmistakable part of a vegetated tropical pond or marsh.

PIED-BILLED GREBE
Podilymbus podiceps

Our most widespread grebe occurs in reed-rimmed ponds from southern Canada to South America and the Caribbean Islands. It resembles a meatloaf with a chicken's head, and the bird's name stems from its stout, black-ringed white bill. Its nest, constructed from decaying vegetation brought up from the pond bottom, is buoyant enough to sup-port both the incubating bird and her clutch of 4 to 6 eggs. On those infrequent occasions

when the female is away from the nest, she conceals her eggs beneath a layer of vegetation.

HORNED GREBE *Podiceps auritus*

Found in both Eurasia and North America, Horned Grebe is named for the rakishly golden-plumed headdress of breeding birds. In North America, it breeds in freshwater lakes and ponds from Alaska south to the northern plains states and east to the Great Lakes. Wholly migratory, the birds may be found along all coasts in winter, including the Gulf of Mexico. Numbers have declined in recent years, and this is a species of concern for future survival.

RED-NECKED GREBE
Podiceps grisegena

Large and dagger billed, this street brawler of a grebe breeds in shallow, well-vegetated lakes and sloughs in temperate regions of the Northern Hemisphere from western Alaska to the northern prairies and east to the Great Lakes. When courting, birds are highly vocal, emitting a torrent of honks, chatters, whinnies, and brays. In winter, they generally prefer deeper water like large, unfrozen lakes or coastal waters. When winter closes its grip on the Great Lakes, the birds' need for open fish-bearing water drives many to seek unfrozen coastal areas or rivers, thus precipitating a sudden late arrival of birds long after other birds have ceased migrating. Breeding males are brighter red than females and have bolder white cheeks.

EARED GREBE *Podiceps nigricollis*

This small, thin-necked grebe of western lakes and prairie sloughs somewhat resembles Horned Grebe, but its breeding plumes are limited to a spray of golden feathers, not

Grebes are lobe-toed divers that breed in freshwater locations, but some may occur in winter in brackish and saltwater habitats. While most grebes have pointed bills suited for fishing, Pied-billed's thick bill is suited for crushing crustaceans as well as catching fish. Clockwise from upper left: Horned, Eared, Red-necked, and Pied-billed Grebes.

Clark's (left) and Western (right) Grebes are large, long-necked waterbirds that occur in the western United States on freshwater lakes and ponds. In winter, they may retreat to brackish or saltwater habitats.

the dense crown adorning Horned Grebe. In winter, Eared Grebes frequently gather in large aggregations numbering from a handful to many thousands on inland western reservoirs and saline lakes, as well as seacoasts.

WESTERN GREBE
Aechmophorus occidentalis

Large and swan necked, this black-and-white grebe with a slender rapierlike bill is celebrated for its spirited nuptial dance. Breeding in western marshes and lakes with emergent vegetation, the birds build their nests amid the bulrushes, with the male often providing the material that the female weaves into a sizable, floating platform. In winter the birds are found mostly along the Pacific Coast, but sizable numbers also occur on unfrozen inland western lakes and reservoirs.

CLARK'S GREBE *Aechmophorus clarkii*

Clark's is very similar to Western Grebe in size, structure, distribution, and habits, but it has a slightly smaller, less daggerlike bill. In winter both species often occur in large rafts. Clark's averages smaller and is slightly paler on the upperparts. However, it is best distinguished by bill color, which is bright yellow-orange (not dull yellow as in Western). In breeding plumage the red eye is completely encircled by white, a feature that distinguishes it from Western Grebe, whose red eye is shaded by a dark mask.

Columbidae: Pigeons and Doves

Absent only in the high Arctic and Antarctic regions, the prodigious total of 309 individual species is a testament to this family's broad ecological reach. Mostly medium to large in size, the group is unofficially divided into smaller birds (doves) and larger birds (pigeons). The group is further divided into those that consume seeds and those that specialize in fruits.

While the greatest diversity of the family is found, by far, in tropical rain forests, pigeons and doves have adapted to an array of habitats, from desert scrub to rain forest canopy to the very heart of urban centers, making them one of the planet's most successful bird families.

All members have plump bodies and small heads with short, blunt bills and short legs. They walk with quick steps and bobbing heads. Their flight is rapid and direct with strong, flicking (sometimes audible) wingbeats. Many are highly social, flying and foraging in flocks. The Columbidae have a rich and pleasing array of cooing songs, and many have iridescent highlights in their otherwise cryptic plumage. The nests are typically twig platforms that support an inner cup nest made of twigs, rootlets, and stems. Nest placement varies among species, and

while most doves are solitary nesters, some nest colonially (the most famous of which was the now extinct Passenger Pigeon, once regarded as the most abundant bird on the planet).

Unique to pigeons is the production of "crop milk," a cottage cheese–like regurgitation of semiprocessed food that adults feed their young.

In North America, we have 17 species, 12 of which are native. Among the non-native species are Eurasian Collared-Dove and the common and widespread Rock Pigeon. Owing to their meaty breasts and strong rapid flight, pigeons are widely hunted throughout their range, with Mourning Dove being North America's most hunted game bird.

ROCK PIGEON *Columba livia*

Large and variably plumaged, Rock Pigeons enjoy a worldwide distribution but herald from Europe, where the ancestors of the millions of Rock Pigeons that infest North American cities, barns, highway overpasses, granaries, and cliff faces originated. Foraging on the ground for seed in small flocks, these granivores came to realize that processed grains in the form of doughnuts, buns, and breads were fine grist for a pigeon's digestive mill, allowing them to infiltrate an urban landscape designed expressly for our species. Rock Pigeon may well constitute the planet's most successful bird species. They breed year-round, and their low, muffled *hoo*ing coo call is part of the urban audio landscape.

WHITE-CROWNED PIGEON
Patagioenas leucocephala

Handsome and dark bodied, this subtropical forest pigeon of the Caribbean is found on a number of islands as well as in coastal forests in Central America from Panama to the Yucatán. Breeding for the most part in mangroves on smaller offshore islands, the birds commute daily over open water to coastal forests, where they find fruiting trees, including poisonwood berries, a fruit toxic to most animals. In North America, White-crowned Pigeon breeds in the Florida Keys and in hammock forests of Everglades National Park, as well as in fruiting trees in suburban areas of south Florida. This inherently very shy pigeon loses its fear of humans in areas where hunting is disallowed, including Key West, Florida.

These six pigeons and doves represent the largest members of this family in North America. Males and females are mostly similar. Clockwise from upper left: Mourning Dove, White-winged Dove, Eurasian Collared-Dove, Red-billed Pigeon, White-crowned Pigeon, Band-tailed-Pigeon.

A large pigeon about the size of Rock Pigeon, it rarely lands on the ground, preferring instead to clamber among the canopy of fruit-bearing trees. Hunted over much of its range, this large meaty bird faces a dubious future due to rising sea levels affecting the many islands where it breeds.

RED-BILLED PIGEON
Patagioenas flavirostris

This large, dark pigeon with a pale-tipped red bill is most often seen in small flocks foraging in the treetops (mostly ebony and mesquite). While a fairly common resident through most of its Mexican and Central American range, this species retreats south from its south Texas breeding range in winter, the northern limit of its range.

BAND-TAILED PIGEON
Patagioenas fasciata

In North America, Band-tailed Pigeon is mostly found in western oak and oak-conifer (typically mountain) forests from southeast Alaska to Peru, where the birds forage on acorns, pine nuts, and wild fruits. Wintering in great numbers in California valleys, they were once slaughtered to the point that it was feared Band-tailed would follow the Passenger Pigeon into extinction. Happily, the bird is now a common component of mature western forests and agricultural fields where flocks gather to feed. While this species is typically shy, a large stable population of tame birds occurs around Los Angeles, California.

EURASIAN COLLARED-DOVE
Streptopelia decaocto

Large, pale, and vocal, this dove is widespread across Europe to Asia Minor. It was introduced to the Bahamas in 1974, where the species flourished and spread throughout the Lesser Antilles to Cuba, appearing in Homestead, Florida, by the late 1970s. Demonstrating the adaptive and reproductive capacity of this family, by the end of the

These three doves are the smallest members of this family in North America. Ruddy Ground-Dove is a rare tropical visitor. From top: male Common Ground-Dove, Inca Dove, male Ruddy Ground-Dove. Male and female Inca Doves are similar in appearance, while female Ruddy and Common Ground-Doves differ from males with less colorful and more muted plumages.

century Eurasian Collared-Dove had spread north to the Carolinas and west to California and southern British Columbia.

Foraging mostly on the ground for grain, the birds acclimate well to rural and suburban habitats with sparse vegetation. The collared-dove's nasal bray call and loud *hoo-hooo-hoo* song is now heard across the United States, except for the Northeast and Great Lakes region, where the bird has yet to colonize.

SPOTTED DOVE *Streptopelia chinensis*

This large ruddy-breasted resident of Southeast Asia was introduced to southern California, where it is now a local resident in suburban habitats from Bakersfield to San Diego.

INCA DOVE *Columbina inca*

Tiny and long tailed, this dove of desert lowland scrub is a fixture on suburban lawns and scrub habitats from the Mississippi in southwest Louisiana and Oklahoma to southern California. Its cooed two-note call, *no hope,* resonates south to Costa Rica. Foraging on open ground for seeds, groups of 3 to 10 are typical. This species has unexplainably recently disappeared or declined greatly from many locations in the South, especially Texas, sparking concern about its future survival in these areas.

COMMON GROUND-DOVE
Columbina passerina

About the size of House Sparrow in length but much bulkier overall, this tiny bird is usually seen in pairs or small groups. These diminutive doves shuffle in search of seed across dry, open, weedy ground near brushy edges, villages, farmyards, and other human habitations. They occur locally across their very limited range in the southern United States from Florida and Georgia to southern California, but they are commonly found throughout Central America to northern South America.

White-tipped Dove (top) is a shy, locally common dove found only in south Texas. Rock Pigeon (center and bottom) is an abundant bird throughout North America and occurs mostly near human habitation.

RUDDY GROUND-DOVE
Columbina talpacoti

Found throughout Central America and much of South America, this small dove of forest undergrowth, borders, and clearings

sometimes mixes with Common Ground-Dove. In the United States, it is a rare but regular visitor to southern California, Arizona, and Texas, and it has bred sporadically in southern California and Arizona.

WHITE-TIPPED DOVE *Leptotila verreauxi*

This plain, compact dove of dry woodland forest floors is more typically heard than seen. Formerly called White-fronted Dove, it is widely found throughout Central and South America, and it reaches the northern limit of its range in the dense, brushy thickets of southeastern Texas. Its distinctive song replicates the sound of wind blowing over a bottle top and is a common component of the audio landscape.

WHITE-WINGED DOVE *Zenaida asiatica*

Large and common, this native species is found from the American Southwest and Texas south through Central America, as well as the Greater Antilles and central and southern Florida (introduced). Occupying a range of forest and thicket habitat, in North America it is most partial to brush-scrub cacti-paloverde desert, well-vegetated suburban and urban areas, and agricultural lands. Formerly highly migratory, this species has settled into its southern United States range in large numbers that are fully resident, including urban areas of Texas.

MOURNING DOVE *Zenaida macroura*

Perhaps the best-known dove to most North American residents, Mourning Dove is mouse colored with a long tail and plaintive cooing song. Found coast to coast and from southern Canada through Mexico, it is as much a fixture at bird feeders in Baltimore as it is in Nebraska cornfields. Mourning Doves are most commonly seen perched shoulder to shoulder on utility lines, where they resemble teardrops on a stick.

North America's most popular game bird, Mourning Dove's reproductive capacity more than compensates for the 16.5 million birds killed annually by hunters, which doesn't include the countless numbers killed by Cooper's Hawks every year.

Cuculidae: Cuckoos, Anis, and Roadrunner

This cosmopolitan but disparate family is united mostly on the basis of skeletal characteristics. They are not closely related to any other living bird families, and the different species might not even be closely related to each other. Instead, they may represent five separate bird families, and most live in tropical or subtropical regions. Six species occur in North America.

All cuckoos are slender, mostly small to medium-sized birds with unusually long tails and zygodactyl feet (with two toes facing backward and two facing forward), a trait they share with trogons, owls, and woodpeckers. Bills are mostly slender with a slight decurve, but flattened in anis.

Plumage is soft and loose in most species, making these birds less water-repellent than other birds, which explains why cuckoos are often seen sunning themselves. Plumage varies, ranging from streaked to solid brown, and from black to metallic green in the Emerald Cuckoo of Africa.

Most cuckoos are forest birds and feed in trees, but all are capable of flight and two are long-distance migrants. They feed mostly on insects, with hairy caterpillars their favored fare.

More often heard than seen, their distinctive calls range from whistles to coos and from clucks to hisses (anis). In many parts of the world, the calls of these "rain birds" are interpreted to portend rain or the onset of the rainy season. The name of the family stems from the familiar "cuckoo" call of the Old World Common Cuckoo, immortalized by German cuckoo clocks.

The family has an array of breeding strat-

Three cuckoos represent this family in North America. Mangrove Cuckoo is limited to southern portions of Florida, Mexico, and the Caribbean. From left: Yellow-billed, Mangrove, and Black-billed Cuckoos.

egies, with some species monogamous and paired, raising their own young, while others resort to brood parasitism (egg dumping in the nests of unwitting hosts). Anis practice cooperative breeding, with multiple females depositing their eggs in a communal nest attended by several members of the flock.

YELLOW-BILLED CUCKOO
Coccyzus americanus

The more common and widespread of our cuckoos breeds across much of the United States and southern Canada but has a patchy distribution west of the prairies where it is experiencing a dramatic population decline. A long slender body and long tail make up the physical profile of this species, with bold white spots on the tail. It breeds in a wide variety of wooded habitats, particularly open woodlands. Its song consists of a hard series of guttural knocking notes. In autumn, birds migrate to western South America.

MANGROVE CUCKOO *Coccyzus minor*

Uncommon and furtive, this tropical and subtropical mostly coastal species is found as a resident in mangroves of coastal Florida and the Caribbean, and mostly as a migrant to southern Texas. The western subspecies occurs from Mexico south to South America. It resembles Yellow-billed Cuckoo but has a dark mask, and the wesetern subspecies has an orangish belly.

BLACK-BILLED CUCKOO
Coccyzus erythropthalmus

This uncommon, slender, shy, and partially nocturnal bird of open forest and forest edge breeds across much of the northern United States and southern Canada and winters in west-central South America. It is smaller than Yellow-billed with a smaller dark bill and has limited spots in the tail. Mostly solitary, it migrates primarily at night, and it may vocalize at all hours of the night or day.

GREATER ROADRUNNER
Geococcyx californianus

Large and pheasantlike, this ground-hugging cuckoo is an uncommon resident of arid regions with patchy vegetation. Found across the southern United States from Louisiana west to California and south to central Mexico, this long-legged, mostly desert species is a strong flier but prefers to run down insect and reptilian prey on foot.

SMOOTH-BILLED ANI *Crotophaga ani*

This disheveled-looking black bird with a high-ridged bill and drooping tail is often seen sunning itself at brushy edges. Found in small groups in second-growth (riverside)

Smooth-billed (left) and Groove-billed Anis (right) occur in Florida and Texas, respectively, with Groove-billed mostly a summer breeder and Smooth-billed a rapidly declining resident of Florida. Greater Roadrunner (center) is a common resident of arid and desert areas of the Southwest.

scrub and forest clearings, this tropical and subtropical resident is found throughout the Bahamas, Caribbean, and parts of Central and South America. In the United States it occurs in southeastern Florida, where it is rare and declining.

GROOVE-BILLED ANI
Crotophaga sulcirostris

A highly social blackbirdlike cuckoo of tropical and subtropical scrub, marshes, and fields, Groove-billed differs from Smooth-billed Ani by its smaller bill with horizontal grooves that lacks the high ridge. Groove-billed is a locally common resident in many locations of Central and South America and occurs as a migratory breeder in parts of southeastern Texas.

Caprimulgidae: Nightjars and Allies

This group of small to large, cosmopolitan, cavernous-mouthed, mostly nocturnal birds is represented by 89 species that are mostly concentrated in the earth's tropical regions, as befits a family of birds that feeds primarily upon large flying insects. Nevertheless, nightjars also occupy temperate regions, migrating south to compensate for periods

when insect activity is low. At least one species (Common Poorwill) is known to enter a state of torpidity in winter.

As befits birds that roost in daytime on the ground or on exposed limbs, the plumage of nightjars is highly variegated, with browns, grays, and buff colors predominating. Since they feed mostly on the wing, their legs are short and their feet small and weak.

While the bills of nightjars are tiny, their mouths are cavernous, capable of expanding horizontally as well as vertically. Bills are fitted laterally (on most species) with long bristles that direct insects into their open mouths. Large sensitive eyes help to locate insect prey in flight in low light. The implications of the name notwithstanding, the birds are most active at dawn and dusk, but some nighthawks forage in daylight hours. Nightjars are accomplished aerialists, using their long slender wings to maneuver when hunting, or, in the case of several species, to migrate great distances.

Spending much of their time roosting on the ground, many species prefer open to semi-open country with a smattering of trees and bushes and a water component. While they are silent most of the year, the advertising song of some species is loud, distinctive, and even the source of the species' common name (such as Whip-poor-will).

Nightjars are mostly monogamous, with

females depositing 1 or 2 eggs on bare earth, the forest floor, or on tree stumps. Both parents care for young.

One of the hallmark traits of this bird group is the luminous eyeshine their eyes reflect when touched by the beam of a flashlight.

LESSER NIGHTHAWK
Chordeiles acutipennis

This New World, blade-winged aerialist is found from the American Southwest south to much of South America, where it wheels, singly or in small groups, over open landscapes, deserts, or water. During the day it roosts on the ground in the shadow of a small shrub. Song is a low whistled trill that recalls a screech-owl or toad. In flight it utters a nasal bleat or laugh. It differs from Common Nighthawk by shorter and more rounded wings and buffier plumage.

COMMON NIGHTHAWK
Chordeiles minor

As the most common and widespread of our nighthawks, this species ranges across most of the United States, Canada, and Central America and winters primarily in South America. Common at dusk and dawn, wheeling over fields, ponds, and in urban skies, its reedy, nasal *peent* call is often heard at night, including over well-lit sports arenas. Displaying males make a whooshing *boom* as they pull out of their dive. Females deposit eggs on open ground, including railroad track beds and gravel roofs. In daylight birds often roost horizontally on branches or fence posts.

ANTILLEAN NIGHTHAWK
Chordeiles gundlachii

Though similar to Common Nighthawk, Antillean has shorter, rounder wings; a shorter tail; and buffier plumage. It is restricted to the Florida Keys, the Bahamas, and Greater Antilles, with the Florida population migratory. The two species are best separated by Antillean's call, a terse sputtering twitter repeated multiple times.

COMMON PAURAQUE
Nyctidromus albicollis

This large, long-tailed tropical and subtropical New World forest nightjar is found in much of South and Central America, reaching the northern limits of its range in the

Nighthawks are expert aerialists that capture their insect prey during extended flights. Three species of nighthawks breed in North America, and two of them (Common and Lesser) are widespread and common. Antillean Nighthawk occurs only in the Florida Keys and the West Indies, including the Bahamas. From left, top and bottom: Common, Lesser, and Antillean Nighthawks.

Our largest nightjar at 11 inches long, Common Pauraque is a permanent resident in the Rio Grande Valley of Texas, and it nests and roosts on the ground.

forested thickets of south Texas where its call is part of the nocturnal audio landscape. Birds forage by making short sallies from the ground. Usually solitary or in pairs, birds frequently hunt over roads adjacent to woodlands at night.

COMMON POORWILL
Phalaenoptilus nuttallii

At 8 inches long, Poorwill is our smallest nightjar. This western denizen of dry, rocky terrain is found in open desert scrub, scrub-oak, sagebrush, and pinon-juniper, a vegetative array that attests to its extensive but exclusive western range, extending from southern British Columbia to northern Mexico. Song is a whistled *poor will,* heard only at night. Birds rest on the ground, often along roadsides, and sally out to catch flying insects.

Poorwill is also the only bird known to hibernate. In 1946–47, a torpid Poorwill was discovered tucked into a rocky crevice in the Chuckwalla Mountains of California, with a body temperature a tepid 64.4° F (42 degrees below normal), and the bird registered no discernible heartbeat. In this state, the bird's slowed metabolism enabled it to conserve its fat reserves, as all animals do when hibernating. Most northern birds retreat to the Southwest and central Mexico in winter.

CHUCK-WILL'S-WIDOW
Antrostomus carolinensis

This large, brown, long-winged southeastern nightjar ranges north to New York and west to southeastern Texas and winters south through Central America to northern South America and the Greater Antilles. At dusk and dawn, this blunt-winged hunter of large moths and insects hunts over open areas surrounded by woodland. Its call is its name but the *chuck* is often faint.

BUFF-COLLARED NIGHTJAR
Antrostomus ridgwayi

A smallish nightjar of dry, rocky scrub and forested hillsides, Buff-collared reaches the northern limit of its narrow Mexico and Central America range in the desert washes of southeast Arizona. Its song is a hurried, ascending, and accelerating series of chirps punctuated by audible wing flaps. It often hunts from the tops of bushes.

Nightjars are nocturnal perch hunters with bulkier bodies and bigger heads than nighthawks. They sally out to catch insects on the wing or forage for moths and flying insects that are attracted to streetlights. From top: Chuck-will's-widow, Eastern Whip-poor-will, and Common Poorwill.

EASTERN WHIP-POOR-WILL
Antrostomus vociferus

Aptly named, this eastern-forest nightjar proclaims its identity in forest habitat from the Carolinas to the Maritimes and west to the prairies. In the Pine Barrens of New Jersey, where Alexander Wilson became acquainted with the species, the loud monotonous chant

of territorial males approaches the level of torture. In winter the entire population retreats to the southeastern states, north to South Carolina and west to south Texas.

MEXICAN WHIP-POOR-WILL
Antrostomus arizonae

Almost identical to Eastern Whip-poor-will, this mostly Mexican species reaches the northern limit of its range in the oak-pine forests of the southwestern United States from southern California east to west Texas, where it occurs at higher elevations than Common Poorwill. The song is similar to Eastern Whip-poor-will's but more trilled.

Apodidae: Swifts

Supreme aerialists, swifts are mostly wings supporting a stubby cigar-shaped body that reduces drag. Indeed, the swift's habitat is arguably open sky. Key to their swiftness is a slender, blade-winged configuration that incorporates long, stiff primaries coupled with a drag-reducing array of shortened secondaries. This wing shape, combined with the bird's enhanced pectoral muscles and oxygen-enriched blood, creates an air-cleaving machine.

Incomparably rapid in level flight, swifts rank among the planet's fastest birds. The White-throated Needletail of New Zealand is reputed to reach speeds of 170 miles per hour, as fast as or faster than the stoop of the vaulted Peregrine Falcon. The birds feed on the wing and drink on the wing, and the only time swifts are not airborne is when they are roosting in some sheltered confine or incubating eggs in their cup-shaped nests affixed to vertical faces by the bird's saliva.

Found throughout the world, 92 species occupy a variety of habitats, including urban areas. They are usually not far from water, which the birds scoop up in their wide

These aptly named speedsters rank among the planet's fastest of birds in level flight. On quivering wings, they wheel and yaw through insect-rich skies, sometimes in loose flocks. White-throated Swift is the only swift that winters in North America. From left: Chimney, Vaux's, and White-throated Swifts.

mouths while skimming low over the surface. This wide mouth also helps them catch insect prey in flight. It seems that a swift's only hard requirement is a dependable plenitude of aerial insect prey and the airspace to pursue them.

The plumage of swifts is typically drab, and their feet are small but powerful enough to secure the birds to vertical cliff faces. The swifts' short, stiff tails also help to anchor and balance the birds, similar to woodpeckers. Their faces are furnished with stiff bristles, a mechanism believed to serve as eye protection. Highly social, they often form large flocks where food is plentiful. Nesting colonially, the birds enter and leave colonies en masse, and some species, most notably Common Swift, are reported to collectively roost in the air, with birds alternating bursts of wingbeats and glides to maintain altitudes of near 10,000 feet. In migration, Chimney Swifts may gather in spectacular numbers. Audubon once estimated that a roosting flock settling into a sycamore near Louisville, Kentucky, numbered 9,000 birds.

BLACK SWIFT *Cypseloides niger*
The largest North American swift, with a wingspan of 18 inches, this all-dark species is an uncommon and local resident of forested montane areas from southeastern Alaska south through Central America and the Antilles. Nesting on cliffs behind waterfalls, adults may travel many miles to insect-rich feeding locations at lower elevations. Winged ants figure prominently in the summer diet. In winter, northern birds retreat into South America.

CHIMNEY SWIFT *Chaetura pelagica*
Small and dark, this swift with a paler belly and more pointed wings than Vaux's is the only swift of the East, where it scours the summer skies on trembling wings east of the Rockies from southern Canada to the Gulf. It winters in the upper Amazon basin. Once confined as breeders to hollow trees and caves, the birds quickly realized that seasonally dormant chimneys in urban areas were an ideal substrate for their half-saucer-shaped twig nests, which are fastened to chimney walls with swift spit, the epicurean foundation of bird's nest soup. Both adults aid in construction of the twig nests.

VAUX'S SWIFT *Chaetura vauxi*
Slightly smaller than Chimney Swift, this mostly dark, crop-tailed swift is a breeding denizen of western skies from southeastern Alaska to central California (also central

Mexico to northern Venezuela). Nesting in hollow trees in mature coniferous forests in North America, the birds are typically seen flying high in small groups over almost any western habitat, but they favor air space over streams and roads, where they often forage with swallows. In winter, birds migrate to central Mexico south to Venezuela.

WHITE-THROATED SWIFT
Aeronautes saxatalis

This distinctive, bicolored, pointy-tailed western swift is a common sight in the skies over montane habitat, especially near cliffs, though it sometimes nests on buildings and highway bridges. Breeding from south-central British Columbia through the Rockies to Central America, this hardy species winters from California and Arizona south to Central America, making it the only swift to winter in the United States.

Trochilidae: Hummingbirds

Simply stated, hummingbirds are magical. We hesitate to say more, fearing that any effort to elucidate will only diminish what little magic is left on earth, but elucidate we must. Hummingbirds are an exclusively New World family whose 330 or so species are second only to the tyrant flycatchers in number.

Tiny to the limits of credulity, the Cuban Bee Hummingbird weighs 2 grams, less than the weight of a penny, and its nest is the size of a quarter. While hummingbirds are celebrated for the male's vivid iridescent plumage, females, who alone rear young, are necessarily more cryptic. A hummingbird's iridescence has nothing to do with feather pigmentation but is the result of refraction

Even perched, hummingbirds lose none of their charm. Note the short legs and nectar-sipping bills. These are some of the most stunning examples of this exciting bird family in North America. Clockwise from upper left, all males: Ruby-throated, Broad-tailed, and Costa's Hummingbirds; Blue-throated Mountain Gem; Buff-bellied and Rufous Hummingbirds.

Anna's Hummingbird is a breathtaking western hummer that has a complete red helmet (males) and is a regular fixture at hummingbird feeders in many locations, including cities and suburbs.

(light bouncing off their platelet-impregnated feathers).

One of the things that most endears hummingbirds to us is their near dependence on flowers for sustenance. Since their metabolism is greater than that of any other life-form, sugar-rich nectar is all that stands between hummingbirds and starvation. So dependent are hummingbirds upon this high-octane fuel that the needlelike bills of some species are calibrated to specific flowers. Obliged to hover to access blossoms, hummingbirds have wings that allow birds to advance, fly backward, rise, descend, and hover. Such unbridled control makes hummingbirds nearly fearless in our presence—another attribute that endears them to us.

The maneuverability of hummingbirds is all in the wings. North American hummingbirds' wings beat an average of 53 times per second (National Park Service, United States Department of the Interior). When a hummingbird is hovering, the wings move in a horizontal plane but the tips rotate in a figure-eight that works much like the stabilizing tail rotor of a helicopter. The Amethyst Wood-star Hummingbird has the fastest recorded wingbeats of any hummingbird at 80 per second (National Park Service, United States Department of the Interior), and estimated level flight speeds of up to 150 miles per hour, a capacity achieved in part by the hummingbirds' ability to gain momentum from both the upstroke and downstroke of the wing. Most birds gain momentum only from the downstroke.

Because of their dependence on nectar, hummingbirds exist where flowers are in bloom. This binds most species to the tropics, although two species are long-distance migrants, penetrating deep into temperate North America in summer and retreating to the tropics by summer's end.

In the Neotropics, hummingbirds are found wherever flowers flourish, from sea level to the edge of Andean snowfields. These tiny dynamos are nearly impervious to cold as long as their nectar supply does not run out. This dependence makes hummingbirds ferocious defenders of "their" patch of flowers, and Blue-throated Mountain Gems have been known to grapple in the snow over rights to sugar water–filled feeders in Arizona.

Insects, which they capture on the wing, also figure in the diet of most species, and some, like the Plain-capped Starthroat, invest much of their time fly-catching. Nevertheless, the nectar reactor that is a hummingbird's power plant must be refueled every 10 to 15 minutes. At night birds sleep, but if they go to roost undernourished, they may lapse into a temperature-induced torpid state to preserve energy until morning.

Hummingbirds depend wholly upon their wings to move about, with wing muscles accounting for one-third of the birds' weight. The feet and legs are so weak that birds can barely shuffle along a perch.

RIVOLI'S HUMMINGBIRD
Eugenes fulgens

This large, regal Mexican hummingbird (formerly "Magnificent Hummingbird") ranges north to Arizona, New Mexico, west Texas, and Colorado. Typically found in montane pine-oak forests, some U.S. breeders migrate south to southern portions of the breeding range, which is southern Panama. Despite the recent name change, this is truly a visually magnificent hummer.

BLUE-THROATED MOUNTAIN GEM
Lampornis clemenciae

This large, handsome Mexican hummingbird of montane evergreen and mixed riparian forest canyons reaches the northern limits of its range in southeastern Arizona. Large size alone distinguishes it from all but Rivoli's

Hummingbird. In winter, some birds remain in northern breeding areas, while others retreat deeper into Mexico, where breeders relocate to lower altitudes.

LUCIFER HUMMINGBIRD
Calothorax lucifer

Small and curve-billed, this beauty with a ragged magenta gorget (male) is an agave specialist. A resident of Mexico, it is a local and uncommon breeder in summer where agave plants flourish in arid montane scrub in southern Arizona, southwestern New Mexico, and western Texas, especially in the Big Bend region.

RUBY-THROATED HUMMINGBIRD
Archilochus colubris

America's hummingbird! As the only hummingbird nesting east of the prairies and breeding across southern Canada, this small, common, and widespread hummer of woodland edge is a celebrated feature in suburban gardens, where it favors red tubular flowers. By the time flowers wither, this animate blossom with the fiery red throat has retreated to Central America, which for many individuals entails crossing the flower-impoverished Gulf of Mexico.

BLACK-CHINNED HUMMINGBIRD
Archilochus alexandri

About the size and shape of Ruby-throated, this western counterpart breeds in riparian and oak woods from south-central British

Like beams of light, hummingbirds flash around gardens with abandon and, unlike other birds, can even fly backward. From left: male Ruby-throated, female Rufous, and male Calliope Hummingbirds.

Columbia to southern California and western Texas. The male's purple throat appears black unless illuminated by direct sunlight. In winter, birds relocate to the Pacific Slope from southern California south into Mexico.

ANNA'S HUMMINGBIRD *Calypte anna*

Named for the duchess of Rivoli, this common, plumpish, raspberry-headed (male) beauty is a mostly coastal resident from southwestern British Columbia to southern California. If you are a gardener in California and have a hummingbird wintering at your feeder, chances are it is this one.

COSTA'S HUMMINGBIRD
Calypte costae

This small, short-billed hummingbird with a purple mutton-chop gorget (male) is common in desert and sagebrush scrub and open chaparral from central California and southwestern Utah south to Baja and southern Arizona. Most winter on the Pacific Slope of Mexico.

BROAD-TAILED HUMMINGBIRD
Selasphorus platycercus

A short-billed, red-throated (male), long-tailed western hummingbird of open montane coniferous woodlands, Broad-tailed breeds from Idaho and western Wyoming south into Mexico, feeding on flowering shrubs and low-growing flowers. Wings of adult males produce a high trill in flight. Most winter in Mexico.

RUFOUS HUMMINGBIRD
Selasphorus rufus

This saucy tyrant of second-growth coniferous forests and riparian woods breeds from

Small and compact in shape, this male Costa's Hummingbird with a striking purple gorget and crown (males) breeds from February to May in far Southwest locations in California, s. Nevada, and s. Arizona. They retreat to Mexico after breeding in locations in the United States.

southern Alaska to western Montana and extreme northwestern California. It winters across the southern United States (California to western Florida) into Mexico. Despite its small size, Rufous is often the most aggressive hummer at feeders.

ALLEN'S HUMMINGBIRD
Selasphorus sasin

Allen's is almost identical to Rufous (except for most adult males), but it is limited to coastal chaparral and oak and riparian woodlands from southwestern Oregon to southern California. In winter, most Allen's Hummingbirds move to southern Mexico, but birds around Los Angeles and a few other areas are permanent residents.

CALLIOPE HUMMINGBIRD
Selasphorus calliope

The smallest bird in the United States and Canada (1/10th ounce, or the weight of a Ping-Pong ball) is an uncommon and local breeder in mountain meadows in montane coniferous forests of the northern Rockies from British Columbia to northern California, western Montana, and Utah, where it finds tubular flowers to its liking. In winter, most migrate to southern Mexico.

BROAD-BILLED HUMMINGBIRD
Cynanthus latirostris

This compact, fairly common emerald beauty with a red-based decurved bill is a resident of Mexico, reaching the northern limits of its range in southeastern Arizona. It frequents riparian woodlands at lower elevations.

BUFF-BELLIED HUMMINGBIRD
Amazilia yucatanensis

This fairly large, curve-billed, mostly Mexican resident reaches the northern limit of its breeding range in southeastern Texas. Locally common in their limited U.S. range, some birds winter from Texas to northern Florida, where they occur mostly at feeders and in flower gardens.

VIOLET-CROWNED HUMMINGBIRD
Amazilia violiceps

Rather slender and long-billed, this purple-capped beauty reaches the northern limits of its Mexican range in southeastern Arizona, where it is uncommon and local along riparian corridors dominated by sycamores and cottonwoods. Its snowy white underparts are distinctive.

Rallidae: Rails, Gallinules, and Coots

This large family (142 species) enjoys a cosmopolitan distribution, and though found mostly in marshes, some species reside in forests. Whatever the habitat, an affinity for tight vegetative confines is nearly universal. While many appear to be weak fliers, this family is celebrated for its ability to disperse great distances and colonize isolated islands.

In North America there are ten species, ranging in size from the sparrow-sized Black Rail to the Fish Crow–sized King Rail. Some have small, chickenlike bills, others long decurved pincerlike bills. Short-billed birds are often called crakes, but this distinction has no official taxonomic designation. The legs of larger rails are generally long, with long, narrow toes. More often heard than seen, rails are mostly secretive and solitary, whereas coots and gallinules are more gregarious and behave like ducks.

Most rails are cryptically colored, with browns and grays dominating, and most lay patterned eggs. All lack crops. Many rails are nocturnal and laterally compressed, allowing them to maneuver through tight vegetation with ease. Walking with quick, precise strides, rails flush reluctantly with legs dangling, and struggle to get aloft on generally short, rounded wings. Once aloft, they prove to be strong fliers, with many migrating great distances. Several species, including Virginia Rail, have a penchant for turning up

These are the smallest rails in North America. Yellow and Black Rails are very secretive and extremely difficult to see. Clockwise from upper left: Yellow Rail, Black Rail, Sora, and Virginia Rail.

hundreds of miles outside their established range.

Some species can climb, and all can swim, although only the coots have lobed toes. Young are precocial and leave the nest soon after hatching. The diet of rails consists of aquatic plants and small animals.

YELLOW RAIL *Coturnicops noveboracensis*

This smallish, speckled, ocher-colored rail is rare, secretive, solitary, and damnably difficult to see. Breeding in the drier portions of sedge meadows and marshes in Canada and northern states, most relocate in winter to coastal marshes of the Gulf and southeastern United States north to Delaware. Some winter in rice fields, and in migration may be found in dry upland meadows and hayfields. Mostly nocturnal, the birds feed primarily on small aquatic invertebrates, including spiders and snails. Observers are usually alerted to the bird's presence by the male's measured "stone-striking" *tick, tick, tick* . . . call, which may be given in April and May in daytime, even away from breeding territory.

BLACK RAIL *Laterallus jamaicensis*

North America's smallest rail, this tiny mouse in feathers creeps through the dense vegetation of shallow fresh and tidal marshes. In migration, it also occurs in dry upland fields. More often heard than seen, the male's growled *kee-kee-kerr* call is the most frequently heard, a vocalization to which females respond with a low, cooing

croocroocroo. Where found, multiple males are not uncommon. While most often heard at night, birds may vocalize in daylight hours in spring and summer from their vegetative confines. The all-black bird with white-speckled back and maroon collar is almost never seen in the open, and in typical matted habitat may lie between an observer's feet in daylight and go unseen.

Resident in Belize, Panama, western Chile, and Peru, Black Rail breeds coastally from New York to Florida and west to Texas (also locally in California, including San Francisco Bay and the Imperial Valley). It is a casual visitor elsewhere, though inland breeding records include marshes in Colorado, Illinois, and Ohio. Winter range includes marshes along the Gulf Coast south to Belize, coastal North Carolina to Florida and Cuba, and from Belize to South America. Food includes small aquatic and terrestrial invertebrates.

RIDGWAY'S RAIL *Rallus obsoletus*

This newly constituted Clapper Rail look-alike was considered a subspecies of Clapper until 2014. This species now includes the former Light-footed Clapper Rail from coastal California and the freshwater Yuma Rail from inland areas of California and Arizona, both of which have brighter orange underparts and faces. Found in freshwater and salt marsh habitats in California, Arizona, Nevada, and coastal western Mexico, the greatest numbers occur in the San Francisco Bay area, where habitat loss and human encroachment threaten its survival.

CLAPPER RAIL *Rallus crepitans*

Clappers are a common, large, grayish to orange, mostly resident species that occurs in tidal marshes along the Atlantic Coast from Connecticut to Florida and the West Indies, and west along Florida's Gulf Coast to Texas and south to Belize. Atlantic Coast birds are

These four rails represent the largest members of this family in North America. Clockwise from upper left: King Rail, Clapper Rail (Gulf Coast subspecies), Clapper Rail (Atlantic Coast subspecies) and light-footed Ridgway's Rail from southern California.

While currently members of the rail family, it is possible that gallinules and coots will share their own separate family in the future. Clockwise from upper left: Common Gallinule (left) and American Coot (right); American Coot running on water; Purple Gallinule; and Common Gallinule (right) and Purple Gallinule (left).

mostly grayish, while Gulf Coast birds are rich orange, similar to King Rail. They prefer regularly inundated wet tidal marshes, where birds forage on mollusks, crustaceans, and small fish.

Calls include the namesake *cac cac cac cac . . .* and a low guttural growl. Best seen at low tide when they may cross tidal creeks, they are also occasionally seen swimming across flooded creeks. When agitated, they may lift into the air and fly short distances before crashing into the marsh.

KING RAIL *Rallus elegans*

This rusty, mostly freshwater rail is often considered a freshwater version of Clapper Rail. It is uncommon and local in marshes across the eastern United States, west to Texas and south to central Mexico. Slightly larger in size, and sharing basic plumage and behavioral characteristics of Clapper, Kings may overlap with Clapper Rail in brackish marshes that border freshwater habitats. Where King and Clapper overlap, they hybridize. In winter, inland-breeding Kings move to the near-coastal resident King Rail range from Delaware south through Texas to eastern Mexico, and all of Florida, Hispaniola, and the Bahamas.

VIRGINIA RAIL *Rallus limicola*

Somewhat resembling a miniature King Rail, this small ruddy rail of freshwater cattail marshes and reedy pond edges is a widespread breeder across the northern and western United States and southern Canada, and a permanent resident in near-coastal areas from British Columbia to Baja, and some mid-Atlantic areas. In winter, it may occur in brackish marshes, with many birds migrating to southern coastal areas and Mexico. In migration, it may occur in roadside ditches, upland meadows, and woodland edges. The birds are best known for their comical calls, which include a piglike *oink, oink, oink, oink, oink* grunt and a stuttering series of metallic *kick* and *kidik* notes. Virginia also frequently gives a guttural grunt

that is very similar to those of King and Clapper Rails.

SORA *Porzana carolina*

Our most abundant and widely distributed rail, this small, black-faced, yellow-billed marsh chicken forages at the intersection of tall rank vegetation and open water. Breeding across much of the United States and southern Canada north to Alaska, it feeds on snails and insects for much of the year. In fall, it gorges itself on wild rice en route to wintering grounds across the southern United States, Mexico, the West Indies, and Central and northern South America. In some locations, the rice-fattened birds are hunted. Their drawn-out, rising *soar-aah* call is a common sound in marshes day and night.

PURPLE GALLINULE
Porphyrio martinicus

This acrobatic, brightly colored, long-toed, aquatic gem is as adept at walking across lily pads as clambering through woody vegetation. It also swims readily, but it flies weakly with legs dangling. Purple Gallinules are celebrated vagrants, often occurring hundreds of miles outside their North American breeding range, even finding their way onto boats many miles offshore. Breeding in freshwater marshes with emergent vegetation, they have an extensive breeding range from Florida to Texas and south to much of South America and the West Indies. They occur in winter in southern Florida and southern Texas, and south throughout their tropical breeding range.

COMMON GALLINULE *Gallinula galeata*

This dark, omnivorous, ducklike waterbird has a red and yellow chickenlike bill. It swims with a bobbing head, and it is equally adept at foraging on land, where it feeds on flowers and seeds and more closely resembles the rails to which it is related. Found in freshwater marshes and ponds with emergent (often dense) vegetation, it breeds across much of the eastern United States and select areas from California to New Mexico. It is resident throughout much of Central and South America, as well as near-coastal southern United States and isolated pockets in California, Arizona, Nevada, and New Mexico. Often seen in vegetated ponds in parks, it shows little fear of humans.

AMERICAN COOT *Fulica americana*

Somewhat resembling a blackish teapot with a white spout, these widespread ducklike rails often leave freshwater ponds and their emergent vegetation to forage on grass in small flocks. Golf courses, with their clipped fairways and abundant water hazards, are near-perfect habitats for this stocky North American bird currently placed in the rail family. American Coots occur throughout much of North America as a breeding species or wintering visitor. Outside the United States, they occur as residents in much of Central America and the West Indies.

Aramidae: Limpkin

LIMPKIN *Aramus guarauna*

Limpkin holds the distinction of being the sole species in a family with genetic ties to both rails and cranes. As large as a Tricolored Heron, this long-legged, somewhat ibislike, brown wading bird with white spots strides through clear fresh water in search of large freshwater snails (primarily apple snails), mussels, and crayfish, which it decants with its long, straight, tweezerlike bill. Ranging from Florida to Argentina (including the West Indies and Central America), Limpkin is best known for its loud, wailing scream (often and unaccountably heard in old Tarzan movies starring Johnny Weissmuller). While mostly nonmigratory, many birds gather in winter in the wet prairies of south Florida, water conditions permitting.

Limpkin is a large waterbird that looks like a cross between an ibis and a large rail, but recent taxonomic changes took it out of the rail family and placed it in a worldwide family of its own. Found in tropical marshes, where it forages with its pincerlike bill for apple snails, Limpkin's range extends north to Florida from its widespread occurrence throughout the tropics. Its name relates to the bird's halting strides. Despite Limpkin's New World origins, its wailing cry long served as the audio backdrop to many a Johnny Weissmuller Tarzan movie.

While heronlike, cranes are not closely related to herons. Sandhill Crane (left) is a common bird that occurs mostly in the western and central United States, while Whooping Crane (right) is highly endangered, with about 650 birds living in the wild (505 in the Texas wintering flock as of 2018) and another 150 in captivity.

Gruidae: Cranes

These large, stately, open-country birds are found on every continent except South America and Antarctica. The 15 species range across shallow wetlands and grasslands from the tropics to the Arctic. With their small heads, straight bills, long necks, large bodies, short tails, and long legs, they appear somewhat heronlike, but cranes fly with necks outstretched, while herons fly with necks tucked. Gregarious outside the breeding season, some species, including both North American species, are migratory,

Every March, tens of thousands of northbound Sandhill Cranes gather along the banks of the Platte River in Nebraska. Their collective calls are very loud, and the spectacle is not to be missed.

Sandhill Cranes perform courtship and posturing displays in late winter, during migration, and on the breeding grounds. These displays involve leaping and bowing with wings raised, as shown here at the Platte River in Nebraska.

while some others are sedentary. Flying in large V-shaped formations (like geese), the birds vocalize frequently and are even known to soar in thermals like some migrating birds of prey. Their loud trumpeting calls are distinctive and exciting to hear.

They feed on an array of food items, including agricultural corn and grains, rodents, and insects. Unlike herons, which often stand and wait for prey, cranes are active foragers. Mating normally involves vigorous dancing, with both adults leaping high off the ground in spirited displays. Pairs are monogamous, and pair bonds typically endure until one dies. Both sexes participate in the rearing of young, and young cranes usually remain with adults through their first winter.

SANDHILL CRANE *Antigone canadensis*

These stately, gray-cloaked cranes with red crowns breed in open marshland and wet meadows across the northern United States and the Arctic from Baffin Island west to Siberia. They winter in several western and southern states, most notably New Mexico and Texas. A Florida population is resident. This species is a celebrated long-distance migrant, with major spring staging along the Platte River in Nebraska. Here numbers approach half a million birds, whose conjoined voices make the spring air vibrate with sound that recalls a multitude of ungreased wooden gates swinging in the wind.

WHOOPING CRANE *Grus americana*

At 52 inches long, Whooping Crane is North America's tallest bird and one of the planet's most-endangered species, with about 650 birds living in the wild and another 150 or so in captivity. Breeding in northern Canada and wintering in coastal Texas, the perpetuation of this iconic bird is a tribute to the ongoing efforts of Canadian and American biologists, and it endures as a conservation success that spans two centuries. Visitors to Aransas National Wildlife Refuge in Texas and to Wood Buffalo National Park in Canada can still thrill to the birds' trumpeting call just as early settlers did when the great white birds were much more common. A very small captive-bred nonmigratory population lives in central Florida.

Recurvirostridae: Stilts and Avocets

This cosmopolitan family of large, elegantly proportioned shorebirds (11 species in 3 genera apportioned across temperate and tropical zones) is represented in North America by Black-necked Stilt and American Avocet. Best known for their exceptionally long legs, these gregarious shorebirds forage and roost in shallow marshes and ponds (fresh and salt). Avocets, as the scientific name suggests, have thin, upturned bills lined on the interior with food-trapping ridges that the birds sweep through the water, seining inver-

Elegant lines and stiltlike legs are hallmarks of these stately shorebirds. Frequenting freshwater and tidal ponds, Black-necked Stilts (right) are pickers, while American Avocets (left) use their scythelike bill for seining prey in a sideways fashion from the water column. In winter, Avocets trade their cinnamon head and neck color for white feathers.

Losing none of their elegance in flight, American Avocets (left) and Black-necked Stilt show the tapered wings characteristic of most shorebirds. Note the long legs of both species that extend well past the tail in flight, and the pied plumage pattern on the upperparts of Avocet.

In winter, American Avocets gather by the thousands in the invertebrate-rich waters of the Bolivar Flats in Texas. The numbers of wintering Avocets in this location have grown from about 8,000 birds in 2010 to 12,000 birds in 2018 (Winnie Burkett personal count).

tebrate prey out of the water column. Needle-billed stilts have bills made for stabbing, but will also bill-sweep, finding invertebrate prey tactilely. The primary prey of both species is the larvae of aquatic insects and small fish. With their long legs, necks, and bills, stilts and avocets are ideally suited to exploit food beyond the reach of other shorebirds, and they typically occur in deeper water.

While stilts may wade in water above the "knee" joint, their long shanks are poorly suited for swimming, whereas avocets swim when water depths exceed their leg length,

thanks to their slightly webbed feet. Next to flamingos, stilts have the longest legs relative to their body length in the bird world.

Stilts and avocets are boldly pied with white bodies and partially or wholly black wings. Some, like our Black-necked Stilt, have black on the head and/or neck.

BLACK-NECKED STILT
Himantopus mexicanus

Striding across a shallow freshwater pond, orange to red legs flashing, the "Lawyer bird," as this long-shanked marsh bird is

known, pauses and starts, emitting a strident, poodlelike yap. This warns its young crouched in the marsh grass that strangers are approaching. While mostly precocial (self-sufficient), young stilts enjoy the protection of adults for several weeks. Black-necked Stilts are high-strung by nature and prone to frequent, noisy squabbles when disturbed, or among themselves.

Less gregarious than avocets, stilts typically occur singly or in small to medium-sized groups. They breed widely in the western United States and from Delaware to southern Florida. Resident populations occur from near-coastal Texas south through Central America and the West Indies to much of South America.

AMERICAN AVOCET
Recurvirostra americana

Standing in packed formation with heads tucked, roosting American Avocets recall an M. C. Escher graphic design. In breeding season, a cinnamon blush on the head and neck enhances the starkly contrasting black-and-white plumage pattern. Avocets breed in loose colonies on shallow lakes and tidal wetlands in the western United States and south-central Canada. They winter south from southern California and southern Arizona deep into Mexico, as well as in ponds and tidal flats from North Carolina to Florida and Cuba, and west along the Gulf Coast from Louisiana south to southern Mexico. They occur as year-round residents in central California and eastern Texas.

Haematopodidae: Oystercatchers

These large, chunky, chisel-billed, mostly coastal shorebirds are nearly cosmopolitan in their distribution, absenting themselves only from some tropical portions of Africa, southeastern Asia, and Antarctica. They

American Oystercatcher is a large, bulky shorebird with a long, carrotlike bill. They inhabit coastal beaches, and they often use their short, sturdy legs to run swiftly from danger. Open sandy beaches with shells are their preferred nesting habitat, and 2 to 4 young are typical. Highly precocial, young leave the nest (scrape) within one day of hatching. Because of their preference for mollusks, adults feed juveniles and immatures for several months, since young birds cannot open hard mollusk shells with bills that are not fully formed. Young oystercatchers stay with their parents for much of the fall and early winter.

American Oystercatchers form small to very large flocks in migration and winter. This group (left) is flying in Broad Channel, New York, in front of the New York City skyline. Oystercatchers perform posturing displays in flight (right) for a variety of reasons, including courtship and just for the sake of posturing to their neighbors.

Black Oystercatcher is limited to the West Coast of North America, where it chisels marine invertebrates off the rocky substrate in the intertidal zone. Hypnotic eyes are an oystercatcher hallmark.

owe their name to British naturalist Mark Catesby, who observed the birds feeding on the salty bivalves in the tidal flats near Charleston, South Carolina. While their diet is not limited to bivalves, the long, straight, laterally compressed bill is ideally suited to shuck oysters from their armor by driving into opened shells and snipping the adductor muscle. The stout bills are equally adept at probing for bivalves, mole crabs, and polychaetes, as well as catching crabs and chiseling limpets off rocks.

While belonging to a single genus, the world's oystercatchers may (unofficially) be divided into those that are mostly blackish and those that are pied (birds with dark upperparts and white underparts). Plumage notwithstanding, all of the world's 11 species have bright orange bills; bright red, yellow, or orange eyes; and sturdy, pinkish legs with feet lacking a hind toe. Birds are monogamous, mating for life, and produce 1 to 4 cryptically patterned eggs. Courtship displays are energetic and demonstrative, usually accompanied by loud, strident, piercing whistles. Group posturing displays involve from 3 to 10 birds and include synchronous flights accompanied by loud, maniacal whistles.

Oystercatchers occur on both rocky and sandy coasts, and in winter they may form loose flocks of several to a hundred or more birds. While most closely related to avocets and stilts, oystercatchers do not typically associate with these or other shorebirds.

AMERICAN OYSTERCATCHER
Haematopus palliatus

The pied oystercatcher of the Americas occurs coastally in North, South, and Central America. Plumage includes a brown back, white underparts, and a black hood. The bill is bright orange, and the eye is yellow with a red orbital ring. In North America, it occurs coastally from New England to Florida and the West Indies, west to Texas, and south to the Yucatán Peninsula in Mexico. They reside from northern Baja on the Pacific Coast to both coasts of South America. In winter, they occur north to New Jersey and southern California. The breeding range of American Oystercatcher overlaps with Black Oyster-catcher's in central Baja, and hybridization has occurred.

BLACK OYSTERCATCHER
Haematopus bachmani

This Pacific Coast oystercatcher is a resident of rocky shores from Alaska to Baja California. Its plumage is mostly dark brown, its head black, and the bill is bright orange. Northern populations are essentially resident but do some relocating outside the breeding season, frequenting mudflats as well as rocky coastlines where the birds may form small flocks in productive shellfish beds.

Charadriidae: Lapwings and Plovers

The plovers are part of the large and diverse scientific order Charadriiformes, which includes shorebirds, gulls, and auks. Sixty-seven species are found worldwide, with nine species occurring in North America. This group of terrestrial and semi-aquatic open-country "shorebirds" includes two of the planet's greatest migratory champions, Pacific and American Golden-Plovers. The other members of the family are more tempered in their approach to migration, but most show some territorial shifts between breeding areas and winter territories.

Small to medium-large in size, these chunky, round-headed, short-necked ground feeders have sturdy legs with hind toes reduced or absent. Their short, blunt, and swollen-tipped bills are adapted for picking their mostly invertebrate prey from the surface of moist or dry land, mudflats, shorelines and lake edges. They are easily recognized by their halting, robinlike walk-stop-tilt feeding behavior (by contrast, sandpipers feed in constant motion), which assists plovers in their location of prey. They also feel worms retracting into the substrate when the plovers walk nearby, and wait patiently for them to return to the surface or probe to find them.

Plover young are mostly precocial, able to stand, walk, and feed within a day after hatching, but are dependent upon parents for protection and warmth for several weeks. The 3 or 4 cryptically colored eggs are laid in bare, shallow scrapes or scrapes ornately lined with grasses and lichen, and both adults incubate them. Plovers are famous for their "broken-wing" display to distract predators and humans from eggs or young.

Plovers hunt mostly by sight and by locating retracting prey with the soles of their feet; their diet consists largely of invertebrates, particularly worms, insects, and small crustaceans. Plumages are typically cryptic and tailored to blend into the surrounding habitat. Piping Plover, which includes a beach-nesting subspecies, is overall pale, the color of dry beach sand. The golden-plovers, which breed on Arctic tundra, have dark but spangled upperparts in breeding plumage that replicates lichen-encrusted tundra, but in fall and winter, when birds forage extensively on grassy surfaces, the duller, more subdued upperparts hark to the color of withered grass, a plumage the highly terrestrial Mountain Plover wears all year.

Outside the breeding season, plovers may gather in flocks, sometimes mixing with other shorebird species. On long, pointed

Plovers are coastal to terrestrial shorebirds that walk, stop, and pick as they feed, similar to American Robin's feeding style. The three large plovers in North America are Arctic breeders whose dappled breeding plumage blends well with tundra vegetation. Clockwise from upper left, all males in breeding plumage: American Golden-Plover, Black-bellied Plover, Black-bellied nest distraction display, Pacific Golden-Plover.

wings, plovers are swift fliers, and many vault hemispheres in their biannual journey between breeding and winter territories.

BLACK-BELLIED PLOVER
Pluvialis squatarola

This large, robust plover breeds in Arctic tundra from the polar deserts to taiga edges across North America and Eurasia, wintering on the coasts of North and South America, Europe, Africa, and Asia. In North America, Black-bellied winters along all United States coasts and in southern British Columbia. Outside of North America, they winter in the Bahamas and coastal Central and South America.

Their preferred winter and migratory habitats include coastlines, tidal flats, tidal marsh, and plowed fields. Called "Grey Plo-

ver" by the rest of the world, these big, bulky plovers with a silvery black back and jet-black underparts (breeding plumage) are perhaps best known for their lonely, whistled call, *pee-oo-eeh*, often uttered just before birds take flight. They are less gregarious than the golden-plovers, and while often solitary, they may occur in small flocks of up to 20 or more birds in migration. On beaches, they are typically well spaced while feeding, but grouped while roosting. While common coastally in winter, Black-bellied Plovers are uncommon to rare inland.

AMERICAN GOLDEN-PLOVER
Pluvialis dominica

This beautiful, golden brown–mantled "black-bellied" plover of the Americas breeds on often-elevated grassy and rocky tundra

Chunky bodies, short stubby bills, and medium-length legs are trademarks of all plovers except Killdeer. All but Semipalmated Plover in this photo array are mostly coastal or near-coastal in all seasons, except for inland breeding populations of Piping and Snowy Plovers. Piping and Snowy have pale, sandy-colored backs, while Wilson's and Semipalmated have darker, mud-colored upperparts. Clockwise from upper left, all males in breeding plumage: Piping, Wilson's, Snowy, and Semipalmated Plovers.

from Alaska east to Baffin Island. In migration it is often found in flocks of up to a hundred or more on short cut grass, mudflats, beaches, and plowed inland fields, where birds forage for small invertebrates, grasshoppers, and both terrestrial and marine worms. It winters mostly in southern South America (primarily Argentina and Uruguay). In spring, the bulk of migrants pass through the plains of North America. Their migration might encompass up to 18,000 miles round trip each year, and they return to the same area of tundra each year. As a biologist working on the North Slope of Alaska, Kevin once found a new Golden-Plover nest marked by a worn, colored tongue depressor that was used for two consecutive years by the same plover, as if a GPS reading was used to locate the exact spot in the middle of an area encompassing 172,000 square miles of similar Arctic tundra habitat!

PACIFIC GOLDEN-PLOVER
Pluvialis fulva

Somewhat similar to American Golden-Plover, with which it was once considered conspecific (the same species), this more cosmopolitan of our golden-plovers breeds in the Arctic from northeastern Russia to western Alaska and winters in coastal Southeast Asia, Australia, Polynesia, and the Hawaiian Islands. To accomplish this migratory feat, Alaskan breeders must fly a minimum of 2,800 miles over open water, assuming they stop in Hawaii to rest and feed. We have good anecdotal evidence that birds may at times

land briefly on the ocean (Sam Orr, personal observation), but plovers are not phalaropes, which are aquatic shorebirds (see p. 58), and must soon resume their migration or become waterlogged. They also winter in small numbers in coastal locations near San Francisco and San Diego. To fuel their migration, birds fatten up on insects, mollusks, worms, crustaceans, and berries prior to their departure.

SNOWY PLOVER *Charadrius nivosus*

This tiny, locally uncommon sand-colored plover breeds both coastally and in the drier interiors of the New World, and in the Old World where it is known as Kentish Plover. Three subspecies breed in separate locations in the United States, including the Pacific Coast, Great Basin, and from Florida to northeastern Texas. Plumage varies among these subspecies, the Pacific Coast birds being darker overall. When surprised, they wheel across the sand at surprising speed. Only Great Basin birds are fully migratory. In winter, birds range coastally from Washington to southern Baja, and from Florida to Texas south to Panama.

WILSON'S PLOVER *Charadrius wilsonia*

Larger, longer billed, and darker backed than Piping and Snowy Plovers, this mostly coastal and typically solitary (or paired) plover of southern coastal beaches and mudflats is the most uncommon and restricted of North American plovers, breeding coastally from Virginia to Florida and the West Indies, and west to Texas and eastern Mexico. A resident population occurs in Baja south to central coastal Mexico. The name was given to a specimen collected by George Ord in New Jersey, where it no longer breeds. The birds are active feeders, sometimes lunging at prey that includes small crabs, insects, mollusks, and marine worms. In winter, Wilson's Plover occurs coastally from South Carolina and the Caribbean to Texas, and south through Mexico and the West Indies to northern South America.

Common and widespread, Killdeer (top and center) is named for its loud call and is found across most of North America at some point of the year in grasslands, parking lots, and marshes. The sand-colored Mountain Plover (bottom) is a western shortgrass prairie specialist and not typically found near water. Fondly called the "ghost of the prairies" because of its cryptic plumage, its population is declining (down 80 percent from 1966 to 2014, per USGS North American Breeding Bird Atlas).

Long winged and graceful, these two plovers are favorites of birders. Note the black wingpits on Black-bellied (left), which helps to separate this species from the golden-plovers. This Piping Plover (right) is molting its wing flight feathers before migrating south from New Jersey, with only four older feathers (the longer ones near the tip) left to replace.

SEMIPALMATED PLOVER
Charadrius semipalmatus

This relatively small, dark-backed "ringed" plover is by far the most abundant member of the plover family in North America and can be seen in virtually every location in North America during migration. Named for the small webs between the outer and middle toes, Semipalmated breeds in a wide assortment of habitats across the northern tier of North America from Alaska to Newfoundland and Labrador. In Arctic and subarctic regions, almost every sizable gravel bar seems to support a pair of these birds. In winter and in migration, singly or from small to very large loose groups, these common shorebirds patrol the worm-rich edges of rivers, ocean beaches, pond edges, and wet fields, where their brown backs match the color of turned earth. Winter range includes all near-coastal areas from northern California and Virginia south to South America.

PIPING PLOVER *Charadrius melodus*

This cryptically colored North American native is named for its plaintive, two-note whistle. A federally endangered species, this plumpish sand-colored beach obligate navigates a fine line between the high beach, where its 3 or 4 sand-colored eggs are housed in a shallow scrape, and the water's edge, which is the source of the bird's mostly invertebrate prey. An inland subspecies breeds along rivers and lake edges, often in rounded-stone habitat.

Piping Plovers use a tactile feeding strategy by vibrating a foot in shallow water to stir up invertebrates or to cause worms or sand crabs to move under the sand. They then grab the prey beneath the substrate after sensing the movement of the prey with the sensitive soles of their feet. Breeding range includes upper Atlantic Coastal areas south to North Carolina, borders of the Great Lakes, and select prairie locations. Coastal winter range is from North Carolina to Texas and a few other locations south to central Mexico and the Yucatán, as well as the Bahamas and Cuba. Despite protection, human recreational beach use is one of the bird's primary challenges, and rising sea levels may eventually extirpate the coastal subspecies.

KILLDEER *Charadrius vociferus*

A landlubber among shorebirds, this highly vocal, very widespread North American plover with two blackish neck bands eschews coastal habitats in favor of grasslands, pastures, plowed fields, gravel parking lots, and even gravel rooftops to establish its territory and deposit the pair's clutch of 3 or 4 brown-spangled eggs. Approach the bird's scrape and the brooding adult erupts in a frenzy of feathered chicanery and plaintive cries—all designed to draw the transgressor away from the eggs. Highly precocial, young resemble puffballs on stilts and forage with adults soon after hatching.

In migration, Killdeer are sometimes found in small to large flocks of up to 50 or more birds. Killdeer are mostly resident from coastal Massachusetts and British Columbia south to Mexico and the West Indies, but vacate interior portions of Canada and the northern United States in winter for areas where water remains open, especially more southern regions. In colder northern areas, birds commonly settle near some limited unfrozen water source in winter, such as a spring, roadside ditch, or leaking water pump.

MOUNTAIN PLOVER
Charadrius montanus

Fondly called the "ghost of the prairies," this prairie endemic nests locally on the short-grass prairies of the western plains (from southern Saskatchewan to New Mexico), and in recent years they have developed a fondness for plowed fields. With their pale brown backs, crouched birds fairly melt into the earth, defeating the eyes of assorted aerial hunters. In winter, birds retreat in small flocks to inland pastures, plowed fields, and grasslands west of the Rockies or in the southwestern United States from central California to coastal Texas, and south to northern Mexico. Their population is declining, and the species is near threatened.

Jacanidae: Northern Jacana

This small but unique family of freshwater birds consists of eight pantropical species, of which one occurs barely in North America. Related to the Scolopacidae (sandpipers), jacanas share with sandpipers not only an affinity for aquatic habitats but young that are highly precocial, or self-sufficient. These medium-sized birds are distinguished by their almost grotesquely long toes that make them one of the only species with mobility over submerged mats of vegetation and lily pads, their substrate of choice. Most are reddish or brown to black above and have a brightly colored crown patch and bill. Some species have a white head and/or neck. Jacanas also have short tails with an abbreviated number of feathers.

Good swimmers but weak fliers, jacanas' long legs sometimes dangle in short flights. Outside the breeding season, the birds are gregarious, but this may relate to reduced

No, they cannot walk on water. Northern Jacanas use their extremely long toes to distribute their weight on lily pads and submerged vegetation.

Among jacanas, which are tropical marsh birds, it is the male who cares for the chicks, and they become mostly independent in as little as four weeks. Yellow underwing feathers and spurs on the forewings are unique to Northern Jacana.

water conditions more than social proclivities. They are often noisy, and the most commonly heard calls are a raucous squawking. Mostly carnivorous, their diet consists primarily of small invertebrates plucked from floating vegetation, and most of the birds' daily time budget is directed toward feeding. While largely sedentary, jacanas do move in response to seasonal wetland conditions, which in the case of some species may result in long-distance relocations.

NORTHERN JACANA *Jacana spinosa*

Found in freshwater wetlands across much of Central America, Mexico, and the Greater Antilles, this rufous-bodied lily pad strider reaches the northern limit of its range in south Texas, where it is an occasional vagrant. A bright yellow crown patch and yellow bill with white base give Northern Jacana a flashy appearance. In flight, the dark-bodied birds show a bright yellow trailing edge to the wing.

Scolopacidae: Sandpipers, Phalaropes, and Allies

This large and diverse bird group is superbly designed to exploit the food riches where aquatic habitats meet uplands. Some are wading birds, while others are more terrestrial, and many are Arctic breeders, using the power of their scimitar-like wings to migrate great distances and thus avail themselves of the food riches of the Arctic summer. Included in this group are some of the planet's long-distance champions, vaulting twice a year the latitudinal dimensions of the planet.

Clad for the most part and for much of the year in cryptic browns or grays, some species don touches of color as breeding season approaches. Composed of six subfamilies— Scolopacinae (woodcocks), Gallinagininae (snipes), Tringinae (shanks), Arenariinae

(turnstones), Calidrinae (sandpipers), and Prosoboniini (Polynesian sandpipers)—this cosmopolitan family is represented on every landmass and has even been recorded (as a vagrant) in Antarctica. The phalaropes also exploit marine environments.

Sandpipers range in size from the diminutive Least Sandpiper (4½ inches long) to the Long-billed Curlew (23–25 inches). This family exhibits an array of feeding techniques, from probing, picking, and flipping stones to herding and chasing. Prey ranges from worms to crabs and small fish, although many species target small aquatic invertebrates. Some species specialize in muddy or sandy substrates, others rocky coasts, and a few forage mostly on dry, upland terrain, where they target insects and berries.

Nesting for the most part in scrapes on the ground, they deposit universally 3 to 4 cryptically patterned eggs. Young are mostly precocial and able to feed themselves soon after hatching, but require protection by one or more parents from predators and temperature extremes for up to several weeks. Some can fly and swim before they fully lose their natal down and are independent within a month of hatching. Shorebirds are highly social, often feeding and migrating in immense flocks, and humans are ever mesmerized by their synchronized, wheeling flight and their use of tightly packed ranks to foil aerial predators.

UPLAND SANDPIPER
Bartramia longicauda

This long-necked, small-headed, straight-billed grassland specialist has a wide but localized North American breeding range extending from the tundra of the Brooks Range of Alaska south to Oklahoma and east to New Jersey. It winters in the grasslands of Argentina, where "Bartram's Sandpiper" finds its favored prey—grasshoppers and crickets. These birds are truly "grasspipers" and occur in grassy habitats year-round.

BRISTLE-THIGHED CURLEW
Numenius tahitiensis

With a world population of fewer than 10,000 birds and a breeding range limited to western Alaska, this tundra breeder leads a precarious existence, exacerbated by its 4,000-mile nonstop flight from Alaska to the Marshall Islands in the South Pacific, where they winter. About the size of a whimbrel, which it closely resembles, it also has a long decurved bill typical of the curlews.

WHIMBREL *Numenius phaeopus*

This large curlew breeds in boreal Arctic and subarctic moorlands of North America, Europe, and Asia, and winters coastally along temperate and tropical coasts, including Oregon and California and the southeastern United States from the Carolinas to Texas and the Caribbean, and south to Mexico and Central and South America. Its narrow, decurved bill is admirably suited for probing for insects, crabs, and other crustaceans. Foraging loosely or in single-species flocks of up to several hundred individuals, it is often difficult to approach, probably because it is hunted in South America and other locations. In winter, birds occur in tidal marsh, beaches, rocky coasts, and mangroves. At night, birds may roost atop palm trees.

ESKIMO CURLEW *Numenius borealis*

Sorry. All gone. You missed it. These enigmatic shorebirds once numbered in the millions but were slaughtered by indiscriminate gunners in the Midwest during their northbound migration in the 1800s. Owing to their tame nature, virtually the entire population was killed for food or sport.

LONG-BILLED CURLEW
Numenius americanus

Breeding widely across the shortgrass prairies of the American West and western Canada, this large, exceedingly long-billed cinnamon-buff curlew spends the winter

along the mudflats and sandy beaches of the West and Gulf Coasts south to northern Central America. Foraging in loose flocks (sometimes with Marbled Godwit) for crustaceans, mollusks, and worms, they also enjoy feeding in marshes and fields and on lawns in search of insects.

BAR-TAILED GODWIT Limosa lapponica

Breeding in rolling tundra close to water in Arctic regions from Scandinavia to western Alaska, the North American population of this large, long-billed champion of long-distance migration passes through the Aleutians en route to wintering grounds from China to New Zealand, where it favors sandy tidal estuaries and mangrove-rimmed lagoons. This is the longest-distance nonstop migrant on the planet, traveling about 7,000 miles over seven to eight days to reach the wintering grounds in New Zealand. The birds' internal organs shrink for the flight as a weight-saving measure to allow them to reach their destination, and they rely on bad weather storms in coastal Alaska to get a tail wind for the first 1,000 miles or so, without which they would not physically be able to reach the wintering area. Males are orange below, and females are a warm buff color.

HUDSONIAN GODWIT
Limosa haemastica

Known to the old market gunners as the "ring-tailed marlin" after the bird's long, slightly upturned bill that recalled the marlin spike sailors used to perforate canvas sails, this smallest of godwits breeds locally in wet tundra near tree line in isolated populations from southeast Alaska east to Hudson Bay. After staging on the shores of James Bay, Hudsonian Godwits fly to wintering grounds in tidal estuaries of southern South America. It is believed that this species also flies nonstop over open water for a good part of its migration, which can take five days or more. Males are a rich chestnut color below, while females are pale orange.

MARBLED GODWIT Limosa fedoa

Unlike the other godwits, this one is something of a homebody, limiting its movements to the Northern Hemisphere, with many wintering in the United States. Breeding in wet meadows in the western prairie states, this large cinnamon-tinged sandpiper winters coastally from Oregon to Mexico and New Jersey to Florida, Texas, and mid–Central America. In winter, it forages extensively on sandy beaches and mudflats, often in loose groups.

RUDDY TURNSTONE
Arenaria intepres

This small, harlequin-patterned, wedge-billed, stone-flipping bird enjoys a Holarctic breeding distribution on coastal tundra in North America, Greenland, northern Europe, and Eurasia. It winters coastally in temperate and tropical regions as far north as Canada on both coasts, and also throughout the Caribbean and West Indies to South America. In migration, they sometimes concentrate by many thousands in areas marked by seasonal food abundance. Otherwise, birds forage singly or in small numbers on sandy beaches and rocky substrates, often with other shorebird species. On its Arctic breeding grounds, this species is territorial and aggressive, often chasing jaegers, gulls, and other predators by flying rapidly and spearing them in the belly from below, all the while issuing a loud, chattering warning.

BLACK TURNSTONE
Arenaria melanocephala

This aptly named West Coast species breeds in coastal meadows of western and southern Alaska and winters primarily on rocky coast from Alaska to southern Baja. It shares its unique chisel-shaped bill only with its cousin Ruddy Turnstone. It uses the bill to pound open periwinkles and barnacles as well as to flip stones and detritus to access food beneath.

Six of the largest sandpipers in North America, all in breeding plumage. Clockwise from upper left: male Hudsonian Godwit, Whimbrel, Greater Yellowlegs, Eastern Willet, female Marbled Godwit, Long-billed Curlew.

RED KNOT *Calidris canutus*

This orange-breasted "super peep" is nearly twice the weight of the next largest *Calidris* sandpiper. It breeds on marshy slopes of montane tundra in the high Arctic, from Canada to northern Greenland and Russia. One North American subspecies is a long-distance migrant with few stopover points, while the other winters from New Jersey to Florida and west to Texas, and along the United States Pacific Coast south to South America. A majority of North American Red Knots winter coastally in Argentina, feeding mostly on small bivalves in tidal areas. It is during their epic spring migration that the birds mass in Delaware Bay by the tens of thousands to fatten up on the lipid-rich eggs of the horseshoe crab, where they double their body weight in about 14 days to allow them to reach the tundra on the next non-stop flight of several thousand miles.

SURFBIRD *Calidris virgata*

This plumpish sandpiper has a foot in two worlds. One world is planted in the rocky tundra above tree line in Alaska and Yukon Territory, while the other is anchored in winter along the rocky Pacific Coast from south-eastern Alaska south to Tierra del Fuego. Here the birds play hide-and-seek with the breakers as they search for barnacles and bivalves, which they open with a stout, sturdy bill. In winter, they often associate with Black Turnstone and Rock Sandpiper.

RUFF *Calidris pugnax*

This ornate, variably plumaged (male) Old World shorebird of wet grassy habitats breeds from coastal to forest tundra in Arctic and subarctic regions across northern Europe and Eurasia, but has also bred in northwest Alaska. The bird is a rare but annual migrant in tidal wetlands along the Atlantic Coast, where it sometimes joins northbound Greater Yellowlegs. On the West and Gulf Coasts, it is a casual visitor. In the Old World, its principal wintering area is Africa, where it favors tidal mudflats, lake edges, and lagoons. Formerly more numerous as a spring migrant in eastern North America, its numbers have declined in recent years.

STILT SANDPIPER *Calidris himantopus*

Long legged and droop-billed, this New World species breeds in moist coastal Arctic to subarctic tundra from the North Slope of

Six medium-size sandpipers in breeding plumage. Clockwise from upper left: male Buff-breasted Sandpiper in courtship display, Spotted Sandpiper, Red Knot, Upland Sandpiper, Surfbird, Stilt Sandpiper.

Alaska to Hudson Bay and winters mostly in freshwater habitats along the United States Gulf Coast south through Central America to Panama. In migration, most birds pass through the North American interior, where they may appear in shallow ponds, sometimes joining Lesser Yellowlegs or dowitchers. World population for Stilt is about 20,000 birds (Morrison et al., 2000).

CURLEW SANDPIPER *Calidris ferruginea*

This ruddy-breasted Old World Arctic sandpiper has bred sparingly in Alaska and is an annual migrant along the Atlantic Coast. Breeding in lowland tundra and foraging on shorelines and mudflats in migration, it tends to favor the higher, drier areas away from the mass of birds.

SANDERLING *Calidris alba*

Most summer beach-goers, upon seeing animate lines of Sanderlings playing tag with the waves, are surprised to learn that the birds breed in the high Arctic regions of Alaska, Canada, Greenland, and Russia. In July and August along both coasts, these medium-sized birds are migrating south. While many spend the winter along North America's beaches (including the Gulf Coast), others travel as far as the tip of South America to wait out the northern winter. Feeding mostly on small marine invertebrates that they pick up in the wake of receding waves, these social peeps seem always on the run. While they're mostly rusty in spring and summer, winter finds them with the palest plumage of all shorebirds, hence the species name *alba*.

DUNLIN *Calidris alpina*

One of the Northern Hemisphere's most widespread and abundant species, Dunlins breed across most Arctic and subartic regions of the world. Formerly called "Red-backed Sandpiper" in testimony to their red upperparts and black belly in breeding plumage, they have longish bills that droop near the tip.

Dunlins winter coastally, often in large flocks, across temperate and tropical portions of the Northern Hemisphere (farther north than most shorebirds), foraging mostly on tidal mudflats for marine invertebrates. In winter, large numbers are found in estuaries, mudflats, and sandy beaches along the Gulf, Atlantic, and Pacific Coasts from Alaska south to central Mexico, and from New

England to north-central Mexico. They also occur on inland freshwater ponds and river edges, especially during migration.

ROCK SANDPIPER *Calidris ptilocnemis*

Hardy and compact, this West Coast sandpiper with a slightly down-turned bill breeds coastally and on islands in marshy coastal tundra in western Alaska, and winters along rocky coastlines from the Aleutians to central California, farther north than any other sandpiper. Rock Sandpiper resembles Purple Sandpiper in winter, but has a slightly shorter bill, yellowish legs (Purple's are orangish), and lacks a purple sheen on the upperparts.

PURPLE SANDPIPER *Calidris maritima*

This dark-plumaged, high-Arctic breeder occupies a range of Arctic and subarctic tundra habitats from the Canadian archipelago to Greenland, northern Europe, and Arctic Russia. Its short legs and longish bill with drooping tip are distinctive. North American breeders winter coastally from Newfoundland and Labrador south to Georgia. It is very discriminating in its choice of habitats, and almost never occurs away from rocky substrates. In the absence of rocky coastlines, Purple Sandpiper forages on rocky jetties and seawalls. Singly or in small groups, feeding birds clamber about the rocks just above the splash zone.

BAIRD'S SANDPIPER *Calidris bairdii*

This dapper New World *Calidris* breeds widely across the New World Arctic in moist coastal and alpine tundra and gravel ridges from northern Alaska to western Greenland, and winters in western South America south to Tierra del Fuego. Not commonly found in large numbers, Baird's often forages singly or in small groups on moist grassy areas near the water's edge. Migration is primarily through the western two-thirds of the United States, but juvenile birds are regular on both coasts in fall. This elegant sandpiper has very long wings that extend past and typically cross behind the tail.

LEAST SANDPIPER *Calidris minutilla*

The world's smallest sandpiper is a widespread breeder in grassy tundra across North America's Arctic and subarctic regions from western Alaska to Newfoundland and Labrador. It winters widely across the southern United States and West Indies south to northern South America. Fondly called "marsh mouse" by Kevin, this tiny shorebird feeds with bent legs near vegetation on mudflats, pond and lake edges, and intermittent pools. Its mostly brown year-round plumage is unique among small sandpipers.

WHITE-RUMPED SANDPIPER
Calidris fuscicollis

This long-winged, medium-sized sandpiper of the Americas breeds in high-Arctic tundra from Alaska to Hudson Bay and winters in southern South America on coastal mudflats, marshes, and flooded fields. With one of the world's longest migrations, it is among our latest spring migrants—some birds are still northbound in June.

BUFF-BREASTED SANDPIPER
Calidris subruficollis

Winsome and dovelike, this New World sandpiper is a polygamous species (male has multiple mates), using a lek system to compete with other males to attract females in moist coastal Arctic tundra habitats from Siberia east across northern Alaska to central Canada. Only the female incubates the eggs and raises the brood.

While it numbered over a million birds in the 1800s, indiscriminate gunning in the prairie states almost caused the extinction of this species in the early 1900s, similar to Eskimo Curlew. The world population now numbers about 20,000 birds (Morrison et al., 2000).

Migrating to the grasslands of southeastern South America, the birds forage on

grazed grasslands, sod farms, and flooded pampas. In spring migration, mostly through the middle of North America, rice fields and wet grassy areas are favorite foraging areas. Attesting to their powers of flight, Pete once saw a small flock of adult birds gaining altitude by soaring in a thermal. This species is, and has always been, Kevin's favorite bird in the world, and he worked with them as a shorebird biologist on the breeding grounds in Alaska during four seasons.

PECTORAL SANDPIPER
Calidris melanotos

This large, burly, bibbed sandpiper breeds widely across the Arctic in moist coastal tundra, and winters in southern South America. Pectoral is a promiscuous species, with a single male having a harem of females in his well-defended territory. In winter and in migration, it is partial to wet habitats with emergent vegetation, and not partial to crowds. Males are conspicuously larger than females, so the typically small flocks may show much variation in the size of flock members.

SEMIPALMATED SANDPIPER
Calidris pusilla

Semis are exclusively a New World species, and the most abundant shorebird by far in the North American Arctic. They breed on moist Arctic tundra from western Alaska east to Quebec Province. In migration, generally east of the Rockies, they can be very common, gathering in the tens of thousands on tidal flats, marshes, and the muddy edges of interior reservoirs. While Semis are similar to Western Sandpipers in winter, the challenge of separating these two grayish peeps is greatly simplified in breeding plumage. Semipalmated Sandpipers winter for the most part along coastal Brazil and Suriname in South America, and along the Pacific Coast from southern Mexico to South America, so any small grayish peep seen in North America in winter north of southern Florida, south Texas and the West Indies is probably a Western Sandpiper.

WESTERN SANDPIPER *Calidris mauri*

Rusty fringed and chesty, this medium-sized peep breeds in western Alaska and northeastern Siberia in low Arctic and subarctic tundra, and winters coastally from Oregon to northern South America in the West, and from New Jersey south along all coasts through Central America to northern South America. While overlapping in size and bill length with Semipalmated Sandpiper at times (small male Westerns and large female Semis), Westerns are often longer billed and longer legged. This species utilizes key staging areas during migration: Cheyenne Bottoms in Kansas (spring and autumn) and Copper River Delta in Alaska (spring) are critical stopover locations.

SHORT-BILLED DOWITCHER
Limnodromus griseus

Its unfortunate name notwithstanding, this pear-sized, pear-shaped New World shorebird in fact has a long bill that it uses to probe the depths for marine worms. Breeding in muskegs and Arctic tundra from Alaska east to Hudson Bay and central Newfoundland and Labrador, it winters coastally in tidal wetlands along the Pacific Coast from Washington State to South America; and from Virginia south to Florida and the Bahamas, and along the Gulf Coast south to South America. These gregarious birds probe shallow water and mudflats with popsicle-stick-like bills and a tireless probing motion. Birds have orange underparts in breeding plumage but are mostly grayish in winter.

LONG-BILLED DOWITCHER
Limnodromus scolopaceus

This more rotund, often longer-billed dowitcher (females) breeds in marshy tundra from northeastern Siberia to Alaska's North Slope and extreme northwestern Canada. It winters mainly in freshwater habitats along

These six sandpipers in breeding plumage represent the smallest members of this family group in North America, including Least Sandpiper, which is the smallest shorebird in the world. Clockwise from upper left: Western Sandpiper, Semipalmated Sandpiper, Sanderling, White-rumped Sandpiper, Baird's Sandpiper, and Least Sandpiper.

the Atlantic, Pacific, and Gulf Coasts (north to British Columbia and Delaware) and across the extreme southern United States and most of Mexico south to Guatemala. Favoring fresh water, it is more likely to be found inland in winter than is Short-billed. Formerly a daunting ID separation from Short-billed Dowitcher, recent ID breakthroughs, including in *The Shorebird Guide* by Michael O'Brien, Richard Crossley, and Kevin Karlson, have mostly solved the dilemma.

AMERICAN WOODCOCK
Scolopax minor

This mostly forest species takes the "shore" out of "shorebird." Uncommon and cryptically patterned to blend in with the forest floor, it breeds throughout most of eastern North America and north to southern Canada. A very long bill and short legs are distinctive, as are very large eyes that can see behind them thanks to their placement on the face. Females deposit their 1 to 5 eggs in an unlined scrape on the forest floor, and both sexes incubate. Woodcocks winter as far north as unfrozen earth allows them to probe for earthworms, and spirited courtship dis-

plays may begin while snow still lingers. The southern limit to their strictly North American range is central Florida and central to southeastern Texas.

WILSON'S SNIPE *Gallinago delicata*

While sometimes considered conspecific with the Old World Common Snipe (*Gallinago gallinago*), this straw-billed stripe-faced marsh bird breeds in fresh and brackish bogs and marshes, widely across northern North America, from Alaska to Newfoundland and Labrador and in the northern United States coast to coast. It winters widely across the United States and parts of British Columbia and Alaska south to northern South America, favoring grassy freshwater wetlands. No seep or unfrozen pool is too small to attract this mostly solitary feeder. While multiple birds may forage in optimal locations, this is not a flocking species like dowitchers and Dunlin.

SPOTTED SANDPIPER
Actitis macularius

This refreshingly distinctive sandpiper is an uncommon but widespread breeder across most of North America, where it breeds

for the most part in open terrain bordering freshwater lakes, streams, or pools. Spotted Sandpipers practice polyandry (the female mates with more than one male) when breeding, with the female dominant and the male incubating and raising the young. A female can lay up to 4 eggs in each of up to 5 different nests per season. Wintering widely across the southern United States, the West Indies, Central America, and much of South America, they favor aquatic edge habitat as well as sandy beach, rocky coast, and mangroves. Usually solitary, the birds (with or without spotted underparts) are distinguished by their compulsive bobbing action and penchant for perching on raised objects.

SOLITARY SANDPIPER *Tringa solitaria*

Living up to its name, this dark, greenish-legged wader is usually alone or in small groups. Our smallest *Tringa*, it is a freshwater obligate that specializes in foraging in small (often temporary) freshwater pools, where it may spend the entire day in a bathtub-sized puddle searching for aquatic insects and their larvae. Breeding in forests from western Alaska across Canada, the birds deposit their 3 to 5 eggs in old songbird nests. They occur in winter from southeastern Texas south to South America, as well as the Bahamas and other islands in the West Indies.

WANDERING TATTLER *Tringa incana*

This short-legged, streamside forager bobs as it walks. Breeding along fast-flowing mountain streams in Alaska, the Yukon, and eastern Siberia, this gray-backed, mostly solitary species winters coastally from British Columbia south to South America and the Galapagos Islands, where it favors rocky coastlines. Breeding plumage includes dense gray barring below, while nonbreeding birds are mostly grayish with paler underparts.

LESSER YELLOWLEGS *Tringa flavipes*

Smaller and more delicately proportioned than Greater Yellowlegs, Lesser Yellowlegs picks its way across shallow ponds, targeting aquatic insects and their larvae. Breeding in loose colonies in forest muskegs from western Alaska to Hudson Bay, this more social yellowlegs sometimes joins dowitchers and Stilt Sandpipers in migration. Among our earliest fall migrants, some birds are southbound by late June. Lesser Yellowlegs winter across the southern United States from Texas to Florida, and along the mid-Atlantic Coast from Delaware south. They also winter from the central California coast south to South America, as well as the West Indies.

WILLET *Tringa semipalmata*

These sturdy, straight-billed shorebirds have two distinct North American subspecies:

One breeds along the tidal marshes of the Atlantic and Gulf Coasts (Eastern Willet), and the other (Western Willet) breeds near lakes and ponds in the Prairie Pothole region of the United States and Canada and the intermountain West. Western Willet winters widely along the U.S. Atlantic, Pacific, and Gulf Coasts south to Argentina, while Eastern Willet winters chiefly in Brazil (Atlantic and eastern Gulf breeders) or along the west coast of South America (western Gulf Coast breeders). While Eastern Willet usually occurs in small flocks, Western Willet occurs in small to very large, loose flocks numbering in the hundreds.

GREATER YELLOWLEGS
Tringa melanoleuca

Striding across a shallow pond, this bird's long yellow shanks flash in the sunlight. Long upturned bill (female) poised, the bird drives small fish into the shallows where retreat is difficult. After breeding in muskeg and marshy taiga ponds across boreal Canada and Alaska, the birds migrate to coastal marshes and inland ponds from Connecticut south to the southern states, where they are found across the United States to Cali-

fornia. In the West, they winter from Washington State south through California and southern Arizona, south to South America, where they forage in fresh or brackish wetlands. During spring migration, birds may gather in single-species flocks of 100 or more in coastal marshes.

WILSON'S PHALAROPE
Phalaropus tricolor

This needle-billed dervish breeds on the edges of shallow, grassy, freshwater ponds across the western prairie region of North America, north to southern Yukon and south to northern California and southern Colorado, where it plucks small invertebrates from the vortex it generates as it spins. After breeding, many thousands gather on brine fly–infested western lakes, but in migration birds are mostly solitary or found in small to medium groups. This species winters primarily in high-elevation lakes in the Andes as well as in the lowlands of Patagonia and Tierra del Fuego, but not at sea, as do other phalaropes. In all phalarope species, males incubate and brood the young while females seek out other males as mates. Females, which are dominant in the pair bond, also have the flashier plumage, with males having a more muted version.

RED-NECKED PHALAROPE
Phalaropus lobatus

This highly pelagic phalarope breeds across Old and New World Arctic regions near lakes and ponds with grassy edges. In migration it frequently gathers on inland brine lakes, often in great numbers. In winter this delicately proportioned shorebird is found far from shores, wintering in small to large flocks in plankton-rich waters of tropical seas, or in small numbers at the Salton Sea in California. All phalaropes practice polyandry, wherein females select multiple mates, and males do all the nesting and incubating duties. Females also have the most colorful plumage.

Phalaropes are sandpipers that are uniquely suited for picking prey out of aquatic habitats. All three of the world's phalarope species are shown here in breeding plumage, and two of these (Red and Red-necked) spend much of the year in far offshore pelagic waters, coming to land only to breed in Arctic locations. Unlike most other bird species, female phalaropes are more brightly colored than the males, and only males incubate the eggs and brood the young. From top: Red-necked Phalarope, Red Phalarope, Wilson's Phalarope.

RED PHALAROPE *Phalaropus fulicarius*

This Holarctic breeder favors marshy coastal tundra with small ponds but, like Red-necked, spends most of its life in cold-water seas from Oregon south to the waters off the west coast of South America, and off the coast of the Carolinas, in small to large flocks. Migration is almost entirely at sea. Red Phalarope females are some of the most striking shorebirds in the world with their bold red color and black and gold upperparts. Phalarope chicks are highly precocial and often leave the nest to feed when only a few hours old, although the male has to brood them for a few weeks until the feathers grow in. Red and Red-necked Phalaropes have webbed, lobed feet to help them swim in ocean waters.

Stercorariidae: Skuas and Jaegers

The skuas are a family of seagoing brigands that breed in Arctic regions and navigate in pirate fashion in pelagic waters off all continents. They are most closely related to gulls, sharing with them a large size; webbed feet; and hooked, flesh-tearing bills.

Of the seven species in this group, four are large-bodied skuas, three of which hail from Antarctic and South Atlantic regions. The outlier, Great Skua, breeds coastally in North Atlantic waters, but its origin appears to be the southern region. Three smaller, slimmer, more ternlike skuas breed in the Arctic and spend much of their life in warmer southern oceans.

The larger skuas are overall brown or grayish; of the smaller skuas, hereafter referred to as jaegers, two have both light and all-dark adult plumages, and the other, Long-tailed Jaeger, has only a light adult plumage. The jaegers also have elongated central tail feathers.

The large-bodied skuas tend to breed in

Skuas are large, bulky, seagoing pirates that use brute force and determination to relieve other seabirds of their prey. South Polar Skua (top and center) breeds in Antarctica and follows migrating shearwaters north to the North Atlantic. Great Skua (bottom) breeds and stays year-round in the North Atlantic.

grassy habitat on islands, while jaegers nest on open tundra. As befits a predatory and piratical group, the skuas are not social. In summer, they steal eggs and hunt fledglings, and some large-bodied skuas also kill adult

Jaegers are predatory seabirds that nest in Arctic habitats and spend the rest of the year in pelagic or near-coastal waters. They spend the better part of their lives at sea, where these nimble brigands use their speed and maneuverability to steal fish from gulls, terns, and other seabirds. From left, top and bottom: Long-tailed Jaeger, Parasitic Jaeger, Pomarine Jaeger.

seabirds. Small mammals, primarily lemmings, are the principal food for jaegers in summer. When lemmings are scarce, insects supplement their diets, and some jaegers, particularly Long-tailed, will forego breeding.

In winter, these oceangoing birds are often found attending gatherings of terns, gulls, and shearwaters, but with piracy, not socializing, in mind. The large skuas tend to target larger seabird species, harassing them to disgorge their fish, while the smaller jaegers, being nimbler, frequently target terns. In short, the skuas are bold opportunistic bullies that excel on land, sea, and air, while the jaegers rely on aerial finesse and tenacity to pirate their food.

Males and females are identical, and pairs are monogamous. Two eggs are typically deposited in a shallow scrape. Aggressive nest defense is a hallmark of skuas and jaegers.

GREAT SKUA *Stercorarius skua*

This northern, large-bodied skua often breeds near seabird colonies from Iceland to Russia, but migrates and winters at sea in eastern North Atlantic waters, as well as waters off northern South America, Europe, and North Africa. Birds are warm or cinnamon brown with white flashes near the wingtips, and larger and broader-winged than Pomarine Jaeger. Great Skua often follows fishing boats and flocks of seabirds and is typically seen well offshore from August to March.

SOUTH POLAR SKUA
Stercorarius maccormicki

Breeding coastally on Antarctica, this large-bodied, cold brown skua with a pale nape or head ranges north into the North Atlantic after breeding. It follows the migration of Great and Sooty Shearwaters, which it parasitizes for food. It is most common off the Atlantic Coast of North America May through October. Some birds are overall paler, particularly on the breast.

POMARINE JAEGER
Stercorarius pomarinus

Pomarine is the largest of the three Arctic-breeding jaegers, ranging from Alaska east to Greenland. Outside the breeding season,

it forages in offshore waters, mostly north of the equator. Adults have a light and dark morph, and have long, spoon-tipped central tail feathers (absent in immatures, which have boldly barred rumps). It is the least likely jaeger to be seen inland.

PARASITIC JAEGER
Stercorarius parasiticus

Breeding across the entire global coastal Arctic region, this medium-sized jaeger with a moderately long spiky central tail (adults) specializes in harassing terns and coastal gulls, and thus is the jaeger most commonly seen from shore during migration. In winter, it is found in coastal pelagic waters off the southern continents.

LONG-TAILED JAEGER
Stercorarius longicaudus

Breeding in dry tundra across all Arctic regions and wintering in southern oceans far from land, this slender-winged, long-tailed seabird is less parasitic than other jaegers. It is also the jaeger most likely to turn up on inland reservoirs during migration. In fall, juveniles have elongated but blunt central tail feathers. Long-tailed Jaegers typically migrate well offshore.

Alcidae: Auks, Murres, and Puffins

These marine birds of mostly cold Northern Hemisphere waters look and behave much like the penguins of the Southern Hemisphere, but the similarities are a matter of biological convergence. Alcids are most closely related to the Charadriiformes (shorebirds), while penguins trace their ancestry to tubenose seabirds. Roughly 23 alcids enjoy a nearly unbroken circumpolar distribution and may for convenience be divided into six species groups: Dovekie (1 species), murres (3), guillemots (3), murrelets (7), auklets (6), and puffins (3). A degree of taxonomic uncertainty reigns, especially with the murrelets.

All of these small to medium-sized pelagic birds have large heads, short (American) football-shaped bodies, short tails, small wings (suited for flight underwater), legs set well back, and webbed feet that serve as rudders, whether swimming or flying. The plumage is dense and waterproof, and birds are typically black above and white below, with many species having plumes and colorful bills or mouth linings. As a whole, the group is admirably suited for a life at sea, whether inshore or in deep, cold, northern waters.

True pelagic birds, the auks come ashore only to breed, typically in large colonies on steep sea cliffs or in crevices or burrows. For most of their lives, the birds are wholly wedded to the sea, resting on the surface and feeding on plankton and fish, which they capture by diving and using their wings for propulsion underwater. The plankton feeders (Dovekie and Cassin's, Parakeet, Least, Whiskered, and Crested Auklets) are smaller with stubby bills.

In short, while they may resemble and behave much like penguins, the auks are a well-defined, cohesive family united by an array of structural and behavioral traits that invite both curiosity and admiration.

DOVEKIE *Alle alle*

The most northerly of the auks, this tiny, compact, black-and-white seabird breeds widely across the entire coastal high-Arctic region in colonies along rocky seacoasts (including those of the Bering Sea and the northern waters of Canada and Greenland). It is generally regarded as the most abundant Atlantic auk, gathering in small groups outside the breeding season over the Grand Banks and the shelf waters east of Nova Scotia, where it finds an abundance of plankton. In the Pacific, it ranges in the waters between Alaska and Siberia.

Murres nest colonially on rocky cliff faces, as shown on the left with some Common Murres in Alaska. Dovekie (right) is our smallest alcid at 8.25 inches long.

COMMON MURRE *Uria aalge*

This fairly large, pointy-billed auk breeds on cliff faces in both the Atlantic and Pacific, generally south of Arctic regions, even to the Farallon Islands off California and coastal Newfoundland and Labrador. In winter it dives for fish in deep water, along the edge of the continental shelf south to New England and central California.

THICK-BILLED MURRE *Uria lomvia*

A pan-Arctic pelagic species similar to Common Murre, Thick-billed has a shorter and heavier bill. It nests on coastal cliffs in crevices or among boulders in northern waters of Alaska and widely in North Atlantic waters from Ellesmere Island to Newfoundland and Labrador, and west to northern Hudson Bay. In winter, it is often seen in offshore northern waters close to breeding grounds, and regularly south to the waters off southeastern Alaska and Long Island. Birds may concentrate in numbers where an abundance of fish occurs.

RAZORBILL *Alca torda*

This blunt-billed, black-and-white fisherman is found only in the North Atlantic, and is highly dependent on capelin, a small smelt that flourishes at the edge of the ice shelf. In winter, Razorbills gather at the edge of the continental shelf, often closer to shore and farther south than other Atlantic alcids. In North America, they breed coastally from Baffin Island and Greenland to Maine and may winter as far south as Florida, but typically only to New Jersey on a regular basis.

BLACK GUILLEMOT *Cepphus grylle*

This all-dark, inshore alcid with a white wing patch and bright red feet breeds along rocky shorelines in northern waters of the Northern Hemisphere, including an isolated population in Alaska, and rarely beyond sight of land. Except for extreme northern populations, this inshore specialist winters close to breeding areas.

PIGEON GUILLEMOT
Cepphus columba

While very similar to Black Guillemot, Pigeon Guillemot occurs only in waters of the northern Pacific and Bering Sea. In North America, it breeds on rocky coasts from Alaska's Seward Peninsula to southern California, wintering offshore close to breeding areas, often in sheltered coves. It differs from Black Guillemot by having a dark slash on the white wing patch.

LONG-BILLED MURRELET
Brachyramphus perdix

Breeding in coastal northern Asia and sometimes considered a subspecies of Marbled

Murrelet, Long-billed Murrelet shows a persistent pattern of vagrancy and has turned up on the Great Lakes and Atlantic Coast, as well as other inland locations.

MARBLED MURRELET
Brachyramphus marmoratus

This small, all–dark brown (breeding) alcid breeds along rocky coasts from the Aleutians to central California. It forages in open waters in pairs or small groups, and breeds on the moss-encrusted limbs of old-growth conifers up to 50 miles inland. In winter, it moves into protected inshore waters near breeding areas south to northern Baja.

KITTLITZ'S MURRELET
Brachyramphus brevirostris

This small brown alcid breeds on rocky coasts above timberline on both sides of the Bering Sea, and in North America south to southeastern Alaska. While somewhat resembling Marbled Murrelet in plumage and feeding habits, this species deposits its eggs on the ground near the crest of unvegetated rocky slopes, never on tree limbs. Birds winter offshore from the Aleutians to Glacier Bay.

SCRIPPS'S MURRELET
Synthliboramphus scrippsi

One of the planet's rarest seabirds (numbering fewer than 20,000 adults), this small (9-inch) black-and-white murrelet of warm southern waters breeds in crevices under large rocks on the rocky islands off southern California and Mexico, and winters coastally from central California to Baja. Formerly called Xantus's Murrelet, which has recently been split into Scripps's and Guadalupe Murrelets.

GUADALUPE MURRELET
Synthliboramphus hypoleucus

Similar to Scripps's Murrelet, with which it was once considered conspecific and called Xantus's Murrelet, Guadalupe Murrelet breeds on islands off southern California and Mexico, and there is little evidence of interbreeding between the two species.

CRAVERI'S MURRELET
Synthliboramphus craveri

While a common breeder on islands off western Baja as well as in the Sea of Cortez, this warm-water murrelet has one of the most limited breeding ranges of any alcid. It is rarely seen off southern California, where confusion with the very similar Scripps's Murrelet is problematic.

ANCIENT MURRELET
Synthliboramphus antiquus

This compact and refreshingly distinctive cold-water alcid breeds on rocky seacoasts adjacent to North Pacific waters in Asia and North America, where the bird is an uncommon but widespread breeder from the Aleutians to coastal British Columbia. In winter, it occurs at sea and along rocky coasts from southern Alaska to central California. Birds are often seen in pairs but may form small to medium flocks.

CASSIN'S AUKLET
Ptychoramphus aleuticus

Plump and lead colored, this auklet with a wedge-shaped bill breeds in burrows in colonies on islands from the Aleutians to Baja, but is often seen far offshore where birds winter, feeding primarily on crustaceans.

PARAKEET AUKLET *Aethia psittacula*

Fairly large and stubby-billed, this alcid of northern Pacific and Bering Sea waters breeds in colonies on offshore islands among boulders. In winter, it remains in ice-free northern waters, feeding on plankton and other marine organisms close to breeding areas, where it never gathers in large flocks.

LEAST AUKLET *Aethia pusilla*

The smallest and most abundant of the alcids is commonly found in small flocks at sea. Breeding on and wintering in waters near

No, these are not penguins; wrong hemisphere. Alcids, like those shown here, behave like and somewhat resemble their Southern Hemisphere doppelgangers. Clockwise from upper left: Common Murre; Pigeon Guillemot; Razorbill, nonbreeding; Thick-billed Murre, nonbreeding; Kittlitz's Murrelets; Common Murre in flight.

These chunky, bulbous-billed alcids are on everyone's short list of favorite bird species. Clockwise from upper left, all in breeding plumage: Horned Puffin; Atlantic Puffin; Tufted Puffin in flight; Tufted Puffin.

talus slopes on islands in the Bering Sea, it mostly forages on planktonic invertebrates and is not known to disperse outside of Alaskan and Asian waters.

WHISKERED AUKLET *Aethia pygmaea*
This small black alcid breeds in dense colonies on cliff faces of islands in the Bering Sea,

where it forages in swift-flowing currents. In winter, it often gathers in large flocks in plankton-rich open seas near breeding colonies.

CRESTED AUKLET *Aethia cristatella*
All black with an orange bill, this alcid nests in colonies on northern Pacific islands off

western Alaska and Asia. It winters in open waters, often in large numbers, near breeding locations.

RHINOCEROS AUKLET
Cerorhinca monocerata

This large, dark, locally common, heavy-billed lump of an alcid breeds coastally in burrows on islands across the North Pacific, and in North America from the Aleutians to central California. Virtually solitary, they are usually seen along seacoasts, diving for small fish. In winter, birds range south to Baja.

ATLANTIC PUFFIN *Fratercula arctica*

This large, iconic, clown-faced alcid nests in burrows on grassy slopes of rocky North Atlantic seacoasts, from Greenland south to Maine, and wanders widely at sea throughout this area. In winter, birds range south over open oceans in waters adjacent to breeding colonies out to the edge of the continental shelf, ranging as far south as the Carolinas.

HORNED PUFFIN *Fratercula corniculata*

This pied, bulbous-billed puffin of the North Pacific and Bering Sea breeds among boulders on rocky coasts and offshore islands from Alaska to British Columbia. Feeding on a variety of small fish, typically within sight of shore, they are usually solitary. In winter they are found offshore adjacent to breeding areas, but some range south to waters off California.

TUFTED PUFFIN *Fratercula cirrhata*

This large and very distinctive black-bodied puffin sports a bulbous bill and rakishly curled golden ear tufts. Found across the northern Pacific Ocean and Bering Sea, it has a widespread breeding range in North America from Alaska to California. Typically solitary, birds winter at sea in the North Pacific, most commonly near breeding areas, providing they find open, fish-bearing water.

Laridae: Gulls

This diverse, cosmopolitan family composed of about 50 species (21 in North America) is found everywhere humans exist, and a few places we don't, such as the Atacama Desert in northern Chile, the driest place on the planet, and the breeding location of Gray Gull. Gulls seem to thrive in habitats modified for our species, including urban areas. With their longish legs, fully webbed feet, hooked bills, and long, narrow wings, no other bird group is more admirably suited to excel on air, land, or sea. Some species spend much of their lives away from coastal and marine environments, so "seagull" is not really a correct nickname. Highly intelligent, wide-ranging, social, and adaptive, gulls exploit a variety of seasonally abundant food resources.

Ranging in size from the aptly named Little Gull, weighing a mere 4.5 ounces on average, to the Great Black-backed Gull (3.8 to 5.8 pounds), gulls are gregarious, breeding in colonies and mixing with other gulls. Clustered predominantly in the temperate zones of the planet, gulls mostly surrender the tropical regions to their close relatives, the terns (Sternidae). Gulls are loosely divided into the larger "white-headed gulls" and the smaller "dark-hooded gulls." As befits a family of opportunistic generalists, many species have a different dietary focus during the breeding and nonbreeding seasons, with some species agile enough to snap insects out of the air and others better suited to tear flesh off larger moribund prey.

BLACK-LEGGED KITTIWAKE
Rissa tridactyla

This mostly pelagic gull is a Holarctic breeder, nesting on sea cliffs in great numbers, spending most of the year in the ocean waters of the North Atlantic and Pacific, where it may sometimes be seen from shore.

It regularly attends fishing trawlers, often in great numbers.

RED-LEGGED KITTIWAKE
Rissa brevirostris

Geographically restricted, this pelagic species breeds on remote island sea cliffs in the Bering Sea and winters in North Pacific waters, mostly beyond the continental shelf and pack ice. The birds are partially nocturnal and mix with Black-legged Kittiwakes at sea. Besides their bright red legs, they differ from Black-legged with darker upperparts, rounder head, and smaller bill.

IVORY GULL *Pagophila eburnea*

This distinctive, all-white Arctic gull breeds on remote sea cliffs and flat shorelines as far north as open water permits. Spending most of the year patrolling the edge of the polar ice, this pelagic species consumes just about anything remotely edible—a dietary array that includes frozen fish, shrimp, algae, carrion, seal placenta, and polar bear scat. Birds follow polar bears for scraps and are reported to investigate anything red.

SABINE'S GULL *Xema sabini*

This beautiful, widespread Arctic nester breeds coastally in small colonies in moist tundra. It breeds in northern and western Alaska and the Canadian archipelago, as well as in Greenland and Russia. In North America, it migrates mostly down the Pacific Coast, singly or in small groups, from August through November and does not typically mix with other gulls. These highly pelagic birds winter coastally in Pacific waters off Central and northwestern South America.

BONAPARTE'S GULL
Chroicocephalus philadelphia

Petite and ternlike, Bonaparte's is a North American specialty, breeding in subarctic and boreal regions from Alaska to southern Quebec, where it builds twig nests in trees bordering taiga ponds and muskeg. The birds winter along all North American coasts, as well as on open inland lakes and waterways, including sewage treatment facilities. Very social and vocal, flocks forage by hovering over turbulent water.

COMMON BLACK-HEADED GULL
Chroicocephalus ridibundus

This dapper Eurasian gull breeds in small numbers in Newfoundland and Labrador, and winters south from the Maritimes to Virginia, as well as around the Great Lakes in small numbers. When they are present,

Five "hooded gulls" and Ross's Gull are some of the smallest gulls in North America. Clockwise from upper left: Sabine's Gull; Franklin's Gull; Bonaparte's Gull; Little Gull, nonbreeding; Ross's Gull; Laughing Gull.

Five white-headed gulls and Ivory Gull make up the medium to medium-large gulls in North America. Clockwise from upper left: Heermann's Gull, California Gull, Ivory Gull, Black-legged Kittiwake, Mew Gull, Ring-billed Gull.

this species typically mixes with Bonaparte's Gulls, which it closely resembles in habits and plumage.

LITTLE GULL *Hydrocoloeus minutus*

Our smallest and possibly rarest gull is a scarce and local breeder in isolated marshy locations around the Great Lakes, Hudson Bay, and other northern areas. It is very uncommon but regular in winter along the Atlantic Coast and the Great Lakes, where it mixes with Bonaparte's Gull. Very rare elsewhere.

ROSS'S GULL *Rhodostethia rosea*

This petite, wedge-tailed pelagic gull is a highly localized breeder in marshy tundra across high Arctic regions, including Russia, Greenland, and parts of Canada. Similar in shape and slightly larger than Little Gull, Ross's winters in northern seas at the edge of the pack ice where it searches for organisms clinging to the ice.

LAUGHING GULL *Leucophaeus atricilla*

This coastal gull is the classic "dark-hooded" summer gull of the Atlantic Coast and at all seasons in Florida, the West Indies, and the Gulf Coast. Breeding in tidal marshes, often foraging offshore, birds migrate in winter

from breeding areas north of the Carolinas and winter as far south as Mexico, Central America, and both coasts of northern South America. They are often seen loafing in monotypic flocks on beaches.

FRANKLIN'S GULL
Leucophaeus pipixcan

These gregarious New World breeders nest along inland lakes in the prairie regions of North America and winter coastally in lagoons and sandy beaches of Chile and Peru. They feed mostly on earthworms and insects in summer, and on fish, krill, and invertebrates in winter. Franklin's is one of our longest-distance migratory gulls.

HEERMANN'S GULL *Larus heermanni*

One of the most beautiful gulls in the world, Heermann's breeds in the Gulf of California and Baja and wanders north coastally to Washington. Nonbreeders are present on the California coast year-round on sandy beaches and offshore over kelp beds, where they specialize in pilfering fish from surfacing Brown Pelicans and sea lions.

MEW GULL *Larus canus*

Petite and attractive, Mew Gull breeds widely from Alaska to central Canada. The birds

nest in marshes and along ponds and rivers in open boreal forests as well as in cities like Anchorage, Alaska, and winter coastally from the Aleutians to Baja.

RING-BILLED GULL *Larus delawarensis*

Possibly the most widespread North American gull, Ring-billed is intermediate in size between Mew and California Gull, and breeds on inland lakes across much of Canada and the northern United States from northeast California to Maine. In winter, it occurs on and near all United States coastlines, and many southern inland locations south through the West Indies and Mexico to Central America. Owing to its nimbleness on land, this opportunistic gull is increasingly found inland in winter, where it roosts on frozen reservoirs and open rivers and feasts on the gastronomic riches of America's fast-food culture in parking lots.

WESTERN GULL *Larus occidentalis*

The classic dark-backed West Coast gull is typically seen within reach of the tide. Breeding on rocky islands and coastal cliffs from southwestern British Columbia to Baja, the birds are common on beaches and garbage dumps and in ocean waters over the continental shelf. Generalist feeders foraging primarily on fish, the birds also haunt seabird colonies and breeding seals, and drop shellfish onto rocks to extract the meat.

YELLOW-FOOTED GULL *Larus livens*

Breeding on the shores of the Sea of Cortez, Mexico, some of these birds wander north after the breeding season to the Salton Sea. Once considered a race of the widespread, dark-backed Western Gull, this large gull continues to walk a fine line with respect to speciation.

CALIFORNIA GULL *Larus californicus*

This slender, white-headed gull is one of the most attractive, with its crisp plumage and dapper features. It breeds along fresh- and saltwater lakes in Canada and the intermountain West and winters along the Pacific Coast from southern British Columbia to Baja and southern Mexico.

HERRING GULL *Larus argentatus*

This widespread Old and New World northern breeder throws much of what we think we know about avian systematics into the blender, with little consensus relating to the fine line between species and subspecies. Common to abundant, this large, white-headed, gray-backed gull with piercing yellow eyes breeds coastally and on large bodies of water across most of northern North America, including Arctic Canada and Alaska. Its winter range is varied across North America and Mexico (though present on all coastlines), with much of the inland West devoid of this species. Herring Gull is a fixture at landfills, where it is often the dominant species. Almost any digestible matter is grist for this omnivorous bird's mill.

ICELAND GULL *Larus glaucoides*

Pallid and petite billed, this elegantly proportioned northern gull breeds in large colonies on rocky cliffs and fjords in the remote Arctic, but ironically not in Iceland, where it winters. In North America, birds winter along the Atlantic Coast south to the Carolinas, and inland to the Great Lakes. On the West Coast, the dark-wingtipped Thayer's subspecies winters from southeastern Alaska to Baja.

LESSER BLACK-BACKED GULL
Larus fuscus

Breeding across coastal northern Europe and Russia as well as Greenland and Iceland, this charcoal-backed gull is typically smaller than Herring Gull and is increasingly common along Atlantic and Gulf near-coastal areas. Far-inland records west to Colorado are less common. It is more pelagic than most gulls and is often seen well offshore. Lesser ×

These six "white-headed gulls" represent some of the largest members of this family in North America. Clockwise from upper left: Great Black-backed Gull; Lesser Black-backed Gull, nonbreeding; Herring Gull; Glaucous-winged Gull in flight; Glaucous Gull, mated pair; Western Gull.

Herring hybrids are being seen in increased numbers, suggesting an unknown remote breeding site in North America.

SLATY-BACKED GULL *Larus schistisagus*

This dark-backed Asian Pacific breeder is a regular visitor to and occasional breeder in coastal Alaska, where it is the only large dark-backed gull.

GLAUCOUS-WINGED GULL
Larus glaucescens

This common, mostly whitish coastal gull breeds from Siberia to the Aleutians and Washington State and winters south to Baja. Somewhat physically similar to Western Gull, with which it freely hybridizes, it produces fertile young with mixed traits where ranges overlap. It also frequently hybridizes with Herring Gull on the Kenai Peninsula in Alaska. Good luck!

GLAUCOUS GULL *Larus hyperboreus*

The "Great White Gull" breeds widely in Arctic coastal regions from Siberia, Alaska, and Greenland to Quebec Province. Second in size only to Great Black-backed Gull in North America, it winters along both coasts

to Virginia and northern California, and on the Great Lakes and surrounding northern inland areas. Large size and pale primaries distinguish it.

GREAT BLACK-BACKED GULL
Larus marinus

The planet's largest gull is the overlord of Atlantic beaches and anywhere else it occurs, where it is unmistakably large and menacing. Its range is strictly eastern, with resident and migratory breeding locations from the Great Lakes to Newfoundland and Labrador and south to Virginia. Migrants are now common in winter south to coastal eastern Florida. Predatory as well as piratic, these gulls harass and kill birds as large as American Coots.

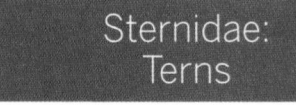

Sternidae: Terns

This cosmopolitan family is closely related to gulls, sharing with them an aquatic lifestyle, colonial-nesting strategy, and basic black, white, and gray plumage. In fact, some

authorities regard terns as a subfamily of the gull family, Laridae.

Terns are typically smaller than gulls and more delicately proportioned, with pointy, not hooked, bills and slender, not broad, wings. Most terns also have black caps, slenderer bodies, and slightly to deeply forked tails, attributes that make them nimbler aerialists. While gulls plop to the surface and swim, terns dive into water or swoop to capture prey from the surface, and many hover adroitly. Also unlike gulls, most terns have short legs, and they walk reluctantly with effort. Many species breed in large colonies near the water's edge, with eggs placed in scrapes on the ground, and are known for their spirited massed defense of nests.

The world's 51 tern species are mostly concentrated around the tropics, although 3 species breed in the Arctic. One of these, Arctic Tern, vaults the planet to winter in Antarctic waters. Many terns are coastal by nature, while others adhere to freshwater environments, and some excel in both environments. North America hosts 17 tern species in 9 genera ranging in size from the tiny 9-inch Least Tern to the 21-inch Caspian Tern.

The principal prey of terns is small fish and aquatic invertebrates. Terns do not typically alight on water, and the Sooty Tern's plumage is not waterproof. As a result, it spends much of its life on the wing.

BROWN NODDY *Anous stolidus*

This large, brown, floppy-winged, spoon-tailed, pantropical tern is common in tropical marine environments where birds swoop and snap fish from the water's surface. Often breeding in large colonies, in North America it breeds on the Dry Tortugas (about 18,000 birds) and winters in warm tropical southern oceans.

BLACK NODDY *Anous minutus*

Smaller and darker than Brown Noddy, this tropical tern of equatorial seas is a rare

Brown Noddy and Sooty Tern are highly pelagic tropical terns that come ashore only to breed on sandy islands. Roseate Tern is also pelagic in nature, spending a great deal of time at sea after breeding. From top: Brown Noddy; Roseate Tern, breeding; Sooty Tern.

vagrant in spring and summer on the Dry Tortugas. Only a few breeding colonies exist in the Americas on islands off the Pacific, Caribbean, and Atlantic Coasts of Central and northern South America.

Often associated with beaches and fish-bearing water, most terns are fish-eating specialists that secure prey by plunge-diving onto sighted quarry. Top, from left: Common Tern nest, Royal Tern courtship, Least Tern copulation with fish prize. Bottom: Forster's Tern coming out of the water after an unsuccessful dive.

SOOTY TERN *Onychoprion fuscatus*

This pantropical pelagic tern spends most of its life aloft over tropical seas. Having no waterproofing, the bird doesn't land or dive into the water, so it snatches fish and squid from the surface. It also sleeps on the wing, with half of its brain resting while the other half is awake. In our region, it breeds on isolated islands in the southern Atlantic and Gulf of Mexico, including about 80,000 birds on the Dry Tortugas, Florida. Storm-driven birds often occur along the Atlantic Coast. Dr. Bill Robertson, one of the finest seabird biologists of his time, mentioned to Kevin in 1999 that he'd recovered a 36-year-old Sooty Tern in the Dry Tortugas, which is remarkable given its hard lifestyle. Sooty Terns are very vocal around their island nesting colonies, and the cacophony gives rise to the colloquial name, "the wide awake bird."

BRIDLED TERN *Onychoprion anaethetus*

Bridled is less pelagic than Sooty Tern and occurs in tropical and subtropical waters, where it is frequently seen perched on floating debris. In North America, it breeds on islands in the Caribbean and West Indies. It follows the warm waters of the Gulf Stream well north of the tropics and is annual off New England.

ALEUTIAN TERN *Onychoprion aleuticus*

This smallish, northern, gray-backed tern with a black cap and white headlamp breeds on the western and southern coasts of Alaska, and its chirping trill and three-note twitter are very unlike the harsh *keeyer* of Common or Arctic Tern. Locally common in coastal colonies on both sides of the Bering Sea, its winter range is unknown, but it is not Alaska.

LEAST TERN *Sternula antillarum*

Breeding near rivers, lakes, on flat rooftops, and on Atlantic and Gulf Coast beaches, this smallest of terns is widespread but local inland east of the Rockies, as well as along coastal California south to Baja, and throughout the West Indies and both coasts of Mexico. In winter, birds extend their range south to South America. Feeding mostly on small fish, diving birds hit the water with an audible *snap*. Breeding in large colonies, birds mass a determined defense against predators, researchers, and beachgoers.

GULL-BILLED TERN *Gelochelidon nilotica*

This somewhat blocky, whitish tern with a black crewcut and black bullet-shaped bill is widespread across near-coastal reaches of the Northern Hemisphere, breeding in a variety of fresh and saline marshes and beach habitats. In North America, it breeds locally from southern California to the Gulf of California and along the Atlantic Coast from Long Island to Florida, and to southern Texas. It occurs coastally in winter from the Gulf Coast through Central America to northern South America. Gull-billed does not plunge-dive for prey, but forages by catching insects in flight or by vertically diving yo-yo style to snatch crabs and other invertebrates from the land.

CASPIAN TERN *Hydroprogne caspia*

Caspian is the world's largest tern at 21 inches long, and it is larger than many gulls. Adults are distinctive, with their extensive black caps and dark-tipped blood-red bills, and their heavy flight style is not buoyant like that of other terns. Enjoying a global distribution, Caspian breeds in colonies on seacoasts and large, inland freshwater lakes in Europe, Asia, Australia, and North America. In North America, it breeds locally in isolated locations from northern Canada to Florida and the western United States. The winter range includes the southern coastlines south into Mexico, and the West Indies south to northern South America. Resident coastal populations occur from Louisiana through Texas and extreme southern California.

BLACK TERN *Chlidonias niger*

This Old and New World breeder has a foot in two aquatic worlds. It breeds in large, well-vegetated, freshwater marshes and lakes, and then this nimble aerialist spends the balance

Arctic Tern (left) travels up to 18,000 miles each year in migration from the Northern to the Southern Hemisphere. Black Skimmers (center) are unusual terns that capture prey by skimming open-billed along the water surface with the lower bill inserted into the water, shutting it after encountering fish or other prey items. Black Tern (right) is a freshwater marsh breeder that does not plunge into the water for fish but picks aquatic invertebrates and fish from the surface without submersing itself.

This intentionally blurred photo captures the dynamic nature of a flock of Royal Terns, which nest colonially and form small to large flocks outside breeding season.

of the year in tropical marine environments. In North America, it breeds in small colonies across much of Canada and the northern states from Nova Scotia to south-central California. In migration, birds may appear over any body of water, swooping to snap prey from the surface.

Kevin once saw a group of 2,500 Black Terns feeding and roosting in early September on Bolivar Flats near Galveston, Texas! Black Terns never plunge into water, and they often roost with other terns. North American birds winter coastally off western Mexico and Central America and the northern coasts of South America.

ROSEATE TERN *Sterna dougallii*

This elegant, medium-sized, very white streamer-tailed tern occurs mostly in warm coastal waters of the world, but it also breeds in temperate regions. In North America, Roseate breeds coastally but locally from Nova Scotia to New York and Florida and south through the West Indies. In winter, it occurs from the West Indies south to northern South America.

COMMON TERN *Sterna hirundo*

Gray backed and medium sized, Common Tern breeds widely in colonies across Europe, Asia, and North America on inland lakeshores, sandy coastal beaches, offshore islands, and floating wrack in tidal marshes. In North America, Common Tern breeds widely across Canada, the Great Lakes, and the Atlantic Coast south to South Carolina. In winter, the birds occur in tropical estuaries and along large rivers in Central America and both coasts of South America. Small numbers occur in winter from Florida to Texas.

ARCTIC TERN *Sterna paradisaea*

This medium-sized, short-necked, petite-billed tern ranks among the planet's greatest voyagers. It breeds widely across temperate and Arctic regions of the Northern Hemisphere and winters in southern oceans south to Antarctic ice. In North America, it breeds across the entire northern tier from Alaska to Newfoundland and Labrador and south to Long Island. This aggressive tern fiercely defends its nest colonies with dive-bombing attacks culminating with pecks by its sharp bill.

FORSTER'S TERN *Sterna forsteri*

This frosty, scimitar-winged, splay-tailed bird is a familiar sight at select freshwater and brackish locations in North America.

It has an affinity for fresh and tidal marshes and occurs as a year-round resident in mid-Atlantic and some upper Gulf Coast to Texas coastal locations. Nesting in small to large colonies on marsh islands and tidal estuaries, these medium-sized terns hover adroitly and plunge for small fish. In winter, they occur coastally from southern New Jersey south to Texas, and from California south to Mexico and Central America. They also occur inland from Texas to Mississippi and Florida in winter.

ROYAL TERN *Thalasseus maximus*

Large, shaggy crested, and with a bright orange bill, Royal Terns are mostly coastal and breed locally from New Jersey south to Texas, and at a few locations in southern California to Baja. They winter widely along the coast from Virginia south to the Bahamas and Caribbean, and from southern California south to northern South America. This is one of most common terns in tropical waters of Mexico and Central America.

SANDWICH TERN
Thalasseus sandvicensis

Slightly smaller but with a shaggy crest similar to Royal Tern's, with which it often associates, Sandwich Tern breeds in the Old and New Worlds, where it occurs in coastal areas. In North America, it breeds from Virginia to Florida and west to Texas at select locations, often offshore islands. In winter, birds range from Florida and the West Indies to Texas and Mexico, and south along Atlantic and Pacific Coasts of Central America.

ELEGANT TERN *Thalasseus elegans*

This medium-large West Coast tern breeds along seacoasts from southern California to Baja but ranges north to Washington. In winter, it occurs along the Pacific Coast from Guatemala to southern Chile. Elegant is similar to Royal Tern, but smaller and with a proportionately longer, slenderer, drooping bill and a shaggier crest.

BLACK SKIMMER *Rynchops niger*

This large, scimitar-winged, highly specialized tern forages with its elongated lower bill slicing through the water and snapping shut when it encounters its fish prey. Breeding in small to large colonies on sandy beaches, it occurs coastally in North America from Massachusetts to Florida and west to Texas. It is resident along both coasts of northern Mexico north to Baja and southern California. Atlantic birds north of the Carolinas migrate south in winter as far as northern South America. Some authorities consider the world's three skimmer species a separate family, *Rynchopidae*.

Phaethontidae: Tropicbirds

Named for the son of the Greek sun god, young Phaethon, according to legend, was allowed to drive his father's chariot across the sky. Unable to control the horses, the hapless youth scorched the earth. To prevent further damage, Zeus, the king of the gods, interceded by throwing a lightning bolt that dislodged Phaethon from the sky. He fell to earth in spectacular fashion, similar to tropicbirds as they dive from great heights into the sea.

The mostly white members in this family of tropical and subtropical seabirds do indeed gleam as bright as the sun, and they dive from great heights for fish and squid, often spiraling as they arrow down. Ungainly on land but superbly designed for life over the ocean's warmer seas, the birds pursue mostly flying fish. Emerging with prey clasped in their large, tooth-edged bills, they struggle aloft on slender wings, streamer tail feathers shedding droplets as they climb. Gaining altitude, the birds head for tall isolated cliff faces where each has a single downy hatchling awaiting in rocky crevices, holes, or caves.

Somewhere near the refined end of Creation, the folks in Research and Development rolled out these flagellum-tailed skydivers: the tropicbirds. Named for Phaethon, the son of the Greek sun god, whose aborted chariot drive resulted in a spectacular plunge into the sea, these gleaming white diving birds do indeed fall upon prey like bolts from the blue. Tropicbirds do not plunge into the water when hunting, but instead pick fish and invertebrates from near the surface. Top: White-tailed Tropicbirds, left and right. Bottom: a Red-billed Tropicbird at a nest site on a cliff face.

The well-fattened young fledge 12 or 13 weeks after hatching, but are initially unable to fly, so they float on the ocean surface until slimming down to flight weight, apparently without parental care. From then on, theirs is a life at sea until sexual maturity calls them back to nesting cliffs.

Two of three tropicbird species occur regularly but uncommonly off the Atlantic and Pacific Coasts of the United States but are rarely seen from shore. The third, the Pacific and Indian Ocean–based Red-tailed Tropicbird, breeds nowhere close to North America and is a casual visitor to pelagic waters off southern California.

WHITE-TAILED TROPICBIRD
Phaethon lepturus

This flagellum-tailed seabird breeds on islands in the Atlantic Ocean and Carib-

bean from Bermuda and the Bahamas to the Greater and Lesser Antilles. In the Pacific, it breeds on the Hawaiian Islands and various isolated South Pacific and Indian Ocean islands. Foraging at sea in warm waters, it regularly follows the Gulf Stream in North America to North Carolina.

Yellowish-billed adults have black wing-tips and bold black braces on their upper-wings. Juveniles have finely barred backs and a hardly discernable eye line. Their graceful flight is not reflective of their powerful flying skills, especially during bad weather.

RED-BILLED TROPICBIRD
Phaethon aethereus

A fairly sedentary tropicbird, with adults mostly remaining in the vicinity of their breeding islands in the Caribbean and eastern Atlantic. Birds of the eastern Pacific nest

Tropicbirds are powerful fliers who move in a graceful, effortless fashion, like this Red-billed Tropicbird.

on islands off Mexico, the Gulf of California, northern South America, and the Galapagos Islands. Immature birds may be encountered in Gulf Stream waters from Florida to New England. In the Pacific, Red-billed ranges irregularly north to California, preferring at all times warmer waters. Adults with bright red bills lack the black wing braces seen on White-tailed Tropicbirds. Yellow-billed juveniles have bold black eye lines that meet at the nape.

Gaviidae: Loons

These large, heavy, aquatic, duck- or goose-sized diving birds with webbed feet and daggerlike bills are ideally suited for capturing fish, their primary prey. Loons (or "divers" as they are called elsewhere) occur across the Northern Hemisphere. There are five species, all of which occur in North America, with the aptly named "Common" Loon being the best known and most widespread. With their legs set well back, loons are excellent swimmers and accomplished divers, with

some species able to dive to depths of over 200 feet and remain underwater for up to eight minutes. The rearward location of the legs makes loons awkward on land, where they must push themselves forward. Owing to their heavy wing load, most loons require a lengthy, labored, foot-slapping running start; only the tundra-breeding Red-throated Loon is capable of taking off without one. Once airborne, they are strong, determined fliers whose steady elastic wingbeats may propel birds to speeds in excess of 70 miles per hour.

Loons carry their young on their backs until they grow too large for comfort. Two young are typical for loons, like this Common Loon.

While agile in the water, loons are awkward on land and push themselves along with their rear-mounted feet. Unlike the other tundra-breeding loons, Common Loon nests on islands and banks (upper left) in temperate freshwater ponds and lakes. Their diet consists primarily of fish. Clockwise from upper left, in breeding plumage: Common Loon, Yellow-billed Loon, Pacific Loon, Red-throated Loon.

Males and females typically mate for life and have identical breeding and nonbreeding plumages. Breeding plumage for all species is mostly gray, black, and white, and nonbreeding plumage grayish to brownish. Nesting primarily in Arctic and far northern regions, loons construct nests of heaped aquatic vegetation on small islands in freshwater lakes or ponds, or on the shores of tidal estuaries, but always close to the water's edge. Downy young (typically 2) can dive two or three days after hatching but often ride on a parent's back. Dependent upon the parents until nearly fully grown, the birds usually spend the first two (nonbreeding) years of their lives in marine environments, where both adults and immatures winter.

Vocalizations include yodels, yelps, growls, and quacks, with the iconic yodel of the Common Loon being synonymous with wilderness and pristine aquatic environs.

Visual hunters, loons require clear, fish-bearing water. This family is particularly vulnerable to lead poisoning arising from lead shot and lead sinkers, and they are also susceptible to entanglement in discarded fishing line.

RED-THROATED LOON
Gavia stellata

This small, slender, rapier-billed loon breeds in northern temperate and Arctic locations, where it nests in shallow lakes and ponds north to the high Arctic. The maroon-colored throat patch is a distinctive feature of breeding birds and is occasionally seen away from breeding areas. Nonbreeding birds are an overall gray and white. In winter, they occur in coastal waters along both coasts from Nova Scotia to Florida and Alaska to Baja. Unlike other loons, Red-throated can take flight without a running start.

Most loons need lots of aquatic runway to get airborne after an effortful, wing-flailing, foot-pattering takeoff (right). Red-throated Loon, however, can take flight from the water without a long, running start. Note the long, angular wings and very large feet on this Common Loon.

ARCTIC LOON *Gavia arctica*

Also called Black-throated Diver, this large, mostly Eurasian species breeds along seacoasts from the British Isles to the Seward Peninsula of Alaska. They winter casually along the Pacific Coast of Alaska south to California, where they are rare. When swimming, most show a white flank above the waterline that is absent on the very similar Pacific Loon, which is slightly smaller and much more common.

PACIFIC LOON *Gavia pacifica*

This medium-sized, widespread Arctic and subarctic breeder favors large, deep tundra and taiga lakes. Breeding across most of northern North America from western Alaska to northwestern Quebec, Pacific Loon winters primarily along the Pacific Coast from Alaska to Baja. It was formerly grouped with Arctic Loon as one species.

COMMON LOON *Gavia immer*

Breeding farther south than other loons, this large loon issues a haunting yodeled call that echoes across the forest-rimmed lakes of North America. Nonbreeding birds winter along both coasts, the Gulf of Mexico, and large inland lakes, making it the most likely loon species to be seen inland. Known elsewhere as the Great Northern Diver, this is the loon made famous in the 1981 film *On Golden Pond,* starring Katharine Hepburn and Henry Fonda.

YELLOW-BILLED LOON *Gavia adamsii*

Our largest loon, weighing nearly 12 pounds, resembles Common Loon but brandishes a large, slightly upturned yellow bill (black to gray on Common Loon). It breeds in freshwater rivers and tundra lakes near seacoasts and away from forested areas. In North America, it breeds in northern Alaska and winters from coastal Alaska to British Columbia. It is rare in coastal California and typically avoids large, interior lakes. In Eurasia it is called "White-billed Diver."

Diomedeidae: Albatrosses

These large, heavy-billed, plank-winged seabirds spend most of their lives getting lift off ocean waves, coming ashore only to breed. Closely related to other "tube-nosed" species, albatrosses are fairly common in southern seas and northern Pacific waters, but infrequently seen from land. Many occur in the South Pacific near Antarctica, and near New Zealand.

Albatrosses, like this adult Laysan, are large, plank-winged, pelagic tubenoses that roam the planet's oceans and come ashore only to breed. While rare in the Atlantic, Laysan frequents northern Pacific waters in North America.

Unmistakably grand, with wings that exceed 11 feet in some species, most adult albatrosses are patterned much like gulls (white below and dark above), but several species are all dark. Feeding on squid, fish, krill, and carrion, they patrol open oceans, often congregating near feeding whales, where sea life is most abundant and concentrated. Some species feed at night, when squid rise to the surface. Like other dedicated seabirds, albatrosses drink seawater and have special glands in their heads that eliminate and excrete excess salt from their blood through tubes on the upper surface of the bills.

The number of albatross species is debatable, ranging from 13 to 24, with 21 species generally accepted by most authorities. These are divided into four groups, or genera, the *Diomedea* (great albatrosses), *Thalassarche* (mollymawks), *Phoebastria* (North Pacific albatrosses), and *Phoebetria* (sooty albatrosses). In North America, three species occur regularly in the waters of the Pacific from Mexico to the Bering Sea, with the waters off Monterey, California, being a particularly albatross-rich environment. Albatrosses are accidental in North Atlantic waters, with few sightings involving mostly two species of mollymawks, Yellow-nosed and Black-browed Albatrosses.

Taking five to eight years to attain sexual maturity, albatrosses compensate for this procreative lag by being very long-lived. One celebrated individual, a Laysan Albatross named Wisdom, was banded as a hatchling on Midway in 1956. Now over 60 years old, she is believed to have reared 40 chicks. Way to go, grandma! To reach this grand old age, Wisdom has had to evade dangers that threaten all seabirds, including fishing nets drawn by trawlers, a gauntlet of baited hooks used in longline fishing, plastic waste that can block a bird's digestive tract, and, peculiar to Midway, collision with military planes on the busy runway.

Due mostly to deaths related to the fishing industry, plus mortality caused by cats and rats introduced to breeding colonies, 19 of the planet's 21 albatross species are threatened with extinction. Dwindling ocean resources due to overharvesting by humans, coupled with changing sea current patterns caused by climate change, are expected to negatively impact albatrosses, as well as other seabirds, in the future.

This mostly brown Black-footed Albatross is fairly common in offshore waters of the Pacific Coast of North America.

LAYSAN ALBATROSS
Phoebastria immutabilis

This smallish (32 inches from bill to tail), slender-winged, pink-billed albatross breeds on assorted Pacific islands, including Wake and Midway Islands and the northwestern Hawaiian Islands. It occurs widely across the northern Pacific from the Bering Sea south to the waters off Baja, mostly beyond the continental shelf. In summer, large numbers occur in Monterey Bay and in the Bering Sea. Adult and juvenile plumage patterns are similar to those of many dark-backed gulls, with white head; dark brown back, upperwings, and tail; white underparts; and a white rump. A large pink bill is obvious at all ages after fledging.

BLACK-FOOTED ALBATROSS
Phoebastria nigripes

This fairly common West Coast species is all chocolate brown, except for a white upper tail and diffused white feathering at the base of a dark bill. It breeds on the Hawaiian Islands, Wake Island, and several islands off southern Japan and southern Baja California. For most of the year, it ranges across the northern Pacific, and is often found in the company of large gulls around fishing boats. Black-footed prefers warmer, inshore waters than Laysan, so it is the albatross most likely seen from land.

SHORT-TAILED ALBATROSS
Phoebastria albatrus

This large, lumbering, all-dark, bulbous-billed albatross breeds on Japan's Tori-shima Island, from which it ranges across the northern Pacific. While extremely rare, the population is responding to conservation measures, and sightings of this pink-billed giant in northern Pacific waters are increasing. Immatures and subadults have white about the face, but the bird's heavy pink bill easily distinguishes it from the smaller, less robust, all-dark but dark-billed Black-footed Albatross.

Hydrobatidae and Oceanitidae: Northern and Austral Storm-Petrels

While these birds cannot walk on water, some can dance on it. The storm-petrels are the smallest pelagic birds and use their crooked wings and webbed feet to skip, dance, patter, or glide across the ocean surface in search of zooplankton and crustaceans. Found throughout the world's oceans, they sometimes rest on the water in dense rafts, but more typically flutter restlessly just above the surface. These small (sparrow to robin-sized) tubenoses spend most of their

Storm-Petrels (a.k.a. sea swallows) are divided into northern and southern families, but ignoring hemispheric boundaries these tiny pelagic birds wander the world's oceans in search of small oceanic organisms that they pluck off the water's surface. Top, left to right: Wilson's, Band-rumped, and Leach's Storm-Petrels. Bottom: a feeding flock of Wilson's Storm-Petrels.

lives at sea, coming ashore only to breed in burrows or natural crevices on protected islands, where their single egg is sheltered from marauding gulls and mammalian predators. Storm-petrel colonies are often large, and pairs show a high degree of fidelity to their natal birthplace and to each other.

Most of the members of this family are overall sooty to blackish brown, with some having a white rump. Divided into two families (Northern and Austral), they are lumped here as a matter of convenience, insofar as several species ignore the distinction of hemispheres.

The name "petrel" is an allusion to Saint Peter and his ability to walk across the Lake of Gennesaret (Matthew 14:30). Sailors regarded "Mother Carey's Chickens," as the birds were known, as birds of ill omen, with their appearance foretelling storms—a myth perhaps linked to the birds' penchant for taking shelter on the lee side of ships during storms.

Sometimes visible from shore, but more often foraging far from land, some species of "sea swallows" face extinction as the result of cats and rats introduced by humans onto breeding isles. One species, the Guadalupe Storm-Petrel, was once abundant on Guadalupe Island near Baja, California, but was driven to extinction in the early 1900s, presumably by feral cat and rat predation. It was last recorded in 1912. While the taxonomy of storm-petrels remains in a state of flux, there are approximately 25 northern and austral storm-petrels worldwide, of which 8 regularly occur in North American waters.

WILSON'S STORM-PETREL
Oceanites oceanicus

This small, brown, white-rumped storm-petrel single-handedly mocks efforts to segregate the storm-petrels by hemispheres. It breeds in Antarctic waters and around Cape Horn, and ranges north mostly through North Atlantic waters, where it is a fairly common to abundant visitor off the Atlantic Seaboard from Florida to Canada from May

to October. One of the most abundant birds in the world, it is famous for its foot-pattering feeding behavior: it slaps the water with its feet as it hovers, perhaps to draw prey to the surface. Despite its Southern Hemisphere designation, Wilson's Storm-Petrel is by far the most common North Atlantic storm-petrel, often gathering in large numbers, and frequently seen from shore. In flight, the bird's feet project beyond the tail.

WHITE-FACED STORM-PETREL
Pelagodroma marina

This distinctive, somewhat solitary, medium-sized storm-petrel breeds widely on islands in assorted southern oceans, as well as Cape Verde and the Canary Islands in the North Atlantic. Foraging at sea, it reaches the nearshore waters of the eastern United States and southern Canada from August through September, where it occurs in small numbers. Overall grayish brown with a whitish face, dark cap, and eye patch, it is easily detected, despite its cryptic plumage, by its low, sailing flight that recalls a stone skipped on water.

FORK-TAILED STORM-PETREL
Hydrobates furcatus

A distinctively fork-tailed, medium-sized Pacific storm-petrel, Fork-tailed is our only gray storm-petrel, breeding along the northern Pacific coasts from northern California to Japan. It regularly occurs in large numbers and is often the only storm-petrel found in cold waters far from shore.

LEACH'S STORM-PETREL
Hydrobates leucorhous

Widespread and mostly solitary, this medium-large, pointy-winged, fork-tailed storm-petrel is mostly brown with a white (often segmented) rump and is distinguished by its bounding flight. It breeds locally on islands in both the Atlantic and Pacific, from the Aleutians to Baja in the Pacific and from Newfoundland and Labrador to Maine in the North Atlantic. From May to October,

Ashy (top) and Fork-tailed (bottom) Storm-Petrels are fairly common in Pacific offshore waters, while White-faced Storm-Petrel (center) is an annual vagrant in mid-Atlantic pelagic waters.

Leach's is fairly common close to its breeding colonies in waters over the continental shelves. In winter, northern breeders retreat to equatorial and tropical waters.

ASHY STORM-PETREL
Hydrobates homochroa

Medium sized and fork tailed, this all–dark brown to ashy gray storm-petrel is virtually endemic to California coastal waters, breeding mostly on the Channel and Farallon Islands from April to November. After breeding, it disperses to adjacent waters south to Baja, staying well offshore.

BAND-RUMPED STORM-PETREL
Hydrobates castro

A large, dark, mostly Atlantic storm-petrel that breeds in the warmer portions of the Atlantic and Pacific Oceans. In the western Atlantic, it occurs in summer north to Massachusetts and south to the Gulf of Mexico. Plumage is mostly blackish with a white rump patch that curls somewhat onto the undertail. Also breeding on the Galapagos and (possibly) Hawaiian Islands, the bird is casual in the Sea of Cortez.

BLACK STORM-PETREL
Hydrobates melania

A large, dark storm-petrel with long wings and forked tail that breeds on islands off southern California and Baja, including the Sea of Cortez. Preferring warm waters, dispersing south to Peru and north to Monterey, it remains common to fairly common over offshore and inshore waters of California from August to October.

LEAST STORM-PETREL
Hydrobates microsoma

This small, dark, wedge-tailed storm-petrel is geographically restricted to islands and warm water off Baja, California, as well as the Sea of Cortez. Birds range north to central California from August to October, where they are rare, and retreat south to the waters off Mexico's west coast in winter.

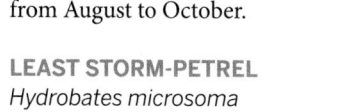

Procellaridae: Shearwaters, Petrels, and Fulmars

Shearwaters are found throughout the world's oceans, often in great numbers. It was evidently the vast numbers of Sooty Shearwaters that unexplainedly crashed into houses and other structures in Bolinas, California, from northern Monterey Bay after ingesting dangerous toxins in 1961 that inspired Alfred Hitchcock's thriller movie *The Birds*. The greatest aggregation of living things Pete ever witnessed involved a feeding flock of 1.5 million Short-tailed Shearwaters in the North Pacific, drawn to a mass of small fish

Shearwaters are tube-nosed seabirds that fly just above oceanic waters on stiff wings. Audubon's (right) is a widespread shearwater of tropical seas, while Black-vented (left) occurs in near-shore waters of Baja and California. Northern Fulmar (center) is a seabird of colder northern Atlantic and Pacific waters and is typically found well offshore, where it often follows fishing vessels.

driven and herded by lunge-feeding hump-backed whales. This mesmerizing tapestry of life was punctuated by intervals of more than 300 Black-footed and Laysan Albatrosses.

Celebrated for their low, gliding flight, which causes banking birds to "shear" the water with their acutely tapered wingtips, shearwaters may also engage in more bounding flights in strong crosswinds. Ranging in size from the 12-inch Audubon's Shearwater to the 19-inch Pink-footed Shearwater, most are patterned like gulls—gray or brown above and white below—but some species have all or mostly dark bodies. Their feathers are tightly packed and waterproof, with an underlying layer of dense down.

Most of the planet's approximately 70 shearwater species breed on islands or headlands in southern waters, but their home is the sea, with some species commuting nearly 8,000 miles on routes that circumscribe the shores of the Atlantic and Pacific Oceans. Seventeen species occur in North American waters, typically beyond sight of land, seeking out fish and squid-rich (generally colder) waters.

After epic months-long journeys, adults return to small but crowded breeding colonies, where they become mostly cave dwelling and nocturnal. They lay a single egg in an excavated burrow or rock crevice as protection from marauding gulls, and forage at night to feed their single chick. All shearwaters have a refined sense of smell that aids them in finding food, and perhaps locating their burrows in the dark. If disturbed, shearwaters can direct a smelly stream of gastric juices from their mouths at offenders.

While sometimes seen in small groups, shearwaters concentrate in vast numbers in areas of food abundance, and multiple species may be present in these concentrations that often occur around feeding whales and commercial fish-processing ships. While most food is plucked from or near the surface, some species can dive to depths exceeding 200 feet.

NORTHERN FULMAR *Fulmarus glacialis*

This stocky, gull-like shearwater has blunter wings and a stouter bill than most other shearwaters. As the name suggests, it is a bird of the Northern Hemisphere, breeding on islands off the coast of Alaska and in the Canadian Arctic south to Newfoundland and Labrador. Wintering from the North Pacific south to Baja, and in the Atlantic from Newfoundland and Labrador to South Carolina, Northern Fulmar is closely related to Southern Fulmar, which is limited to southern waters. With a plumage that ranges from white to light and dark gray, this very abundant species has been increasing in numbers for the last 50 years or more.

BLACK-CAPPED PETREL
Pterodroma hasitata

A large, boldly patterned seabird that has a dark-capped white head and broad white band on the upper tail. This is the *Pterodroma* most likely to be seen off the Atlantic Coast. It breeds on Hispaniola (Haiti and Dominican Republic) and wanders at sea in the Caribbean and western Atlantic regularly to North Carolina, and irregularly farther north. Its high, arcing flight style is distinctive.

HERALD PETREL *Pterodroma heraldica*

This medium-sized, slender-winged gadfly petrel breeds on islands in the South Atlantic and occurs mostly in Gulf Stream waters off the Carolinas. Found in both light and dark plumage, it often resembles a jaeger, from which it can be distinguished by its dynamic, bounding flight, a *Pterodroma* signature trait.

MURPHY'S PETREL *Pterodroma ultima*

Fast flying and streamlined, this overall grayish gadfly petrel shows a faint, dark *M* pattern on its upperparts. Nesting on a handful of South Pacific Islands, it was not described to science until 1949, and not until the 1980s was it learned that it may be a regular visitor far off the west coast of North America.

Sooty Shearwater (left) is common off both coasts, while Short-tailed (center) occurs in vast numbers in the North Pacific in summer. Both breed in the Southern Hemisphere but spend much of the year in Northern Hemisphere waters. Black-capped Petrel (right) breeds in the Caribbean and follows warm Gulf Stream waters north to Long Island. Unlike Sooty and Short-tailed, Black-capped is usually solitary or in small groups.

FEA'S PETREL *Pterodroma feae*

Medium sized and slender winged, this gadfly petrel breeds on the Cape Verde Islands and Madeira and occasionally wanders west across the Atlantic to the Gulf Stream waters off the Carolinas. Similar to the more commonly seen Black-capped Petrel, it is separated by a gray nape, pale gray tail, and dark underwings.

MOTTLED PETREL
Pterodroma inexpectata

This compact and distinctly marked gadfly petrel breeds in southern New Zealand but is fairly common in the cold waters of the North Pacific, where it is the only *Pterodroma* likely to be encountered. Its dark belly makes it appear oiled, and a strong *M* pattern on the wings is distinctive.

BERMUDA PETREL *Pterodroma cahow*

Very rare, this medium-sized gadfly petrel breeds in sandy burrows and reconstructed artificial burrows on the Castle Harbour Islands, Bermuda, and it is presumed to wander over subtropical waters of the eastern Atlantic, but a few birds are regularly recorded off the Carolinas. The world population is about 300 birds (All About Birds).

CORY'S SHEARWATER
Calonectris diomedea

This common, large, broad-winged, long-billed shearwater breeds on barren islands in the Mediterranean and eastern North Atlantic and wanders widely across the North Atlantic. It generally prefers warm waters. The pale brown upperparts and heavy yellow bill easily separate it from Great Shearwater, with which it often forages.

PINK-FOOTED SHEARWATER
Ardenna creatopus

Fairly common and large, this stocky, broad-winged shearwater breeds on islands off Chile and, while preferring warm waters, wanders north along the eastern Pacific to the south coast of Alaska. Gray-brown upperparts give way to smudgy flanks. It has mottled underwings and dusky head in flight. The dark-tipped pink bill is long and slender, and the legs are pink.

FLESH-FOOTED SHEARWATER
Ardenna carneipes

This large, fully dark Pacific shearwater has a dark-tipped pink bill and pink legs. It breeds in the southern Indian and southwest Pacific Oceans. It ranges east across the Pacific to

waters off North America in late summer to fall, where it is rare in warm ocean waters from northern Baja to the south coast of Alaska.

GREAT SHEARWATER *Ardenna gravis*

A large bird with grayish upperparts, black cap, and slender black bill, Great Shearwater breeds on islands in the South Atlantic. It ranges north primarily over warm waters above the continental shelf along the western Atlantic Coast from Florida to Newfoundland and Labrador and to Greenland. It is common to very common in late spring to fall along the East Coast of North America, with many adults in heavy wing molt at this time.

BULLER'S SHEARWATER
Ardenna bulleri

This large, strikingly patterned Pacific shearwater breeds on islands off New Zealand and ranges across the Pacific to the West Coast of North America in late summer. Its gray and black-and-silver upperwing pattern is unlike that of any other West Coast shearwater.

SOOTY SHEARWATER *Ardenna grisea*

This common to locally abundant medium-large, dark brown shearwater with silvery underwings and a long, slender dark bill breeds on islands in the South Atlantic and South Pacific and ranges across northern oceans off both North American coasts from late spring to autumn, often in very large numbers. In 1986, Kevin saw over a million Sootys in one hour at Grays Harbor, Washington, in August, but the huge numbers have declined somewhat since then.

SHORT-TAILED SHEARWATER
Ardenna tenuirostris

Short-tailed is a common to abundant medium-large, all-brown Pacific shearwater that breeds off southern Australia and ranges north across the northern Pacific in summer, where it may be found in great abundance in cold northern waters of the Bering Sea (May to October). Occasionally seen in summer off California, with sightings increasing in late fall as birds return south to breed, it is very similar to Sooty Shearwater but slightly smaller with a shorter bill, steeper forehead, and duskier underwings.

MANX SHEARWATER *Puffinus puffinus*

This small black-and-white Atlantic shearwater breeds on islands in the northeast Atlantic (mainly the British Isles) from spring through summer (also from Newfoundland and Labrador to Maine), with a few birds wintering off the Atlantic Coast of North America. It is casual on the Pacific Coast.

Cory's Shearwater (left) breeds on islands in the Mediterranean and the eastern Atlantic and regularly occurs in Atlantic Seaboard waters. Great Shearwater (center) breeds in South Atlantic waters but forages off the Atlantic Coast in large numbers. Manx Shearwater (right) is a small shearwater that nests on offshore islands in the cold waters of the northern Atlantic region.

BLACK-VENTED SHEARWATER
Puffinus opisthomelas

This small, dull brown-and-white Manx-like shearwater breeds on islands off Baja California and ranges north along the coast to northern California into autumn. Black-vented also occurs in the Sea of Cortez. Dark undertail coverts help distinguish it from Manx. Large numbers of this species are often seen from shore in fall.

AUDUBON'S SHEARWATER
Puffinus lherminieri

Our smallest North American shearwater with dark brown upperparts has relatively short wings and a longish tail and prefers tropical and subtropical waters. It breeds on a number of Caribbean islands and ranges north over warm Gulf Stream waters off the East Coast from Florida to southern New England from spring through fall. It is similar to Manx but has paler upperparts and a whitish undertail (dark on Audubon's).

Ciconiidae: Storks

This well-known and widely distributed bird group traces its lines back to the late Eocene, with the earliest fossil evidence found in France. North America's sole representative, the Wood Stork, harks back to the Pleistocene era, when much of North America was under ice and mammoths roamed the landscape. Therefore, "Old Flint Head," as the bird is called in the South, looks old because it is. It is only one of 19 stork species distributed across the planet, including one of the world's largest flying birds, the five-foot Marabou Stork of Africa, and the European White Stork, which, according to German folklore, was the bearer of human newborns.

All storks are large to medium-sized, long-legged and long-necked birds with heavier bodies and bills than the herons. Several species have bare skin on the head

Ungainly as they might be, in the air these long-legged wading birds show a mastery that harks to their close relatives, the vultures.

Nesting in colonies, Wood Stork's breeding success is tied to drought and water levels. The two nests on the left attest to a successful breeding season. Immature Wood Stork (right) has a yellowish bill and lacks the gray head scaling of adults. Wood Stork numbers have increased dramatically in the last 25 years, due in part to proper water management policies.

and neck, which, in the case of Wood Stork, is a refinement that allows birds to forage in turbid waters. While always heavy and broad based, the bills of different stork species are specialized to accommodate different feeding habits. Most storks are resident, but the White and Black Storks of Europe and central Asia are highly migratory, flying in massed flocks numbering at times in the tens of thousands as they make their way south into Africa and southern Asia. Unlike most other birds, storks lack a syrinx (bird voice box) and communicate by clattering their bills.

WOOD STORK *Mycteria americana*

Our sole stork species has seen its population climb in recent years owing to conservation efforts and regulated water levels in its feeding sites. It is currently listed as federally threatened, but the number of nests in Florida and Georgia have increased greatly over the last 30 years. Limited and localized in its North American distribution to the southeastern United States (specifically east Texas to Florida and north to South Carolina), some birds disperse northward after breeding.

Wood Stork also resides in Central and

Panhandling is right out of the Wood Stork playbook. This angler better mind his bait or lose it to North America's only native stork species.

South America and the Caribbean. Nicknamed "Old Flint Head" because of the bare bony plate found on the noggin of adults, this stately, white-bodied, black-winged bird is a fixture in mangroves, wet grasslands, shallow standing (often muddy) water, and roadside sloughs. Feeding mostly on small fish, this tactile feeder also dines on crayfish, amphibians, small snakes, and even hatchling alligators. It appears to favor waters that are drawn down by drought and where food is

concentrated. Wood Storks also concentrate around anglers and visit backyards, where they passively beg for handouts. They breed in large colonies and may sometimes forage in concert with other storks. Powerful fliers and soaring birds, they have a widespread pattern of vagrancy, occasionally reaching Canada.

Fregatidae: Frigatebirds

The five members of this small family are mostly limited to the planet's tropical and subtropical regions. Since they range widely across coastal pelagic waters outside the breeding season, often far from land, it is perhaps inaccurate to call frigatebirds marine birds as they rarely land on the water. They spend much of their time aloft, where they soar effortlessly for long periods, including searching for food in tropical waters. With their streamlined bodies, six- to seven-foot wingspan, and extremely light wing load, frigatebirds are supremely specialized for a life aloft, where their soaring and gliding prowess makes light of distances. They are the only seabird whose males appear quite different from females.

Contributing to frigatebirds' refinements are their fused pectoral girdle (for structural strength), unusually large pectoral (flight) muscles, and extremely porous bones, whose combined weight constitutes less than 5 percent of their total body weight. The bird's forked tail contributes to this incomparable aerialist's maneuverability, an attribute that is the foundation of the family's name.

Since the days of ships under sail, frigates have been warships that sacrifice armor and armament for speed and mobility. Frigatebirds' range, maneuverability, and long hook-tipped bills make them likewise near-invincible buccaneers, able to pirate prey from other seabirds, with boobies and Royal Terns their favorite targets. Frigatebirds are also adept at plucking prey directly from the ocean's surface, particularly flying fish and squid. Their piratical reputation notwithstanding, they obtain most of their food this way. Frigatebirds, however, require a dependable flow of air for extended flight, which may explain the family's equatorial distribution. The air above tropical waters is stirred by the same trade winds and thermal development that early sailors depended upon to navigate the seas.

Four of the five species are large (approximately 40 inches in length), with wings extending to 90 inches. All are mostly black with iridescent greenish or purple highlights. Juveniles have white heads and females white breasts. While equipped with webbed feet, like other members of the order Pelecani-

When not soaring, which frigatebirds do for hours on end, they usually perch on slender branches owing to the small size of their tiny feet. Left to right, all Magnificent Frigatebirds: adult male, juveniles, adult female.

Two male frigatebirds show off their bright red inflated throat pouches while trying to impress the ladies at the breeding colony in Florida. An immature Red-footed Booby is in the lower right corner.

Among the ultimate flying machines of the bird world, frigatebirds often soar for long periods. On the left are adult male (upper) and female Magnificent Frigatebirds; on the right are two white-headed immatures.

formes, frigatebirds rarely swim, and when settled on the ocean they quickly become waterlogged. When not flying, frigatebirds perch on land, ship rigging, bridges, tree branches, or channel markers. Even in modest winds, they need only open their wings to be drawn aloft.

When breeding, for the most part on remote islands and isolated coasts, often in mixed breeding colonies with other pelagic species, frigatebirds secure their stick nests in bushes or trees, particularly mangroves, as well as on the ground. The single chicks require constant guarding from marauding by other frigatebirds. Frigatebirds do not breed every year, as the female raises the chick for about a year. Because of their single-chick strategy and protracted development to adulthood, frigatebirds have very low productivity, a detriment mitigated somewhat by the bird's longevity, with adults sometimes living 25 years.

MAGNIFICENT FRIGATEBIRD
Fregata magnificens

North America's sole representative of the family is found mostly in warm southern waters and is a year-round resident of southern Florida, where it is a common fixture perched on elevated man-made structures near water. The birds also breed on islands off Baja south to South America and on the Marquesas Keys, Dry Tortugas, and Lesser Antilles in the Caribbean Basin. After breeding, birds wander at sea north to central California, the Gulf Coast, and the Carolinas. Owing to the birds' habit of flying solo above the range of the unaided eye, it is likely that many more frigatebirds penetrate northern waters than are reported. Vagrants occur as far north as Canada.

Sulidae: Boobies and Gannets

This worldwide pelagic family of large, plunge-diving, fish-eating birds is composed of ten species. Boobies are mostly limited to tropical and subtropical waters, whereas gannets breed in the earth's temperate regions. Highly social and breeding in colonies on cliff faces and remote islands, boobies may share breeding locations with frigatebirds and cormorants, while some gannet colonies number in the tens of thousands. Sulid courtship is elaborate, involving wing waving, bill elevating, head bowing, stick passing, and, in several species, the presentation of their colorful webbed feet. Most species lay 1 to 3 eggs in scrapes on the ground. Lacking brood patches, parents warm hatchlings by placing them on the tops of their feet. Rarely does more than one hatchling survive.

Tireless fliers, sulids patrol fish-bearing waters on long pointed wings set well back, using binocular vision to spot and gauge the depth of prey. When they sight prey, they stall, turn, and fold their wings like hands in

Nesting on cliffs in eastern Canada, Northern Gannet is the most common sulid in Atlantic and Gulf waters, where many spend the winter. These very large seabirds with long, pointed wings often fly in tandem during migration. From top: juvenile (first year), subadult, adult.

prayer, plunging 3 to 100 feet to the surface. Northern Gannets reach speeds in excess of 55 miles per hour. They sometimes dive to depths of 30 feet and deeper if they deploy

All four booby species found in North America appear here in breeding condition with bright facial skin and colorful feet. Clockwise from upper left: Masked Booby, Brown Booby, Blue-footed Booby, Red-footed Booby in dark plumage.

their wings for an assist. To accommodate the jarring impact, sulids' neck muscles are particularly strong, and flight muscles are reduced, giving birds a slender, laterally compressed profile. The bases of the pointed bills are also spongy to absorb shock, and the nostrils open into the mouth so that water is not forced into them when they dive. On shallow-angled dives, boobies often chase prey underwater, using their wings and feet for propulsion.

Sulids are occasionally persecuted for their consumption of commercially viable fish. In some parts of the world, the nitrogen-rich guano at their nest sites is harvested for fertilizer.

NORTHERN GANNET *Morus bassanus*

By far the best-known sulid to most East and Gulf Coast birders, this large, common Atlantic seabird breeds in massed colonies on rocky coastal cliffs in the Gulf of St. Lawrence and on islands off Quebec, Newfoundland and Labrador, and northern Europe. Outside the breeding season, it wanders at sea over the continental shelf from Newfoundland and Labrador to Florida, frequently close to shore. In migration, birds travel in strings of a few to more than 20 birds, whose rising and falling flight recalls the tandem cars on a roller coaster. Kevin recently saw a flock of over 6,000 Northern Gannets feeding near Cape May, New Jersey, in late February. Adults are mostly white with black wingtips and a peach blush to the head. Immatures and subadults are mostly grayish brown above with a white base to the tail, while first-year birds are mostly brown.

MASKED BOOBY *Sula dactylatra*

This warm-water species resembles a small Northern Gannet, with a white head and body and black wingtips, but differs with a completely black trailing edge to the wing. A

Note the long, narrow wings; wedge-shaped tail; and long, straight powerful bill on these adult boobies. Clockwise from upper left: Masked Booby, Brown Booby, Blue-footed Booby, Red-footed Booby in white-morph plumage.

wedge-shaped yellowish bill is bordered by the bird's namesake dark face mask. While gannets commonly occur within sight of land, Masked Booby often forages well off-shore.

In North America, Masked Boobies breed on islands in the Atlantic–Caribbean region and off the Yucatán Peninsula. They are occasionally seen along the Gulf Coast and in the Atlantic north to the Carolinas. In the Pacific, Masked Boobies breed from south-western Baja California south to Peru. They are casual off California north to the central coast. Nazca Booby, formerly a subspecies of Masked, breeds in Mexico and occasionally strays to the California coast. It differs by having an orange versus yellowish bill.

BLUE-FOOTED BOOBY *Sula nebouxii*

Large and lanky, this brownish-backed sulid with a gray bill and bright blue feet breeds on islands in the Gulf of California and along the coast of South America from Colombia to Peru, and in the Galapagos in large num-bers. It ranges across the eastern Pacific and is a casual visitor to coastal California. It sometimes strays to interior lakes and res-ervoirs as well as the Salton Sea. Young birds have brownish heads and necks and white bellies and lack blue feet.

BROWN BOOBY *Sula leucogaster*

This small, brown-backed, dark-bibbed sulid with relatively short wings and a long tail breeds on islands in the Caribbean and occasionally the Florida Keys. In the Pacific, it occurs on islands from the Sea of Cortez to Honduras and Colombia. Unlike most other sulids, Brown Booby builds stick nests. Some birds wander annually north to New England and northern California. When not swim-ming or flying, birds often perch on chan-

nel markers, lighthouses, and buoys. Brown Booby is the booby most often found on inland lakes, usually after big storms.

RED-FOOTED BOOBY *Sula sula*

Our smallest booby breeds on islands in the Atlantic–Caribbean region and in the Pacific off Mexico, Costa Rica, and Ecuador. In the United States, it wanders casually to southern California and the Sea of Cortez, and in the Atlantic, it is accidental north to South Carolina. Polymorphic, adults may be mostly white with black wingtips like gannets, or overall brownish with a white tail. In all plumages, note distinctive red feet, which are dull red in young birds. Red-footed Boobies either build stick nests or lay eggs in scrapes on the ground.

Phalacrocoracidae: Cormorants

This large family of highly aquatic fish-eating birds of mostly marine environments and large inland seas has a worldwide distribution, including Arctic and Antarctic regions. Taxonomy is somewhat sketchy, but approximately 40 species relating to a single genus, *Phalacrocorax*, are recognized, though some authorities place the flightless cormorant of the Galapagos in a separate genus. In North America, there are six cormorant species, with three restricted to the Pacific Coast.

Cormorants are long-necked, heavy-bodied birds with long, laterally flattened, hook-tipped, flesh-tearing bills. Long stiff tails aid in balance and locomotion on land and navigation in the water. When perched, necks are usually retracted in an S-shaped configuration, giving birds a hunched appearance.

Most (including all North American species) have dense, dark plumage with an iridescent blue or green sheen on the upperwings. Many also have a featherless gular pouch and facial skin that ranges in color according to species.

While especially designed for swimming and diving, cormorants are strong fliers, despite their relatively short wings. They are capable of migrating great distances and soaring in thermals. Migrating birds typically form V-shaped configurations that are less orderly than those of geese, and foraging birds often fly low over the water in lines. Takeoffs from land and water are effortful, involving much foot pattering and labored

Cormorants are large, fish-eating birds that are strong fliers, expert swimmers, and even soar at high altitudes. Their feathers are not waterproof, so they must perch and extend their wings out to dry after swimming. Clockwise from upper left: Double-crested Cormorant, Double-crested drying its wings, immature Great Cormorant, Pelagic Cormorant in flight, breeding Pelagic Cormorant, breeding Neotropic Cormorant.

Three common North American cormorants and one uncommon one (Red-faced) with a very restricted range. From left, in breeding condition: Double-crested, Neotropic, Red-faced, Brandt's.

Cormorants sometimes catch very large fish for their meals, which they eat whole, like this Great Cormorant (left). A Pelagic Cormorant (right) is taking flight using a fast, running start on the water to get airborne.

flapping. While awkward on land, some species are capable of perching on limbs and even utility lines. In the water, they swim and maneuver well enough to pursue and capture small to large fish, which they swallow whole. Out of the water, cormorants are frequently seen with wings open, benediction-wide, to dry sodden feathers that help cormorants remain underwater when submerged.

Very social, cormorants breed in large colonies, placing their stick-and-guano nests on cliff faces, low brush, or dead (or soon to be dead) trees. On inland bodies of water, islands are the substrate of choice, and often shared with herons and egrets.

Persecuted at times for their focus on fish, cormorants consume large quantities of small fish whose commercial value is low, including herring and eels. Cormorant guano is harvested in some places for fertilizer.

BRANDT'S CORMORANT
Phalacrocorax penicillatus

This large West Coast cormorant is limited to rocky coasts and occurs from southern Alaska to Baja. Very social, it sometimes fishes cooperatively. It differs from the smaller, less social, and thinner-necked Pelagic Cormorant by its larger size and the buffy patch at the base of the bill (which is dark on Pelagic).

NEOTROPIC CORMORANT
Phalacrocorax brasilianus

While geographically restricted in the United States, this small, long-tailed resident of saltwater bays and freshwater lakes and ponds is widespread from Mexico to South America, as well as in the Caribbean. In North America, it occurs mostly in the eastern half of Texas and the Panhandle, with small num-

bers breeding in Florida. This species has a widespread pattern of vagrancy and is rapidly expanding its range. It often associates with the larger Double-crested Cormorant.

DOUBLE-CRESTED CORMORANT
Phalacrocorax auritus

Our most widespread cormorant breeds widely across much of the United States and coastal Alaska and much of southern Canada. While common in coastal marine environments through much of its range, it is the cormorant most likely to be seen on inland bodies of water (except for Texas, where Neotropic Cormorant is common inland). The Double-crested has an all-dark body and orange face, and the namesake crests are visible only in breeding plumage. The immature is mostly brown with a paler breast.

GREAT CORMORANT
Phalacrocorax carbo

This large, bulky, cosmopolitan cormorant breeds in cold water habitats from Newfoundland and Labrador to Maine and winters coastally from Maine south to the Carolinas, with some birds occurring on inland lakes. It also occurs globally on many continents. This heavy-billed bird has a white throat, which is obvious in breeding season. Young are brownish with brown upper breasts and white bellies.

RED-FACED CORMORANT
Phalacrocorax urile

This marine cormorant is resident from Siberia through the Pribilof Islands to the Gulf of Alaska. It differs from the more slender and dark-faced Pelagic Cormorant by its larger size, bright red face (breeding), and yellowish bill.

PELAGIC CORMORANT
Phalacrocorax pelagicus

A slender, snaky-necked cormorant of rocky northern Pacific coasts, Pelagic breeds from northern Japan to the Aleutians, and south to southern California. It winters in much the same coastal waters. Rarely far from shore, it prefers to feed in sheltered coastal waters, often alone. Breeding birds may form small colonies, but pairs may also select isolated ledges or caves.

Anhingidae: Darters

Limited to only three species but found throughout most tropical and subtropical regions of the world, these snaky-necked, spearfishing water birds spend more time in the water than most birds, except possibly the grebes. Able to submerge without a ripple, and swimming with only their heads and necks above the surface, these submarines of the bird world absorb water into their body feathers like diving submarines take water into their ballast tanks. Sometimes swimming through vegetated freshwater habitat less than two feet deep, the birds combine stealth and concealment to secure their mostly fish prey.

Moving forward on webbed feet synchronized like oars, a submerged bird stalks or waits for fish to approach within range of its harpoonlike bill. Neck muscles cocked and ready, the bird releases its harpoon with a powerful forward thrust, impaling its prey. Surfacing, it then tosses the prey into the air and catches it as it falls, swallowing it

Breeding male Anhinga has bold, iridescent colors around its eyes.

Anhinga's feathers are not waterproof, so they must dry their wings after swimming by holding them open while perched. They are strong fliers and often soar high in the sky, sometimes joining kettles of vultures and raptors. Anhingas use their daggerlike bills to spear fish, which they take to the shore to eat.

headfirst. While it somewhat resembles a slender cormorant, the spearfishing technique of a darter is more reminiscent of herons, whose bills are similarly pointed.

Making use of their stout, claw-tipped webbed feet, successful darters earn the right to clamber onto waterside branches, where they spread their wings with heads drawn back to dry and warm up. The downside of water-soaked plumage is heat loss, which the tropical and subtropical sun soon restores. Because of their need for drying perches, darters prefer aquatic habitats with forested edges where they spend the non-hunting hours, often in the company of other darters. Swamplands and sluggish rivers cutting through forests are ideal habitats.

While less social than cormorants, darters roost and breed in the company of other waterbird species, most notably herons and egrets. Their perch-borne nests are ramshackle affairs constructed of sticks and leaves. Ungraceful out of water, darters are excellent fliers, alternately flapping and gliding with fanlike tail spread and neck outstretched.

While most darters are resident, some inland and northern breeders are migratory. In March and April, we have seen flocks in excess of 200 birds soaring and wheeling at extreme altitudes over the Rio Grande in Texas. Unlike migrating hawks, Anhingas soaring in thermals all turn in the same synchronized direction.

ANHINGA *Anhinga anhinga*

Our only darter of the New World occurs from near-coastal Carolinas south and west through near-coastal Texas into Mexico, and south to South America. It is resident throughout Florida, Hispaniola, and some Bahamian islands.

Shunning estuarine habitats, it much prefers freshwater swamps and sluggish streams. Its preference for freshwater habitats notwithstanding, Anhinga also occurs in brackish lagoons with mangroves. In winter,

Anhingas build large stick nests in bushes and trees and on top of broken palms, like the one shown here. While it seems as if they are showing sensitivity to each other, they are primitive waterbirds that squabble with each other every time they change nest duties. (Male is on left; female right.)

northern and many inland breeders move south into Mexico. Demonstrating a widespread pattern of vagrancy, individuals have been reported as far north as Ontario and as far west as California.

Slimmer and longer tailed than cormorants, with a pointy (not hooked) bill, male Anhingas have all-black bodies and silvery wings. Females and juveniles appear like males but have buffy brown necks. Anhinga is often referred to as the "snake bird" because it swims with only its snakelike neck and head above the water.

Pelecanidae: Pelicans

These large, fish-eating birds rank among the heaviest of the flying birds. Found on every continent except Antarctica, all seven or eight species are in a single genus, and for convenience, the clan can be grouped into white pelicans and Brown Pelican.

Almost grotesquely proportioned with their elastic, inflatable throat pouches, pelicans are truly among our most iconic and readily identifiable birds. Although pelicans are clumsy on land, their short, widely spaced, rearward-set legs and paddlelike feet make them well suited for swimming in all aquatic environments. Once airborne, no small feat for birds that may weigh as much as 20 pounds, pelicans are transformed into accomplished aerialists, able to soar in thermals and tease lift out of wave-driven air. Few can fail to be transfixed by the sight of White Pelican flocks wheeling in the deep blue of a western summer sky, or the sight of Brown Pelicans gliding in tandem across the kelp beds of coastal California.

Highly social and nesting in large colonies, pelicans must breed close to rich, fish-bearing waters. The larger White Pelican breeds on islands in shallow western lakes, rivers, and freshwater marshes, while Brown Pelican is mostly coastal and generally prefers warmer waters. Foraging White Pelicans often exhibit a measure of teamwork

and coordinated effort as they drive fish into the shallows by gathering in U-shaped formations or converging interception lines. Brown Pelicans are plunge divers, diving up to 60 feet to engulf swimming fish. In neither case do the birds carry fish in their bills. The pouches of pelicans serve as dip nets,

White (top) and Brown (bottom) Pelicans in flight, and both in the middle. Note White Pelican's larger size and the differences in plumage and bare parts between these two species.

not holding tanks. Prey secured, the birds squeeze the water out of their bills, raise their bills skyward, and swallow the fish whole. The bills of pelicans also help cool the birds through gular fluttering.

AMERICAN WHITE PELICAN
Pelecanus erythrorhynchos

Weighing in at 10 to 19 pounds, this grand yellow-billed white bird with black trailing wing feathers breeds on islands in lakes of the western interior. White Pelicans nest in colonies, with the largest recorded being in Chase Lake National Wildlife Refuge in North Dakota (more than 35,000 birds in 2006). They winter along the Pacific Coast from central California and southern Arizona south to Central America as well as all the Gulf Coast states. White Pelicans surround and herd their fish prey into shallow-water corners, where they feast at will.

BROWN PELICAN
Pelecanus occidentalis

Weighing at an average of 8 pounds, the world's smallest pelican is a coastal resident found in the Pacific from central California south to Panama, and along the Atlantic from the Carolinas south along all coasts to South America. They breed in colonies, with stick nests placed on sandy beaches or in elevated mangroves. Each pair feeds its 2 or 3 young a regurgitated fish porridge, offered in open bills that serve as feeding troughs. Typically seen flying single file just offshore or perched on docks, this plunge-diving aerialist is also something of a panhandler, eagerly snapping up the bait of fishermen, whether offered or not.

Adults have gray upperparts and black underparts. Necks of nonbreeding adult birds are white. Bills are gray, becoming orange and yellow when breeding. Young are grayish brown with white bellies.

Attesting to the universal acclaim of pelicans and the distribution of this species, Brown Pelican is the national bird of St.

White Pelicans (top) swim as a group and herd fish into shallow edges of ponds and estuaries, where they scoop up the fish in their large, porous throat pouches. Brown Pelicans (bottom) plunge-dive into coastal waters after spotting fish concentrations from the sky. Both species drain their pouches of water through the porous pouch membrane. White Pelicans often soar (center) in large groups at very high altitudes.

Maarten, Barbados, St. Kitts and Nevis, and the Turks and Caicos, as well as being the state bird of Louisiana. In 1903, President Teddy Roosevelt named Pelican Island in Florida as the nation's first National Wildlife Refuge, a move necessitated by plume hunting.

Ardeidae: Herons, Egrets, and Bitterns

Found worldwide except for polar regions and some Pacific islands, this family of long-legged wading birds is most concentrated in the tropics. While the classification of this group has undergone and continues to undergo revisions, at this writing there are 60 or so recognized species, 12 of which occur in North America. For convenience and with some taxonomic foundation, these are divided into the "day herons," whose ranks include the egrets and most herons; the night-herons; and the bitterns. Nomenclature aside, there are no genetic or taxonomic differences between herons and egrets.

Most are united by their dependence on shallow water suitable for stalking afoot, and prey is captured largely, if not exclusively, on foot. Legs and necks of herons are uncommonly long, with pointed bills serving as harpoons. Feet are fitted with long toes well suited for perching and striding in slippery substrates, although some species forage on dry ground while others clamber through reeds and foliage. Males and females are similar in size and plumage, although some species have dark and light plumages.

Virtually all are social, roosting and breeding in large colonies, but the bitterns and a few herons nest in mostly solitary fashion. Wings are typically broad and rounded, and some species are migratory and capable of traveling great distances. They differ from cranes in flight with necks drawn back, not projecting.

Differing markedly in size, American Bittern (top) and Least Bittern (bottom) are ferocious reed- and grass-dwelling herons that specialize in the slow stalk-and-stab foraging method. Least Bittern (male, left; female, right) is our smallest heron at 13 inches long.

"Day herons" are typically the largest and most aquatic of the group, feeding largely on fish, which they capture with stabbing thrusts of their bills, but some hunt using different techniques. The large 39-inch Great Egret and larger Great Blue Heron (46 inches) are stately stalkers. The smaller Snowy Egret is a more active feeder and guilefully uses its bright yellow feet to attract prey. Reddish Egret is an active, aggressive feeder, charging across tidal flats with much wing flapping and splashing. Green Heron, small and mostly dark, is a bushwhacker, crouching at the water's edge or balanced atop a branch within stabbing distance of submerged prey.

Night-herons, as the name suggests, are partly to mostly nocturnal, and while they feed on fish, these stocky birds vary their diets to include crustaceans, especially crabs and crayfish.

Bitterns, which are more cryptically plumaged, forage mostly in reed beds for a variety of prey, including insects, small birds, mammals, reptiles, and fish. Solitary hunters, bitterns are perhaps best known for their vocalizations.

Several species (most notably the egrets) are celebrated and were once killed for their fine, filamentous breeding plumes that emanate from the head, neck, and back, and confer upon birds a rakish appearance that translates to sexual attractiveness. Taking the hint, well-dressed Victorian ladies incorporated egret plumes into their often outlandish headgear. The resulting slaughter

of birds gave rise to the National Audubon Society, whose direct confrontation with the millinery trade is responsible for the wealth of herons we enjoy today.

As breeding season approaches, many herons' and egrets' bare parts change color and become brighter and more visually arresting.

Stick nests are usually seated in trees or bushes adjacent to or surrounded by water. Many species nest communally with other herons and some non-heron species, most notably cormorants, Wood Storks, and Roseate Spoonbills. Bitterns, which are solitary nesters, weave nests of the marsh reeds among which they hide the nests. Clutch size ranges from 3 to 7 eggs among herons, with 3 the average for larger species. Competition for food among nestlings is acute, with the largest, first-born chick surviving while smaller siblings may not. Rookeries are raucous, odoriferous affairs made frenetic with the comings and goings of adults.

AMERICAN BITTERN
Botaurus lentiginosus

This large, stripe-necked hunter of fish and vertebrates is a master of camouflage, often standing erect with bill pointed skyward, blending into the surrounding reeds. Found in fresh, brackish, and tidal wetlands across most of the United States and Canada, it is celebrated for its loud gulping call. The "bog pumper," as it is sometimes called, is so confident of its cloak of concealment that it will freeze in an erect posture when standing in plain sight, even swaying with the breeze in imitation of the presumed reeds that are not concealing it.

Mostly solitary and nocturnal, American Bitterns withdraw from northern breeding grounds in winter. Many winter in coastal states north to southern British Columbia and New Jersey. Others winter south through Mexico to Panama and the West Indies. Frogs, crayfish, and fish are favorite foods, but they also eat insects and small invertebrates.

Six of North America's stunning and commonly occurring herons and egrets. Coming in different shapes and sizes, these long-legged wading birds fill a variety of niches from deep water to upland edge. Clockwise from upper left: Snowy Egret, Great Blue Heron and nest, breeding Cattle Egret, Green Heron, Black-crowned Night-Heron, Tricolored Heron.

Always inspiring in stature and beauty, these long-legged wading birds were nearly hunted to extinction at the hands of plume hunters in the late 1800s and early 1900s. This slaughter sparked the conservation movement in North America. Clockwise from upper left: Reddish Egret, Snowy Egret, Tricolored Heron, Cattle Egret, Great Egret, Great Blue Heron.

LEAST BITTERN *Ixobrychus exilis*

Our smallest heron is as ferocious a predator as any in this family. Residing mainly in tall aquatic reeds, this pigeon-sized caramel-colored heron clambers through reeds in fresh, brackish, and sometimes tidal marshes. It breeds widely across most of the eastern United States, southern Oregon and southern California, and very locally in a few southwestern states. While a weak flier, it is able to compress its body and slip through narrow vegetative gaps as thin as a rail. Weak fliers or not, northern birds migrate at night in winter to the southern United States and the Caribbean, and as far south as Panama.

GREAT BLUE HERON *Ardea herodias*

Our largest and most widespread heron breeds across most of the United States and southern Canada, and from coastal Alaska south through British Columbia to southern Mexico and the Caribbean. Winter range extends to northern South America. Great Blue is a four-foot giant, towering over other members of the family, and these stately stalkers prefer to hunt alone. Preferring freshwater habitats, the all-white-plumaged subspecies known as "Great White Heron"

haunts the marshes of extreme southern Florida.

Typical birds are mostly slaty blue with white faces, long legs, and strong, stabbing bills. They patrol shallow water for fish, eels, and frogs, but also hunt uplands for mice, voles, snakes, and small birds. Northern birds are migratory, vacating regions locked in winter ice. Great Blue migrates day and night in flocks that may number 50 or more, but Pete and Kevin once saw a flock of more than 1,000 birds migrating along the shoreline of Cape May, New Jersey, after a strong cold front in November. It took ten minutes for all the birds to pass by.

GREAT EGRET *Ardea alba*

This large, yellow-billed all-white heron is one of the planet's most widespread birds, occurring in temperate and tropical regions on all continents except Antarctica. Four subspecies are recognized, but they differ little except for bare-part coloration during courtship. Feeding in shallows of fresh and tidal waters (including mangroves) or on dry, open ground (particular agricultural lands), Great Egret is a stalker, covering ground in long strides with head usually elevated

and neck outstretched. Prey includes fish, frogs, snakes, insects, and small mammals. In North America, it breeds across most of the United States and extreme southern Canada, except for northern New England and the prairie states. Winter range includes southern New Jersey south to Florida and central Texas, and from Oregon and California south to South America.

SNOWY EGRET *Egretta thula*

Medium sized and hyperactive, this all-white heron with black legs and yellow feet occurs widely across the central and southern United States south to South America and is resident on most of the West Indian islands. It is casual inland in the United States and reaches greatest densities in coastal locations, where it frequents tidal marshes, small ponds, and mangroves. Snowies often hunt in small to large groups and employ a unique feeding style in which they run/fly across shallow water and grab small fish as they move. Kevin calls this technique "fly-fishing."

LITTLE BLUE HERON *Egretta caerulea*

Breeding primarily in the southeastern United States north to central Kansas and southern New Jersey, Little Blue is a local resident in near-coastal Mexico and the West Indies. While partial to woodland swamps, it also forages in tidal marshes and freshwater wetlands. A solitary feeder, its slow movements and habit of craning its extended neck with one eye turned down helps distinguish the all-white immature birds from the similarly sized but more active Snowy Egret. Adults are cobalt blue with reddish hues on the neck and a grayish-based bill. Late first-year and second-year birds are piebald, white with intrusions of blue.

TRICOLORED HERON *Egretta tricolor*

Slender and snake necked, this mostly subtropical heron of the New World moves like a feathered ninja, creeping along shallow edges or muddy channels in stealth fashion. Its dark, tricolored neck and white belly are unique among North American herons. A resident in mostly coastal and some inland marshes from the southern United States to northern South America, Tricolored breeds in smaller numbers from southern New Jersey to North Carolina, and postbreeding birds disburse north to southern California from coastal western Mexico.

REDDISH EGRET *Egretta rufescens*

Medium-large and shaggy necked, these highly animate subtropical herons feed primarily in shallow coastal waters, where they

Herons and egrets perform a variety of elaborate courtship displays, which continue during the nesting cycle. From left: Great Blue Heron, Great Egret, Yellow-crowned Night-Heron.

prey on fish, frogs, tadpoles, and crustaceans. Famous for their open-winged, water-thrashing, foraging antics, they are either all white or mostly bluish with a reddish head and neck, similar to the smaller Little Blue Heron but with a shaggier neck and longer, pink-based bill. They are resident from coastal South Carolina south to Texas and Mexico, and locally uncommon in the West Indies. Reddish is also resident from coastal western Mexico south to Honduras. In winter, some birds move from coastal Mexico into California. Pacific birds are primarily dark plumaged.

CATTLE EGRET *Bubulcus ibis*

This small, stocky, social egret forages mostly in dry habitats, including roadsides, but most commonly among grazing animals that stir up large insect prey. However, mammals and reptiles are also prey for this formidable hunter. Native to Africa and Asia, they breed across much of the southern United States from New Mexico to Virginia, and locally from central California south to Central and South America, where they are very common. The all-white birds with stout, stabbing, yellow to orange bills don splashes of orange on head, back, and neck during the breeding season.

GREEN HERON *Butorides virescens*

Football sized and shaped, this overall dark heron occurs along edges of vegetated fresh- and saltwater bodies across much of the central and eastern United States and southeastern Canada, and from southern British Columbia south to Panama. Migrant and wintering birds occur in southwestern states. It is typically seen crouched on a limb or stump adjacent to fish-bearing water with its head drawn back. Bright orange legs contrast with its dark greenish back and rufous throat. It is similar to the Striated Heron of South America. Its distinctive *skeew* call is usually given in flight. Green Heron typically nests high in trees, and sometimes nowhere near other herons or egrets.

BLACK-CROWNED NIGHT-HERON
Nycticorax nycticorax

This short, stocky, gray-bodied heron has a black back and crown, and the red eyes of adults are arresting. Breeding birds brandish a single white head plume. Widespread throughout tropical and temperate regions, they range in North America from southern Canada to Mexico. More crepuscular (most active at dawn and dusk) and social than Yellow-crowned, they forage day and night in fresh- and saltwater habitats. Black-crowned either sits on banks and waits for fish to swim by, or slowly stalks its prey, often standing still for long periods.

YELLOW-CROWNED NIGHT-HERON
Nyctanassa violacea

This gray-bodied heron with a strikingly patterned face and short stabbing bill is particularly fond of crustaceans, especially crabs and crayfish. Typically feeding alone and at night, this New World species is common in warm, mostly coastal areas but also breeds in near-coastal areas from Massachusetts south to South Carolina, and inland from Illinois south through Texas. It is resident from coastal Georgia to Florida, southern Texas south to South America, and western Mexico south to South America. Unlike Black-crowned, it actively stalks crabs on the Gulf Coast beaches day and night.

Threskiornithidae: Ibis and Spoonbills

While ibis and spoonbills are closely related to storks, the grouping of these two subfamilies is as much a matter of convenience as genetic convergence. Both are medium to large, long-legged, long-necked waterbirds, but here the similarities end. Ibis, with their

Our two dark ibis are adapted for foraging in aquatic environments. Both have reddish brown bodies with glossy hues. White-faced Ibis (left, top [breeding] and bottom [nonbreeding]) has a red eye and rosy color to the wings. Glossy Ibis (right, top and bottom) is nimble enough to perch and capable of soaring flight. All ibis have long, decurved bills.

long, narrow, decurved bills, are picking and probing birds. Spoonbills, with their spatula-tipped bills, are swishers, sweeping the water in search of aquatic prey, fish, insect larvae, tadpoles, crabs, and crayfish. Both locate prey by touch. They are typically found in small to large feeding flocks and prefer freshwater habitats, but also occur in brackish water locations, where they freely associate with each other and other wading birds. Shallow ponds and flooded fields constitute ideal habitats. Found on every continent except Antarctica, both ibis (28 species worldwide) and spoonbills (6 species) reach their greatest species diversity and numbers in the tropics and subtropics.

WHITE IBIS *Eudocimus albus*

This handsome, snowy white bird with black wingtips and red to orange legs and bill is a common fixture in coastal southern marshes and wet fields. Roosting birds festoon islands of trees like large white Christmas tree ornaments. White Ibis is closely related to the stunning Scarlet Ibis of South America, and both are known to interbreed where their ranges overlap. White Ibis is especially common in coastal marshes, tidal estuaries, mudflats, and mangroves, and its numbers have increased dramatically in the southeastern United States in the last 20 years, with many birds wandering as far north as Connecticut in spring and summer.

White Ibis are highly social, feeding and bathing in groups, and have become increasingly urbanized in recent years, foraging on lawns and roadside ditches. They are resident from coastal Virginia south to all of Florida and the coastal Panhandle to eastern Texas, as well as the West Indies and coastal Mexico south to South America. Young birds show a persistent pattern of vagrancy and may

With long necks and legs, Roseate Spoonbill (top) and White Ibis (bottom) are aquatic birds that frequent fresh-water ponds and shallow lakes. While both are tactile feeders, the bills of ibis are specialized for probing and picking, whereas the spatula-shaped bills of spoonbill are designed for swishing and straining.

wander north to eastern Canada and west to the plains states.

GLOSSY IBIS *Plegadis falcinellus*

Glossy is the only ibis with a worldwide dis-tribution, but it is oddly absent from much of Mexico, Central America, and most of South America. In North America, it is the dark ibis of the Atlantic and Gulf Coasts. This curve-billed, bronze-colored wading bird flashes iridescent hues of purple and green as it turns. Mostly coastal, it forages in fresh- and saltwater ponds. Glossy breeds from Maine to Florida, and from Alabama to east Texas, where it overlaps and hybridizes with the very similar White-faced Ibis. It is resident from South Carolina to east Texas.

WHITE-FACED IBIS *Plegadis chihi*

The dark ibis of the west, this New World species has separate North and South Amer-ican populations. Found mostly in shallow freshwater marshes and ponds, in North America it is the ibis of the western interior, primarily west of the Mississippi. Recent eastward expansion of White-faced and western expansion of Glossy Ibis in southern states has resulted in an increase of hybrid birds in southern locations. While similar to Glossy Ibis in plumage, breeding adults have pinkish facial skin bordered by white, and their plumage flashes golden and rosy iridescent hues. Immature birds are similar to Glossy. In winter, they occur in southern California and from the western Florida Pan-handle coast south to Belize (very rare). The resident South American population occurs in southeastern Bolivia, Paraguay, Brazil, Argentina, and Uruguay.

ROSEATE SPOONBILL *Platalea ajaja*

This large, resplendent, rose-hued wad-ing bird is especially admired by everyone thanks to its stunning beauty and unusual pink color. Perched in mangroves or rising above the ibis with which it sometimes feeds,

The male of this mated pair of Roseate Spoonbills is vigorously defending their newly built nest against the more aggressive Great Egret at a breeding colony in Texas. He was successful in his defense. Spoonbills often nest in colonies that contain Wood Storks, herons, and egrets.

this pink-bodied bird with the scarlet slash across the upperwing commands instant recognition. From the neck up, it looks positively prehistoric. The bird's namesake spatula-shaped bill is often not in evidence as hunched, foraging birds stride along while sweeping their bills through the water. Younger birds have paler bodies and lack the crimson slash.

Formerly hunted to near extirpation in the South, in 1939 there were only 30 spoonbills remaining in Florida. In 2018, Florida Audubon recorded over 1,200 nests in the state, with biologists estimating possibly double that number. They also occur as near-coastal residents from Louisiana south through Mexico, and from coastal western Mexico south to South America. Spoonbills often breed alongside Wood Storks in large waterbird colonies.

Cathartidae: New World Vultures

Something of an ornithological hot potato, the nine species in this family were historically ranked among the Falconiformes (falcons), despite morphological and behavioral differences. In 1990, DNA analysis confirmed close genetic ties to the storks. The vultures were accordingly stripped of their raptorial standing and relegated to the order Ciconiiformes (storks), only to be later placed in their own order, Cathartiformes. They sit adjacent to the newly constituted Accipitriformes (birds of prey), which does not include falcons, who are also taxonomic outliers.

Regardless of how they are ranked, New World vultures constitute an accomplished

While the taloned feet of New World vultures are too weak to grasp prey in proper raptor fashion, they are adept at perching and biped locomotion. Note the hooked, flesh-rending bills and unfeathered heads that allow vultures to reach deep into carcasses without fouling their feathers with gore. Turkey Vultures (top) have a keen sense of smell that helps to locate carcasses of dead animals, while Black Vultures (bottom) have no sense of smell.

and widespread group of soaring birds with a dietary focus on carrion, thus filling the ecological niche of Old World vultures, whose genetic lines bind them directly to birds of prey. The nine New World vultures (three in North America) are further distinguished by the absence of a syrinx (avian voice box) and their habit of defecating down their legs, a mechanism for evaporative cooling.

Characterized and unified by bare, unfeathered heads; short, sturdy legs; broad, stiff wings; and hooked, flesh-tearing bills, New World vultures are celebrated for their mastery of flight: birds can soar aloft for hours using thermal and orographic lift as opposed to powered flight. They also share uncommonly keen eyesight, a penchant for depositing their 1 to 3 eggs on the ground, often in some sheltered confine, and well-developed social proclivities, with birds roosting, foraging, and even feeding communally. Some species, including Turkey Vulture, are able to locate carrion by smell, a useful advantage for a carrion feeder.

While some regard the vultures as loathsome, they do not lack for charm and are handsome, if not endearing, at close quarters.

BLACK VULTURE *Coragyps atratus*

The smallest of the New World vultures (with a wingspan of a mere 49 inches) is a common resident across much of Mexico and Central and South America. During Audubon's time in the United States, it occurred only in the southeastern states, where this carrion feeder performed the useful task of chief sanitation engineer, ridding hot southern cities of offal, animal carcasses left on the streets, and the fetid remains of carnal houses and hospitals.

In the last half of the twentieth century, Black Vulture initiated a northward expansion, perhaps in response to climate change but probably to capitalize on the increase of road-killed animals (particularly deer) that flourished in response to suburban sprawl spawned by the new interstate highway system. Today, this efficient carrion feeder breeds as far north as southern New England and is mostly nonmigratory except for limited movements in winter.

Rarely solitary, Black Vultures patrol the highways, pulling smaller prey away from traffic lanes and rending flesh from larger carcasses by combining the leveraging force of their short sturdy legs with flesh-tearing bills. Capable of killing small animals, most notably piglets and chickens, two or more vultures hold their struggling prey between them and "make a wish," using cooperation to offset their inability to grasp prey individually in raptor fashion. They have no sense of smell, so Black Vultures rely on their keen eyesight or Turkey Vulture's acute sense of smell to locate carrion.

TURKEY VULTURE *Cathartes aura*

Widespread throughout the United States and southern Canada, Turkey Vulture is arguably one of North America's best-known birds. Its large size, V-winged configuration, bare red head, and wobbly flight render instant recognition, though in many quarters it is mistakenly called a "buzzard." True buzzards are Old World raptors in the genus *Buteo*. By any name, from western ranchers

The wings of vultures are designed for soaring, with their length and breadth capable of squeezing every ounce of lift out of rising air. California Condor (top and center) may travel over a hundred miles in search of food. Adult Turkey Vulture (bottom) needs a running start to take flight, whereas condors prefer landscapes with a bit of pitch to get airborne.

to northeastern suburbanites, most are familiar with this large, dark, soaring bird with silvery underwings. Able to locate carrion by scent as well as sight, this species has benefited from the proliferation of road-killed deer. Northern and western populations are highly migratory, and any individual bird's winter destinations may vary greatly from year to year.

CALIFORNIA CONDOR
Gymnogyps californianus

Fossil remains suggest that during the age of the great mammals, about 10,000 years ago, California Condor was widespread across North America. By the time Lewis and Clark went exploring, our largest soaring bird was relegated to a vestigial strip of land between coastal Oregon and Baja, where this carrion feeder dined on moribund sea mammals and dead cattle introduced by Spanish landowners. Its numbers were perilously low and reaching the point of genetic impoverishment by the mid to late twentieth century,

when the world's remaining 27 California Condors were placed in protective custody as part of a captive breeding and release program. This resulted in free-flying condors once again patrolling the skies over California and the Grand Canyon. Visitors to the Grand Canyon now thrill to the sight of these Pleistocene relics, easily distinguished by their immense size and near-ten-foot wingspan, as the birds navigate the updrafts of the canyon. The total world population, including captive birds, is approaching 500 individuals, with released birds now reproducing in the wild.

Pandionidae: Osprey

This unique cosmopolitan raptor occurs on every continent except Antarctica and is most closely related to the kites. "Fish hawk" or "fish eagle," as it is fondly called, is dis-

Ospreys are fish-eating specialists that hunt by plunging feetfirst into the water to catch fish near the surface. Their toes are situated with two talons in the front and two in the back to facilitate the grasping and holding of fish. Other birds opportunistically wait patiently for Ospreys to drop a few scraps of food when they are eating on beaches with no perches nearby.

Ospreys build their large stick nests close to clear, fish-bearing waters. Two chicks are typical, but in years of abundance, adults may rear three or four to fledging. Adults are dark backed, while juveniles have pale-tipped feathers, imparting a scaly-backed impression.

tinctive enough to warrant not only its own genus, *Pandion*, but its own family. A large bird of prey, its five-foot wingspan makes it almost eagle sized.

OSPREY *Pandion haliaetus*

Ospreys are almost wholly dependent on fish for food and are anatomically refined to capture and consume aquatic prey. Their feet are equipped with fish-grabbing spicules in the pads, which affords small to medium-sized fish little chance of wiggling free of an Osprey's grasp. Their crooked wings are designed to withstand the jarring impact of a large bird striking the water, and Osprey's outer feathers are tightly packed and exceedingly oily, allowing birds to penetrate to depths of 10 feet and emerge dry. While sea eagles pluck fish from the surface, Ospreys dive talons first and emerge often as not with prey. They then fly to a perch to feed or ferry their prey to their large stick nests with 2 to 4 hungry young. Found all across North

Plumage of a juvenile Osprey, which is retained until spring, includes a buff wash on the underwings and white fringing on the upperpart feathers.

America, Ospreys are reliant on clear, open, fish-bearing water (salt or fresh) for successful hunting. Ospreys are leapfrog migrants, with northern breeders wintering much farther south, sometimes to South America, than more southerly breeders. Southern breeders are typically resident.

Accipitridae: Diurnal Raptors

This large, diverse, widespread family is represented by 23 species in 13 genera in North America. All are gifted fliers with visual acuity and capable of grasping prey with their taloned feet, then tearing it apart with hook-tipped bills. It is the ability to bind prey that defines raptors (from the Latin *raptar*, "one who seizes by force"). Their taloned feet are specialized for grasping their primary prey, and the feet of bird-catching hawks like Sharp-shinned and Harris's Hawks have elongated middle toes, extending their reach. Rough-legged Hawk's feet are small and calibrated for small rodents, while those of Golden Eagle are large and well suited for killing prey as large as coyotes. This grouping does not include New World vultures, whose feet are incapable of grasping, nor does it include the falcons, whose genetic lines are not related to the Accipitridae.

Birds of prey are widely represented in human religion, legends, and lore, and continue to inspire us today. North American raptors range from the robin-sized Sharp-shinned Hawk to the turkey-sized Bald and Golden Eagles. This family enjoys a pronounced degree of reverse sexual dimorphism, with females slightly to much larger than males.

WHITE-TAILED KITE *Elanus leucurus*

An angelic black-and-white bird with demonic eyes, White-tailed ranges widely across the Americas, but in North America is limited to the Pacific Coast from Oregon to Baja, eastern Texas, and extreme southern

Kites are nimble aerialists whose flight is like the wind given form. The splay-tailed Swallow-tailed Kite plucks prey off the forest canopy, while Snail Kite feeds almost exclusively on large freshwater snails. White-tailed Kite parachutes down onto its mostly small mammal prey, and Mississippi Kite plucks large insects out of thin air. Males and females are similar in plumage, except for Snail Kite. Clockwise from upper left: Swallow-tailed, Snail, Mississippi, and White-tailed Kites.

Florida. Feeding primarily on small rodents, hunting birds hover over appropriate habitat and then parachute slowly down upon prey with wings uplifted in a V, using surprise rather than speed to grasp prey.

HOOK-BILLED KITE
Chondrohierax uncinatus

This feathered sloth spends much of its life below the forest canopy. Hook-billed feasts on tree snails that it plucks from trunks and branches with a large, snail-crunching bill, and transfers prey to its talons only after landing on a favored perch. Widely distributed in tropical and subtropical forests from Mexico to central South America, it reaches the northern end of its range in the Rio Grande Valley of Texas, where numbers have declined in recent decades. The bowling pin–shaped birds are dimorphic, with males having gray barring below, and females rufous.

SWALLOW-TAILED KITE
Elanoides forficatus

A large, graceful, splay-tailed aerialist, Swallow-tailed is on everyone's shortlist for most beautiful bird in North America, where it dominates the insect-rich skies over southeastern riverside forests and suburbs. Ranging from Central and South America (where it is resident) to the United States, it occurs from northeastern Texas to all of Florida and north to South Carolina. United States breeders depart for winter territories in Central and South America in August and return from late February to April.

GOLDEN EAGLE *Aquila chrysaetos*

Large and powerful, this golden-crowned raptor of mostly high, open country occurs throughout the Northern Hemisphere, but it is primarily a western and Arctic breeder in North America. Northern birds move south in winter, where they may hunt waterfowl to augment their principal diet of rabbits and medium-sized mammals up to the size of coyote. Smaller numbers breed in eastern Canada.

NORTHERN HARRIER *Circus hudsonius*

Closely related to the Old World Hen Harrier *Circus cyaneus* (considered conspecific [same species] by some), Northern Harrier is the sole representative of this genus of ground-hugging prey interceptors in North America. It is a bird of open, often grass-covered habitats (wet and dry). In North America, it breeds across most of the northern and interior western United States and Canada and winters across much of the United States south to northern South America, as well as the West Indies. Its primary prey is small rodents, but birds also make up a part of its diet in winter.

SHARP-SHINNED HAWK
Accipiter striatus

This small, agile forest raptor is scarcely larger than some of its avian prey. Nesting mostly in northern mixed forests, it breeds across most of Canada and the northern United States south along the Appalachians and the Rockies to Mexico. Mostly vacating northern breeding areas in winter, the birds fan out across the United States and Mexico. Readily attracted to birds concentrated at backyard feeders, the "blue darter" is a winter resident in suburban and urban habitats that have trees.

COOPER'S HAWK *Accipiter cooperii*

Larger but otherwise somewhat similar to Sharp-shinned Hawk, Cooper's breeds across much of the United States and southern Canada to the mountains of western Mexico. Cooper's is less a woodland raptor than a bird of broken and edge habitat. Targeting generally larger prey than the smaller Sharp-shinned Hawk, including small mammals and domestic chickens, Cooper's shows a special fondness for doves and pigeons, which enables it to penetrate urban environments. Cooper's numbers have grown

These four agile fliers share somewhat similar physical traits of slender bodies, narrow wings, and long tails. Accipiters are forest raptors that specialize in killing birds for their meals, while Northern Harrier hunts small mammals and birds as it courses over open spaces with a dipping, foraging style. Clockwise from upper left: adult male Northern Harrier, adult male Sharp-shinned Hawk, adult Northern Goshawk, adult female Cooper's Hawk.

dramatically in the past few decades, and it is increasing northward. In winter, northern breeders may move as far south as southern Mexico.

NORTHERN GOSHAWK *Accipiter gentilis*

Unlike the previous accipiters, Goshawk occupies temperate old-growth forests across the entire Northern Hemisphere. Slightly to much larger than Cooper's Hawk, this perch-hunting raptor specializes in hunting grouse and snowshoe hare to the point that Goshawk populations rise and fall in response to their prey's population cycles. When hare and grouse numbers crash (about every ten years), these smoke-colored hawks stage migratory eruptions that propel large numbers of birds south of their breeding range and across much of the United States, except for Texas and the Deep South.

BALD EAGLE *Haliaeetus leucocephalus*

One of eight "sea eagles," this emblematic bird of the United States occurs only in North America, where it is widespread and concentrated along seacoasts, large inland lakes, and major river systems. Northern breeders are migratory, but they winter as far north as open fish-bearing waters. Waterfowl and carrion are important food items. The adult has a white head and tail, while the immature is mostly brown. It takes four years for Bald Eagle to acquire the full white head and tail.

MISSISSIPPI KITE
Ictinia mississippiensis

Once limited to the skies over riparian woodlands of the southeastern United States, this nimble aerialist has acclimated to suburban woodlots and golf course forest tracts. It occurs locally from Arizona to Florida and

north to Virginia, with breeding documented as far north as New Hampshire. Soaring or gliding in dragonfly- or cicada-rich skies, the birds swoop upon unsuspecting prey and snatch them out of the air. Where prey is abundant, multiple kites may hunt the same airspace. In winter, birds withdraw to South America. As opportunistic vagrants, they will appear and breed in new locations after cyclical outbreaks of cicadas, only to possibly disappear in subsequent years. Population numbers have increased dramatically since 1998, from 186,000 to just under 370,000 in 2014 (HawkWatch International).

SNAIL KITE *Rostrhamus sociabilis*

This large, highly specialized predator of big freshwater snails is locally common in marshes from central Mexico south to South America. In the United States, it occurs in central and southern Florida, where it feeds on apple snails and introduced Asian snails. Adult males are slate gray; females and immatures are brown and heavily streaked below. Federally listed as an endangered species, its numbers and distribution depend on consistent water levels and snail availability. While

nonmigratory, some birds are nomadic in their search for snail-bearing waters.

COMMON BLACK-HAWK
Buteogallus anthracinus

This large, coal black buteo-like hawk of tropical and subtropical forests ranges from Texas and the southwestern United States to northern South America and is usually associated with water. In the United States, it has one of the most limited breeding ranges of any raptor, being confined to portions of Arizona, New Mexico, and Texas, where it is mostly found in riparian forests bordering freshwater streams and rivers. A fairly sluggish raptor, it spends much of its time perched on limbs or rocky outcroppings overlooking watercourses. Small fish, reptiles, and amphibians constitute much of its diet. Pairs show a high degree of fidelity to breeding areas, but the United States population, estimated at about 250 pairs, is partially migratory and expanding northward.

HARRIS'S HAWK *Parabuteo unicinctus*

From Argentina to the southwestern United States, rabbits and medium-sized birds quake

While noble looking, our nation's emblematic bird is not above squabbling over discarded fish prey, and immature Bald Eagles (lower right) are given to adolescent jousting.

at the shadow of this lanky, tenacious hunter. Some hunt alone, while others hunt together as a pack, with multiple birds chasing prey until it is exhausted. After catching the prey, they share the bounty, which is very unusual among birds of prey. Hunts are often preceded by ritual gatherings of the pack, typically made up of an alpha pair and young of one or more seasons. This handsome, long-tailed, dark brown and russet-plumaged hunter occurs from Texas to Arizona in the United States, and south to South America, and most frequently occurs in brush woodlands where rabbits and jackrabbits abound.

WHITE-TAILED HAWK
Geranoaetus albicaudatus

In the United States, this large gray-mantled beauty is restricted to eastern and southern Texas, but this aerial hunter of tropical and subtropical shrub-steppe habitat ranges south through near-coastal Mexico to South America. As a prey generalist, White-tailed feeds extensively on cottontail rabbits and small mammals and often concentrates in numbers above grass fires to capture prey flushed by the flames. Its long, tapered wings extend well beyond the tail when it is perched, and it is our only buteo with a distinctive second-year plumage.

GRAY HAWK *Buteo plagiatus*

While currently assigned to the genus *Buteo,* this smallish tropical and subtropical forest raptor has at times been assigned its own genus, *Asturina.* Adding to the confusion, it is also known as "Mexican Goshawk," based on its resemblance to Northern Goshawk and its spirited manner.

While found widely from Mexico to central Panama, this dark-eyed, gray-cloaked beauty is limited in the United States to riparian woodlands in southeastern Arizona, southwestern Texas, and the lower Rio Grande Valley. Despite a world population estimated at about two million, only about 2,000 or fewer birds occur in the United

States. The descending whistled call is often heard before a bird is seen. When one is spotted, it's often perched on a limb, fence post, or utility pole near a permanent stream. This perch-hunting raptor feeds primarily on vertebrates, including lizards, snakes, small birds, and small mammals, as well as some insects.

RED-SHOULDERED HAWK
Buteo lineatus

This colorful medium-sized forest buteo is something of a harbinger of spring for northern areas. From riparian woodlands in California to forested hillsides in New England, the lusty *keeyer* cries of this russet-shouldered beauty ring out before buds begin to swell. Found mostly across the eastern half of the United States and southeastern Canada as well as California north to southern Oregon, the "singing hawk" is most commonly seen perched at mid-heights along forest edges, where it searches for small mammals, reptiles, amphibians, birds, and insects. Migratory in northern portions of its range, Red-shouldered Hawk carries its colors south just as the oaks begin to turn.

BROAD-WINGED HAWK
Buteo platypterus

This small woodland buteo was chided by both Audubon and Wilson for its lack of spirit, a view not shared by eastern chipmunk and other ground squirrels. Breeding widely across Canada and much of the United States east of the Corn Belt, Broad-wings migrate to wintering areas in Central and South America, with increasing numbers wintering in southern Florida, Louisiana, and southern Texas. They travel in September and October in celebrated mass movements involving tens of thousands of birds; one million birds were documented in one day at Veracruz, Mexico, where Kevin once saw 700,000 Broad-wings in one morning. Invertebrates figure prominently in the birds' diet, which also includes reptiles and small birds. Population numbers

North America's buteos target a variety of prey. The large feet of Harris's Hawk (upper left) can handle animals the size of jackrabbits, while the smaller feet of Rough-legged Hawk (top right) are calibrated for smaller mammals. Adult White-tailed Hawk (lower right) is a generalized feeder, but odds say this bird is standing on a cottontail rabbit, while this Florida Red-shouldered Hawk (lower left) hunts small mammals, snakes, and lizards.

of this species have increased from about 1.7 million birds in 2002 to over 2 million in 2014 (HawkWatch International).

SHORT-TAILED HAWK *Buteo brachyurus*

A compact aerialist, Short-tailed is a master of stop-and-go control, able to move forward, stop, and control its elevation with nimble manipulation of its wings. In this manner, Short-tailed Hawk is able to fashion perches out of thin air, whether soaring over the canopy of a Brazilian rain forest or the super-heated air over south Florida. But let a cotinga linger atop the canopy, or a Red-winged Blackbird flair its epaulets, and Short-tailed descends to within striking distance, which ends in a spectacular stoop and often a bird wrapped in buteo talons. Residing in tropical and subtropical Americas, it occurs north of Mexico in Florida and the mountains of southeastern Arizona. Short-tailed has both light and dark plumages, and its numbers in Florida are increasing.

SWAINSON'S HAWK *Buteo swainsoni*

This handsome, polymorphic (having multiple forms), long-winged buteo of open grasslands vaults the forested interior of South America in its biannual commute between the prairies of the western United States and the grasslands of Uruguay and Argentina. To accomplish this feat, Swainson's apparently fasts along much of the up to 6,000-mile route, relying upon energy-saving thermal lifts and fat reserves laid down prior to migration. This long-distance migration champion spends so much time aloft that its principal habitat might be said to be air. While its diet includes small mammals, birds, and reptiles, in winter and prior to (and sometimes during) migration it feasts upon grasshoppers and locusts.

These three common buteos are some of the most abundant members of this family in North America. From left: Red-tailed Hawk, Swainson's Hawk, Broad-winged Hawk.

ZONE-TAILED HAWK *Buteo albonotatus*

This medium-sized aerial hunter courses over a mix of tropical and subtropical forests and adjacent open country, incorporating stealth and versatility to capture prey ranging from small mammals to reptiles and birds. A Turkey Vulture mimic, this buteo soars and glides in the unhurried fashion of vultures (and often in their company) to lull prey into a false sense of security before stooping in unvulturelike fashion. While it is common from Mexico to South America, the United States population of fewer than 2,000 birds is spread across southern and western Texas, New Mexico, and Arizona.

RED-TAILED HAWK *Buteo jamaicensis*

With 14 subspecies typically recognized, this large, burly buteo is found across much of North America south through Mexico to Costa Rica. Most adults are recognized by their namesake red tails, but the Harlan's subspecies has a grayish to whitish tail, and the Krider's subspecies a pink-washed tail. Mostly an open-country perch hunter, this versatile hunter is also capable of kiting (holding its place in the sky), thus fashioning perches out of thin air from which it stoops upon prey ranging from small mammals and medium-sized birds to reptiles. Red-tailed plumages in the western United States are especially complex, ranging from a pale light plumage to an all-dark one, with many variations in between.

ROUGH-LEGGED HAWK *Buteo lagopus*

Rough-leggeds are lanky, small-billed, and small-footed, and have consistent light and dark plumages, as well as uncommon intermediate ones. This Holarctic breeder withdraws entirely from northern breeding areas from Newfoundland and Labrador to Alaska to open areas in southern Canada and the United States, where standing snowpack does not conceal its mostly rodent prey. It often perches on fence posts or irrigation wheels, or hovers with deep wingbeats over open terrain.

FERRUGINOUS HAWK *Buteo regalis*

This large "eagle" of the American prairies hunts prairie dogs and ground squirrels in sagebrush and grazing habitats. Large billed and flat headed, it often perches on the ground or on a hill overlooking prairie dog towns. It has feathered legs and small feet, and can have light, dark, and intermediate plumage. Its huge stick nests are situated in isolated trees, cliffs, or on the ground. Breeders in Canada and northern states withdraw south in winter, but not farther than northern Mexico.

Tytonidae: Barn Owls

A cosmopolitan family, Tytonidae is represented by 16 species divided into two subfamilies: typical barn owls (Tytoninae, 14 species) and bay owls (Phodilinae, 2 species). The Tytonidae are mostly a tropical forest family, with some species geographically restricted, unlike the Barn Owl, *Tyto alba*. It is one of the planet's most widely distributed land birds, and a bird at home in temperate as well as tropical locations. Among Barn Owl's 28 recognized subspecies, many are geographically isolated, poorly studied, and may in fact constitute distinct species.

The Tytonidae are medium-large, big-headed, long-legged owls with heart-shaped, sound-amplifying facial disks. With offset ears (for sound triangulation), large eyes, and sound-dampening modifications to feathers, they are supremely adapted to nocturnal hunting and are able to locate prey in total darkness as well as under a blanket of grass or snow. Most feed on small to medium-sized mammals, although birds, reptiles, amphibians, and insects figure prominently in the diet of some species. Solitary hunters, they employ two strategies—perch hunting and cruise hunting—which may incorporate quartering, gliding, and hovering.

Most are cavity nesters, but where tree cavities are absent some nest underground in abandoned mines or caves. Barn Owls do not construct nests but deposit their eggs directly on a chosen substrate. Clutch size varies, with some species averaging 2 eggs per clutch, while the Barn Owl may lay as many as 14 eggs, although 4 to 7 is typical. The implications of the name notwithstanding, barn owls nest in natural cavities as frequently as in man-made structures, and birds show a high degree of fidelity to prime nest sites.

BARN OWL *Tyto alba*

Medium-large and "monkey faced," Barn Owl is cosmopolitan and widespread across the United States, except for some northern areas. Mostly a resident species, it favors open country, including marshes, grasslands,

Large broods keep the "Monkey-faced Owl" (Barn Owl) working late into the night in search of mostly mammalian prey that they can locate in total darkness. Enjoying a worldwide distribution, Barn Owls do indeed breed in barns and abandoned structures, as well as abandoned mineshafts.

Barn Owls often have large clutches of young, as this group of fledglings can attest to. This group of curious youngsters was located in the attic of an abandoned building in Texas.

and deserts, often near human habitation, including urban areas. Almost fully nocturnal, birds roost during the day in natural cavities and sheltered woodland canopies as well as man-made structures, including bridges and stacked hay bales. The call, uttered only at night, is a breathy, spine-tingling shriek.

Strigidae: Typical Owls

A large worldwide family (189 species) of mostly nocturnal hunters, typical owls occur on every continent except Antarctica. While most are forest dwellers, various species are adapted to habitats from the Arctic to tropical rain forests to the Sahara. One species, the North American Burrowing Owl, is partially subterranean. Ranging in size from the diminutive Elf Owl (1.4 ounces) to Eurasian Eagle-Owl (5.9 pounds), owls are characterized by large round heads (with and without "ear" tufts), which can rotate as much as

270 degrees to compensate for their fixed, forward-looking eyes. These eyes are surrounded by feathered facial disks that catch, amplify, and direct sound to the birds' offset ears, whose configuration enables owls to triangulate prey in darkness and under concealing vegetation.

As befits a meat-eating predator, bills are hooked and toes taloned. The outer toe is capable of being directed back, presenting prey with a four-cornered net of talons. Small to medium-sized mammals are key ingredients in the diets of most owls, but reptiles, frogs, fish, insects, earthworms, and birds figure in the diets of some species.

Most owls are cryptically patterned (with grays and browns dominating) to conceal birds at roosts in daylight hours. Feathers are velvety to facilitate silent flight, and the feathers on the leading edge of the wing of most species are fringed to further reduce sound. Owls do not build nests per se, but appropriate those of other large birds or place eggs in natural or man-made cavities.

In the absence of visual courtship dis-

plays, owls have evolved a varied and complex vocal array to attract mates and establish territories. These range from hoots, whinnies, and shrieks to toots, moans, and barks. Some species duet, including Eastern Screech-Owl, with females joining the party.

FLAMMULATED OWL
Psiloscops flammeolus

A secretive western owl, Flammulated is our only small owl with dark eyes and blunt ear tufts. Breeding locally in open mountain coniferous forest from British Columbia to Guatemala, it feeds mostly on nocturnal insects. The male's call is a low, soft *whoo*, repeated every few seconds.

WESTERN SCREECH-OWL
Megascops kennicottii

Small and compact, this tufted owl of western open woodlands is resident from southeastern Alaska to Baja and central Mexico. Found in both gray (dominant) and brown plumages, this nocturnal hunter preys mostly on insects and small mammals. Its distinctive song is a series of *churring* hoots that accelerate at the end.

EASTERN SCREECH-OWL
Megascops asio

This small, nocturnal, tufted forest owl found in gray, reddish, and intermediate plumages is a common resident of open woodlands east of the Rockies. It spends the daylight hours in tree cavities or nest boxes. Songs include a low, whistled trill on a single pitch (tremolo song) and a descending whinny. Its varied diet includes songbirds, rodents, insects, crayfish, and earthworms.

WHISKERED SCREECH-OWL
Megascops trichopsis

Slightly smaller and with less-defined breast streaks than Western Screech-Owl, this small gray-brown or rufous owl is resident from Nicaragua to southeastern Arizona, where it favors open oak woodlands at high elevations. Only the gray-brown plumage morph occurs in the United States. The song is a series of low, spaced toots that slow at the end and recalls Morse code.

GREAT HORNED OWL *Bubo virginianus*

Great Horned is named for its large size and feathered ear tufts and is everyone's picture

Small they might be, but those taloned feet are needle sharp. These owls all show the fixed, forward-staring gaze that identifies them as predators and gives them the binocular vision needed to precisely calibrate the location of prey. From left to right: Boreal Owl, Northern Saw-whet Owl, Eastern Screech-Owl.

Large they might be, but the favored prey of Snowy Owl (left), Great Horned Owl (center), and Great Gray Owl (right) is small rodents. This would be a bad time to be a vole.

of what an owl should look and sound like. It is found in a variety of woodland and desert habitats from North to South America, and the only place it is absent is treeless tundra. Eastern birds are darker and brownish; western ones paler and gray; and northern ones are almost white. Prey includes small to medium-sized mammals, birds, and reptiles. While mostly nocturnal, they become vocal and active up to an hour before sunset. Their deep 5- to 7-note hoot is iconic.

SNOWY OWL *Bubo scandiacus*

These large white owls have a Holarctic distribution and forage day or night, feeding mostly upon lemmings and voles from tree line to polar seas. They navigate the edge of the ice cap in winter, hunting sea birds and waterfowl. Some birds regularly winter south to the northern prairie states and coastal New England, but in years of low food availability (irruption years) Snowy wanders farther south and in greater numbers. Southern wintering Snowy Owls prey on small mammals and birds, some as large as Great Blue Heron.

NORTHERN HAWK OWL *Surnia ulula*

Square faced and long tailed, these perch hunters of open taiga forests range across all of northern North America and Eurasia.

Feeding mostly in daylight and mainly on voles, they wander south of their boreal forest stronghold when prey numbers crash, and their diet becomes more varied to include birds as large as grouse. Mostly nomadic, they breed where voles are abundant. The song is a rapid tooting chatter. Calls include a Barn Owl–like shriek.

NORTHERN PYGMY-OWL
Glaucidium gnoma

Predators need not be large to be formidable. At 2.5 ounces, Northern Pygmy-Owl weighs less than some of the birds it hunts, and it is one of the toughest predators in the clinches. Ranging from southeastern Alaska to Central America, this western diurnal hunter prefers montane oak-coniferous forests, and in winter also occurs in riparian woodlands and forested cemeteries in urban areas. It can be easily overlooked because of its small size (6.5 inches long) and cryptic gray, brown, or reddish plumages. Observers are often alerted to a pygmy-owl's presence by a single- or doubled-tooted song or by mobbing chickadees, whose ire for this perch-hunting raptor is unsurpassed. From behind, the dark nape has two dark spots that resemble eyes to fool predators into thinking it is watching them, but its real eyes are bright yellow.

FERRUGINOUS PYGMY-OWL
Glaucidium brasilianum

Enjoying a range that extends from southeastern Arizona to southern South America, this small, ruddy, long-tailed tyrant haunts arid oak-mesquite and riparian woodlands in Texas and saguaro-mesquite desert in Arizona. Perch hunting day or night, its prey includes insects, scorpions, reptiles, birds, and small mammals. The song is a lengthy series of hurried, high-pitched, even toots. This bird also has fake eyes on the back of its head.

ELF OWL *Micrathene whitneyi*

The world's smallest owl (5.75 inches) inhabits cactus desert, mesquite, and wooded canyons in the American Southwest from Texas to southeastern California south to central Mexico. Locally uncommon, this tiny, tuftless owl hunts at dawn and dusk almost exclusively for moths and insects. Its song is a short, hurried, squeeky chatter punctuated by a softer mew.

BURROWING OWL *Athene cunicularia*

These crepuscular (most active at dawn and dusk), long-legged hunters of reptiles and insects are often seen perched in open grasslands infested with prairie dogs, whose burrows they appropriate for roosting and nesting, or they dig their own using strong, unfeathered feet and legs. Fence posts are also favorite perches. Burrowing Owls breed from southwestern Canada south across most of the western United States and east to eastern Texas. A separate population occurs in Florida and the West Indies, and they use old tortoise burrows for nest sites. Their song is a hurried chatter often punctuated by a plaintive squeal. Northern birds are migratory.

SPOTTED OWL *Strix occidentalis*

Dark eyed and heavily marked, this large owl has two separate populations—one associated with mature, coastal, old-growth

These three owls have very different physical appearances and hunting styles. Ferruginous Pygmy-Owl (top) is a small, long-tailed tropical species that inhabits open brushy habitats and hunts birds and other prey in daylight hours, while Burrowing Owl (bottom) is a terrestrial owl that nests and roosts in underground burrows and hunts lizards and large insects. Long-eared Owl (center) is a nocturnal species that lives in mature forests and hunts small mammals.

Five common North American owls in flight. Clockwise from upper left: Snowy Owl, Great Gray Owl, Great Horned Owl, Short-eared Owl, and Barred Owl. All hunt during daylight hours, but Great Horned is a nocturnal owl that may also hunt around dawn and dusk.

(hemlock-fir) forests from British Columbia to California, and another in shaded wooded canyons from Utah south to north-central Mexico. Nest sites are tree cavities or topped-off trees. A perch hunter preying mostly on small mammals, including flying squirrels, its song is a short series of low nasal hoots, with northern and southern populations having different patterns. Southern birds are paler and less heavily marked below.

BARRED OWL *Strix varia*

Closely related to Spotted Owl, this large, dark-eyed owl of mature eastern coniferous and mixed forests occurs throughout most of the United States east of the Great Plains and ranges west across Canada and south to northern California. A segregated population occurs in Mexico. In the East, Barred Owl shows a particular fondness for swamps with trees large enough to support the large cavities it uses to nest. Its diet is varied, but it feeds primarily on small mammals, birds, frogs, and crayfish. While mostly nocturnal, this species calls and hunts in daylight. Its song is a series of deep, measured hoots phonetically rendered *who cooks for you; who cooks for you all.*

GREAT GRAY OWL *Strix nebulosa*

This very large, gray owl of northern and montane western forests south to the Sierra Nevadas is branded with a white X between its yellow eyes and known for its near-hypnotic gaze. Occurring in dense taiga and coniferous forests in the Old and New Worlds, it is mostly resident but nomadic, and sometimes irrupts south when rodent populations crash. Its song is a series of deep, resonant well-spaced hoots.

LONG-EARED OWL *Asio otus*

Slightly resembling Great Horned Owl, but smaller and slenderer, Long-eared breeds in a variety of forest types in temperate North America and Eurasia. Strictly nocturnal and often migratory, they roost communally in winter in dense foliage and conifers near hunting areas, where they capture small mammals and birds by coursing and hovering. Their song is 3 or 4 long, low, sustained hoots.

SHORT-EARED OWL *Asio flammeus*

Occurring widely across northern North America, Eurasia, and parts of South America, this tawny, mothlike owl of open habitats

wheels and hovers in search of mostly mammalian prey, often in daylight hours. Roosting and nesting on the ground, it often jousts with Northern Harrier, whose habitat and prey it begrudgingly shares. Vocalizations include a series of nasal snarls and barks.

BOREAL OWL *Aegolius funereus*

This medium-small, nonmigratory owl of boreal forests across the Northern Hemisphere is sparsely distributed in mixed forests and ranges widely across Canada, Alaska, and isolated pockets in the Rockies south to Colorado. A perch hunter, Boreal Owl targets birds and small mammals, especially voles and shrews. Its song is a series of 10 to 12 whistled toots that grow in volume.

NORTHERN SAW-WHET OWL
Aegolius acadicus

A winsome tiger of coniferous forests, Saw-whet breeds widely but sparingly from Alaska south to western Texas and east to New Jersey and Tennessee. This coffee mug–sized owl hunts mammals and birds and can be a resident or long-distance migrant, occupying a variety of woodland habitat types. Its song is a monotonous series of high toots that recalls a file drawn over a saw.

Trogonidae: Trogons and Quetzals

This small family (39 species) of arboreal fruit and insect feeders occurs in tropical and subtropical regions of Asia, Africa, and the Americas. They are medium-large with tubular bodies, long narrow tails, and large neckless heads that can swivel an owl-like 180 degrees, an adaptive concession to the bird's peculiar feet, which have two toes facing forward and two backward, a configuration well suited for perching but little else. The feet of trogons and quetzals are so poorly suited for locomotion that the birds cannot

Elegant Trogons are birds of Neotropical and subtropical forests that sally out to snap insect prey out of the air. They sit quietly near tree trunks while surveying their territories. Top to bottom: female and male Elegant Trogons.

turn on their perch without applying their wings. And perching is what each of these sluggish birds does for most of the day. It sits upright on a horizontal limb beneath

the canopy and turns its head in slow motion in search of fruits, insects, and occasionally small vertebrates, which it engulfs with its short but strong hook-tipped bill after a short sallying flight.

Sedentary hunting is also advantageous from a defensive perspective. Immobility does not draw a predator's eye; and keeping a cryptic green or brown back toward a potential threat that may be studied with a rearward-turned head while the bird directs its bright yellow or red underparts away from hunting eyes has obvious advantages.

ELEGANT TROGON *Trogon elegans*

A green-headed, red-bellied bird of tropical forests and sycamore-riparian woodlands in the United States, Elegant Trogon reaches the northern limit of its range in southeastern Arizona, where it is locally uncommon. Its call is a series of soft croaks.

EARED QUETZAL *Euptilotis neoxenus*

This large, robust-bodied, red-bellied Mexican quetzal with a white undertail resides in montane pine-oak forests lining canyon watercourses. Feeding on both insects and fruit, it is a rare visitor to the Chiricahua and Huachuca Mountains of Arizona, and there is a breeding record for Ramsey Canyon. It is possible that a small resident population exists in the remote canyons of Arizona's sky islands. Its call is a loud, squealing *skreeee-chuck*.

Alcedinidae: Kingfishers

Implications of the name notwithstanding, not all kingfishers eat fish. Many species outside the Americas are forest birds that do not live near water. However, all kingfishers are predatory, dropping from elevated perches onto fish, insects, or vertebrate prey that the birds secure in their knifelike bills. The plan-et's tropical forests are home to the greatest diversity of these worldwide birds, and while some are desert dwellers, many occur near aquatic environments. Most nest in chambers at the end of tunnels excavated by both sexes in earth cliffs or banks that may be far from water. Some nest in tree cavities.

Ranging in size from the African Dwarf Kingfisher, weighing about 0.3 ounces, to the Australian Laughing Kookaburra, weighing nearly a pound, most kingfishers are between 1 and 3.5 ounces, with North America's most widespread Belted Kingfisher weighing 5 ounces. All kingfishers have long, pointed, daggerlike bills, relatively large neckless heads, compact bodies, and short legs, and the majority have four toes—three forward and one back. Most have green or blue backs, and many show a degree of brilliance. Males, females, and juveniles are mostly similar.

Like owls, kingfishers have limited eye mobility, so they are obliged to search for prey by turning their heads. Fish-eating members of the family that plunge-dive for submerged prey must adjust their dives to account for light refraction. While most are perch hunters, some are adroit at hovering.

Kingfishers are mostly shy; some species vocalize as soon as humans appear, and many riverside species flush well ahead of approaching watercraft. While not accounted among the bird world's most accomplished musicians, 92 kingfisher species enjoy a vocal repertoire from rattles and ticks to peeps and loud, raucous yodels. The laugh of the Australian Laughing Kookaburra ranks among the most recognized animal sounds on the planet.

RINGED KINGFISHER
Megaceryle torquata

This very large (11-ounce), boisterous, tropical and subtropical New World resident of freshwater lakes, ponds, rivers, and coastal mangroves ranges widely throughout Central and South America, reaching the northern limit of its range in south Texas. Distin-

These diving, fish-eating specialists have a broad distribution. Belted Kingfisher (top center, male; lower right, female) ranks as one of the most widely distributed bird species in North America. Ringed Kingfisher (upper and lower left) is a tropical and subtropical species that reaches the northern limit of its range in south Texas. The diminutive Green Kingfisher (top right) is another tropical species limited to south Texas and southeastern Arizona.

guished by its massive bill, rufous belly, and diet of mostly fish, a Ringed Kingfisher will plunge steeply for prey before returning to a perch, where it stuns the prey by repeated thrashing and then swallows it headfirst.

BELTED KINGFISHER *Megaceryle alcyon*

One of the most widespread North American birds, this large, shaggy-crested, blue-backed, fish-eating bird breeds across much of forested North America, except from southern California to eastern Texas. Belted Kingfisher winters widely across North America (mostly the United States) wherever water remains open, including coastal Alaska south to Washington State. Winter range also includes Central and South America and the West Indies. It is the only kingfisher of the Americas whose females are more colorful than the males.

GREEN KINGFISHER
Chloroceryle americana

These 11-inch darts in feathers are almost half bill. Perched in tangles of roots or branches hanging low over the water, they appear dark backed, an illusion that ends when the darts flash into sunlight, revealing emerald green upperparts. The birds are shy and retiring by nature, and observers are usually alerted to their presence by their Geiger counter–like clicking call. Ranging from South America to central Texas and southeast Arizona, Green Kingfishers favor sluggish, often turbid water bodies and flooded ditches, where they hunt small fish, crustaceans, and aquatic insects.

Picidae: Woodpeckers and Allies

If not the planet's most accomplished bird family, woodpeckers are certainly the most specialized. They boast an array of physical refinements that allow them to exploit food resources that are literally beyond reach of other bird species, such as insects and larvae barricaded within a fortress of wood. These small to medium-large birds occur in both temperate and tropical zones on every continent except Australia but reach their greatest species diversity in the forests of Southeast Asia and South America (216 species). Most are forest dwellers, but some thrive in open deserts and grasslands. In North America, there are 22 woodpecker species, ranging in size from the 7-inch Downy to the 17-inch Pileated Woodpecker.

Woodpeckers align in having sturdy, pointed, chisel-like bills and stiff tail feathers that anchor birds as they cling to trees with their strong, sharply clawed zygodactyl feet (two toes forward, two backward). To reduce the impact of driving bills into wood, woodpecker bills are equipped with a spongy, shock-absorbing base as well as nostril-covering feathers to prevent wood splinters from penetrating.

Woodpeckers may chisel prey out of wood, flake away bark, excavate earth, or fly-catch in search of food. All are equipped with remarkably long, retractable tongues, which expand the birds' reach and secure prey. Tongues are fitted with back-pointing barbs and aided by a sticky secretion of sublingual glands, such that some species use them as glue sticks more than stabbing instruments. While most feed primarily on insects and their larvae, many routinely consume fruits, seeds, nuts, tree sap, and even flower nectar.

As a rule, woodpeckers are not overly colorful. Most are gray, black, brown, and white, with bright red and greens mostly limited to heads and necks. Plumage of males, females, and juveniles is mostly similar, except for sapsuckers.

Most species communicate by "drumming" on resonating surfaces (most often wood), with the drumming of various species having differentiating patterns, tempos, and lengths. Typically used to communicate between partners, drumming is performed

Pileated (left), the aptly named Red-headed (center), and Red-bellied (right) Woodpeckers all have the black, white, and red colors that are woodpecker trademarks. Pileated is our largest and only crested woodpecker.

These three woodpeckers occupy different ranges and habitats. Golden-fronted (left) is a permanent resident of south Texas in arid, brushy habitats, while Black-backed (center) is a burn specialist that occupies localized northern and high-elevation coniferous forests and forages for insect larvae in fallen or standing trunks. Ladder-backed Woodpecker (right) is a resident of open woodlands in southern locations from western California to Texas. All are males.

by both sexes. Almost all woodpeckers nest in tree cavities they've excavated themselves, but a few species nest underground. Most woodpeckers are resident, and only a handful are truly migratory, but many routinely relocate to take advantage of seasonal food abundance.

LEWIS'S WOODPECKER
Melanerpes lewis

This large, broad-winged, darkish woodpecker occurs in open habitats with standing dead trees across the forested West from southern British Columbia to New Mexico. Perching on treetops, it sallies out to snap up flying insects, but also forages on the ground. It also consumes fruits and berries as well as acorns and other nuts in winter. Northern and interior populations are migratory.

RED-HEADED WOODPECKER
Melanerpes erythrocephalus

Handsome and tricolored, Red-headed is locally common east of the Rockies in open habitats with scattered trees and in forests with scant understory. It was the first specimen collected by Alexander Wilson upon his arrival in America. Red-headed feeds on a variety of insects and other invertebrates in spring—targeting flying insects more often than wood-boring insects—and switches over to a diet of mostly seeds, nuts, and berries in winter. Northern populations are migratory.

ACORN WOODPECKER
Melanerpes formicivorus

Raucous, rambunctious, and boldly patterned, this highly social western woodpecker occurs mostly in oak woodlands from the far West to the Southwest, and south to Panama. It is generally common where acorns abound, which it caches in holes in walls for later retrieval, much to the dismay of some homeowners with wood siding. Insects figure prominently in the diet of nestlings.

GILA WOODPECKER
Melanerpes uropygialis

Mostly solitary, this ladder-backed woodpecker of arid lowland scrub with a large cactus component is omnivorous, as befits a bird adapted to a desert environment. It consumes an array of animals and assorted fruits. Range extends from southwestern California to New Mexico and south into Mexico.

GOLDEN-FRONTED WOODPECKER
Melanerpes aurifrons

This common, geographically restricted, ladder-backed woodpecker with a golden nape occurs in dry woodlands from southwestern Oklahoma south through Texas to Mexico. The birds mostly consume fruits (including cactus), nuts, insects, and larvae secured by gleaning and probing in crevices and openings in trunks and limbs. They also engage in ground feeding and fly-catching.

RED-BELLIED WOODPECKER
Melanerpes carolinus

A fairly tame eastern ladder-backed woodpecker with a rose blush on its belly, it occurs mostly east of the Great Plains. Ongoing range expansion finds it now established in Maine and southeastern Canada. Found mostly in deciduous woodlands, it has acclimated well to suburban neighborhoods with trees and visits feeders that offer peanuts, suet, and sunflower seeds.

SAPSUCKERS

The next four species are members of the genus *Sphyrapicus* and similar in size and structure. They share not only a taste for sugar-rich tree sap but also a common means of extraction. Sapsuckers circumnavigate tree trunks and bore a series of shallow holes into the sap-bearing inner bark, returning later to drink up the bounty of their endeavors and consume insects that are drawn to the sweet fluid. Sapsuckers also share a common drum pattern—an initial burst of taps followed by a faltering series of loud, spaced taps. Until the latter twentieth century, Red-breasted, Red-naped, and Yellow-bellied Sapsuckers were grouped as a single species, differing only in plumage and range.

WILLIAMSON'S SAPSUCKER
Sphyrapicus thyroideus

This onyx-colored western beauty is a common but generally quiet and retiring denizen of (mostly mature) western montane pine forests from British Columbia south to Mexico, with some northern birds wintering in western Mexico. They secure mostly insect prey by gleaning and probing crevices and bark openings. Nest holes are often in aspens.

YELLOW-BELLIED SAPSUCKER
Sphyrapicus varius

A highly migratory and wide-ranging sapsucker, Yellow-bellied breeds in northern coniferous and mixed forests from Alaska east across Canada to the Maritimes, and south to Pennsylvania and North Carolina. They winter in the central and southern United States east of Colorado to New Jersey and south to Panama and the West Indies. Resident populations occur in Jamaica and Cayman Brac. They consume a variety of insects, including ants, beetles, and larvae, as well as large amounts of sap. In winter, their diet includes fruits, nuts, and berries, including poison ivy. Their call is a soft mewing, and their stuttering drumming is reminiscent of Morse code.

RED-NAPED SAPSUCKER
Sphyrapicus nuchalis

Breeding in Rocky Mountain forests, often with aspen, from western Canada to western Texas, Red-naped's diet combines arthropods and tree sap, especially in spring. Highly migratory, its winter range extends deep into Mexico, where it favors woodland edges dominated by oaks. Its plumage is very similar to that of Yellow-bellied Sapsucker, except for the red on the nape.

RED-BREASTED SAPSUCKER
Sphyrapicus ruber

This red-cowled, westernmost sapsucker breeds in montane coniferous forests with aspens from southeastern Alaska south to central California. Nests are usually high in a conifer. Birds vacate northern breeding areas in fall, retreating into southern portions of

their breeding range and south to northern Baja.

AMERICAN THREE-TOED WOODPECKER *Picoides dorsalis*

This burn specialist occurs in mature boreal and montane conifer forests from Newfoundland and Labrador to Alaska, and south in the Rockies to northern New Mexico. Lacking an inner rear toe, these specialists flake bark off fire-scorched, insect-infested dead trees. They may be fairly common where their exacting habitat occurs. This species is an important predator of spruce-bark beetles.

BLACK-BACKED WOODPECKER *Picoides arcticus*

This large woodpecker shares with Three-toed Woodpecker an abbreviated foot and a fondness for burned-over or insect-riddled coniferous forests, where it forages for wood-boring insect larvae on standing and fallen trunks. A northern species of montane and Boreal forests, it ranges across Canada to Alaska, but is only patchily distributed in the Rockies.

DOWNY WOODPECKER *Dryobates pubescens*

This smallest, very common, widespread woodland woodpecker shows a measure of geographic variation across its extensive and exclusive North American range, which excludes only tundra regions, southern California, and the Southwest east to southern Texas. Feeding mostly on insects and larvae excavated by boring, it also forages on reed stalks and consumes berries. It is a staple at bird feeders and often joins mixed feeding flocks.

NUTTALL'S WOODPECKER
Dryobates nuttallii

Essentially a California endemic, Nuttall's is closely related to, and has an overlapping range with, Downy Woodpecker. This oak-loving woodpecker feeds mostly on insects that it gathers by gleaning and probing. Like Downy, it enjoys suet and sunflower seeds at bird feeders.

LADDER-BACKED WOODPECKER
Dryobates scalaris

Slightly larger than Downy, this woodpecker of semi-open woodlands ranges from southern California to east Texas and south to southern Mexico. Foraging mostly on tree trunks and branches, where it gleans most food from bark surfaces rather than excavation, it augments its diet of insects and larvae with fruit. It bred with Downy Woodpecker in Galveston, Texas, in 2017, which is extremely unusual and probably represents a stray bird. Brenda Dawson of Galveston photographed the birds and their young, and Kevin reviewed the photos and confirmed the hybrid offspring.

RED-COCKADED WOODPECKER
Dryobates borealis

This rare and federally endangered black-and-white woodpecker is limited to open mature pine forests from the Carolinas to Florida and east Texas, where they are resident and consume mostly wood-boring beetles. Highly social and living in family groups, the birds excavate nests in living pines, which are distinguished by a ring of sap encircling the opening.

HAIRY WOODPECKER *Dryobates villosus*

Unlike Downy Woodpecker, which it closely resembles, this larger, longer-billed, black-and-white woodpecker occurs in mature forests of all types. It forages on trunks and large branches for wood-boring beetles, which it excavates with determined drilling. It is usually found singly or in pairs. Hairy's broad range extends from Alaska to Newfoundland and Labrador south to Central America, though it is absent from Texas and the extreme Southwest.

WHITE-HEADED WOODPECKER
Dryobates albolarvatus

This large, striking woodpecker with a white head is limited to the far West, where it occurs in mature, mixed conifer, montane forests. It forages mostly near the base of trunks for adult insects and larvae. Its range extends from the southern interior of British Columbia to the mountains of San Diego County, California.

ARIZONA WOODPECKER
Dryobates arizonae

Fairly common and subtropical, this brown-backed woodpecker of pine-oak and riparian forests reaches the northern limit of its mostly Mexican range in the sky islands of southeastern Arizona and southwestern New Mexico. Feeding mostly on beetles and grubs in pine trunks, it forages mostly by flaking bark away with its bill and feet.

PILEATED WOODPECKER
Dryocopus pileatus

This grand, crested woodpecker of mature forests is North America's largest, and it ranges across eastern forests and southern Canada to the Rockies and south into central California. Found year-round in pairs in mature coniferous and deciduous forests, it forages on trunks, limbs, and fallen timber, where it industriously chisels for carpenter ants and beetle larvae. The bird's deep, oblong excavations sometimes cause trees to topple. It also thrives in suburban habitats with mature trees and consumes berries and suet in winter.

NORTHERN FLICKER *Colaptes auratus*

This large, gilded-winged, ground-foraging woodpecker ranks as one of North America's most common and widespread breeding

Three widespread and common woodpeckers. Downy (right) and Hairy (Rocky Mountains race, center) occur throughout most of North America, while Acorn (left) is a woodpecker of the western United States.

Flickers are large, vocal woodpeckers whose chisel-like bills excavate nesting cavities that are used by a number of bird species in subsequent seasons. Flickers spend much time on the ground foraging for ants, their favored prey. From left: Red-shafted Flicker, Yellow-shafted Flicker, Yellow-shafted in flight.

birds, ranging from the edge of the Arctic tundra south to Central America and the Greater Antilles. Birds from Canada and Alaska are migratory, retreating in fall to southern portions of the breeding range. They specialize in ants, which they find in insect-riddled trees or on the ground, and their yellow (eastern) or reddish (western) underwings render the birds unmistakable in flight. The eastern subspecies, Yellow-shafted Flicker, has suffered an almost 80 percent decline since 1990, partly due to Starlings taking available nest holes or evicting flickers from theirs.

GILDED FLICKER *Colaptes chrysoides*

While similar to Northern Flicker, this geographically restricted desert specialist flourishes in the cactus-enriched deserts of southern California, Arizona, and northern Mexico where Northern Flicker is absent. In these habitats, it adds berries and cactus fruits to its diet of ants and other insects, which it locates primarily on the desert floor.

Falconidae: Falcons and Caracaras

Recently split from the Accipitridae, in whose family the falcons were historically allied, this exciting and dynamic bird group continues to be evaluated and modified. Some authorities divide the 63 or so species into three or four subfamilies, two of which (Caracarinae [caracaras] and Falconinae [true falcons]) are represented in North America. All members are powerful fliers and have hooked bills and large, taloned feet. Their aerial finesse is aided by fused thoracic vertebrae, which adds stability, and large pectoral muscles, which may constitute up to 20 percent of body weight.

Another distinguishing trait is the "tomial tooth," a cutting spike at the tip of the upper bill that fits into a corresponding notch on the lower bill. This refinement facilitates the decapitation of prey, a falcon forte. A bony protuberance seated in the nostril (absent in forest falcons) is believed to facilitate air flow during high-speed dives.

All falcons, except pygmy falcons, have heavily blotched reddish brown eggs that are among the handsomest of all birds' eggs, with larger species having clutches of 3 to 7 eggs, and smaller species 3 or 4. Falcons do not build nests, so they lay their eggs on bare substrates, in cavities, or in other birds' nests from previous years.

Falcons enjoy a worldwide distribution and occur on every continent except Antarctica. Many species are concentrated in tropical regions, but Gyrfalcon and Peregrine breed in Arctic environs. They are adapted to almost every habitat, from forest to desert, urban centers to grasslands, and even Arctic marine environments, where many Gyrfalcons spend the northern winter.

North America's nine falcons include one caracara, and one species (Prairie Falcon) that is found exclusively in North America. Prey is captured mostly in the air, and ranges from insects to large birds, though some species also target small mammals.

CRESTED CARACARA *Caracara cheriway*

This large, plank-winged generalist is sometimes chided for its dietary focus on carrion, but our only caracara is also a fast, deter-

While not closely related to diurnal raptors, falcons are consummate predators, as the flesh-tearing bills and taloned feet attest. American Kestrel targets large insects, while Merlin and Peregrine are bird-catching specialists. Aplomado Falcon hunts birds and large insects, while Gyrfalcon favors ptarmigan and other large birds. Crested Caracara consumes almost anything edible, including snakes, lizards, carrion, and small mammals. Clockwise from upper left: male American Kestrel, male Merlin, Peregrine Falcon, Crested Caracara, Gyrfalcon, Aplomado Falcon.

Falcons are celebrated for their aerial finesse, and these mostly open-country interceptors range in size from the Killdeer-sized American Kestrel to the Osprey-sized Crested Caracara. Peregrine Falcons have been clocked at over 200 miles per hour in their celebrated stoops. Clockwise from upper left: American Kestrel, Prairie Falcon, Aplomado Falcon, Crested Caracara, Peregrine Falcon, adult male Merlin.

mined predator capable of overtaking and capturing birds the size of Little Blue Heron in flight, and it regularly kills small mammals. This long-legged, heavy-billed bird is nimble afoot and clever enough to flip cow pies in search of edible treasures hidden below.

Opportunistic, they attend grass fires to capture mammals and reptiles flushed or trapped by the flames. At road kills, caracaras typically arrive early and often in large numbers. Caracaras have been documented harassing vultures and pelicans, forcing them to disgorge the contents of their crops. While widespread across the Americas, they occur and are resident in North America only in central Florida, eastern Texas, and southern Arizona.

AMERICAN KESTREL *Falco sparverius*

A small, jaunty, colorful falcon, American Kestrel occurs throughout most of the Americas. It is widespread in North America, with northern breeders migratory. Most migrants winter in the southern United States. Kestrels are cavity nesters, often appropriating old flicker holes, but they also find nooks and crannies in bridges, buildings, and rock cliffs suitable housing for their 4 or 5 young.

Feeding mostly on large insects (particularly grasshoppers and dragonflies), kestrels are also accomplished mousers and will capture small birds, especially in winter. Males and females have different plumage, evident even in newly fledged young. Kestrels have experienced a dramatic decline in the United

Merlins are fierce predators that target small- to medium-sized birds for their prey, but they also eat dragonflies, especially during migration. This adult male Merlin has just finished a meal and is balancing himself in a strong wind.

States since 1990 (over 80 percent in some areas), with causes incompletely known.

MERLIN *Falco columbarius*

This small, pugnacious, bird-hunting falcon of open habitats ranges across the Northern Hemisphere, breeding across most of northern North America and wintering across much of the United States south to South America. It targets mostly flocking birds in winter, including shorebirds, Horned Lark, blackbirds, starlings, and waxwings. Males have bluish upperparts and are fondly called "Blue Jacks" by raptor enthusiasts. Females and young are brown. There are three sub-species of Merlin in North America, with one (*F. c. suckleyi*) having a mostly black plumage.

APLOMADO FALCON *Falco femoralis*

A colorful, limber, long-tailed, tropical and subtropical bird and insect-catching falcon, Aplomado occurs from the Texas coast, where it was successfully reintroduced, to South America, where it occurs from alpine tundra to moist tropical lowlands. Locally uncommon in the United States, it occurs mainly in coastal prairies of Texas and desert grasslands of New Mexico. Occasionally hunting cooperatively in pairs, the flushing

bird may pursue prey on the ground or in brush while the mate waits overhead. This species also uses perch hunting.

GYRFALCON *Falco rusticolus*

Large, robust, and long tailed, Gyrfalcon has three distinct plumages—gray, brown, and white. While a fairly common Arctic and subarctic breeder, this northernmost falcon winters in much of its breeding range, except for extreme northern areas. Some navigate the edge of the seasonal ice cap in winter, taking advantage of the bounty of alcids, gulls, and sea ducks that winter in the food-rich waters. Returning to nest sites on rocky cliffs or old bird nests long before less-hardy raptors return, they feed their clutch of 1–5 young a diet of mostly ptarmigan, augmented by the occasional lemming, hare, jaeger, or gull. Taking most prey in the air after a one-sided pursuit, Gyrs are fast enough to overtake even the fastest-flying waterfowl (an amazing feat).

PEREGRINE *Falco peregrinus*

Medium-large, mostly bird-catching raptors, Peregrines are celebrated for their spectacular stoops on prey, a plunge that may reach speeds in excess of 200 miles per hour, making Peregrines among the fastest-flying birds. They occur on every continent except Antarctica and breed in the North American Arctic from Alaska to Newfoundland and Labrador, as well as in a wide variety of locations from coast to coast, especially on cliff ledges in the West. DDT eradicated the eastern population (*F. p. anatum*) by 1964, and an introduced population (a genetic mix of multiple subspecies) is now flourishing in urban landscapes where Rock Pigeons, among Peregrines' favorite prey, are abundant. Additionally, after the release of captive-bred birds of *F. p. tundrius*, this subspecies is now once again flourishing in the eastern U.S. Northern and high-mountain breeding birds are migratory, with many wintering in the American tropics.

PRAIRIE FALCON *Falco mexicanus*

Implications of its scientific name notwithstanding, most Prairie Falcons reside in the hills and mountainous grasslands and steppes of the western United States and southwestern Canada. While closely related to Peregrine and similar in size, this medium-large sand-colored falcon feeds primarily on small mammals. It is something of a street brawler among falcons, with birds reported to ricochet off the ground after missing their mostly ground squirrel prey. In winter, Prairie Falcons also target open-country birds like Horned Lark, which are captured after a low-angle stoop followed by short, swift pursuit. While mostly resident, some birds vacate breeding territories in winter, with eastward expansion onto the prairies or the upper West Coast noted.

Psittaculidae: Parrots

This large, cohesive group of small to medium-sized birds varies enormously in size and color. While many are bedecked in extravagant colors, some are mostly monochromatic, with greens dominating. A cursory review of ranges indicates that most of the 300 or so members are tropical by nature or herald from the Southern Hemisphere.

Parrots have in common stout, hooked, fruit-tearing bills (with fleshy ceres), with the upper bill movable. They have large heads, thick necks, short legs, and zygodactyl feet (two toes facing in either direction) to facilitate perching and maneuvering in the canopy, a focused mobility that is often assisted by the bill. Wings are commonly pointed and the keel well developed, morphological traits they share with their close relatives, the falcons. Parrot tails may be long and pointed or fan shaped. They are intelligent, gregarious, garrulous, and given to raucous screeching.

Parrots and parakeets are highly social, mostly tropical species. While the family is poorly represented in North America, Green Parakeets are locally common in the Rio Grande Valley of Texas, and their mostly Central American range extends south to Nicaragua.

Many have considerable vocal arrays, and some can imitate human speech.

Parrots are so distinctive as a group that their taxonomic affinities remain uncertain.

One dubious distinction is that no other large bird group has a greater proportion of threatened or endangered species, with the illegal pet trade contributing to this dilemma.

While the Northern Hemisphere was slighted in its apportionment of parrots, there were formerly two native species in the United States—Carolina Parakeet, which is now sadly extinct, and Thick-billed Parrot, now a rare visitor from Mexico. Nevertheless, scores of non-native species have been introduced or escaped, with many established in mostly subtropical portions of the United States. Monk Parakeet enjoys a wide distribution since its accidental introduction.

MONK PARAKEET *Myiopsitta monachus*

This large, noisy, greenish parakeet and South American native was introduced into the United States and has established itself widely across eastern North America, with colonies reported north to Boston and Quebec and south to Texas and Florida. Active control measures were implemented in several fruit-growing states, but the highly urbanized birds are not a threat to agriculture.

GREEN PARAKEET
Psittacara holochlorus

All green and smallish, this Mexican native has established a significant naturalized population in border communities of south Texas, where it is commonly found in flocks in fruiting trees.

THICK-BILLED PARROT
Rhynchopsitta pachyrhyncha

Large and green, this red-fronted resident of Mexican oak-pine forest breeds in the mountains of northern Mexico and was formerly reported as far north as central Arizona. A recent attempt at reintroduction to the Chiricahua Mountains of Arizona failed.

WHITE-WINGED PARAKEET
Brotogeris versicolurus

A small green parakeet with white trailing edge to the wings, this native of South America is established in small numbers in southern Florida and southern California.

Red-crowned Parrots (top and center) are large, stocky *Amazonas* that now occur in California, southern Texas, and southern Florida, where native populations may have existed. Monk Parakeet (bottom) was introduced to the United States from South America, and it has spread widely across the eastern United States, even to cold climates as far north as Canada.

RED-CROWNED PARROT
Amazona viridigenalis

Native to Mexico, this stocky green and red-trimmed *Amazona* is established in California, Florida, and south Texas, where some birds may be of native origin. The thriving Texas population may exceed the indigenous population in Mexico.

Tyrannidae: Tyrant Flycatchers

At first glance, this eclectic assemblage of four somewhat disparate subfamilies has little in common above the submolecular level other than their geographic estrangement to the New World, where the family finds its greatest diversity in the forests of South America. With 429 species in 104 genera, ranging from the Amazon rain forests to the North American Arctic, where Say's Phoebe breeds, it is expected that diversification should be apparent. However, some binding generalities do exist.

While most members target insect prey (as the name flycatcher implies), many consume fruit during their annual cycle, and some species (manakins) are dedicated fruit eaters. A variety of hunting methods ranges from gleaning and hovering to sally-type fly-catching. One habitat the family has not broadly mastered is the ground, although Great Kiskadee, the family's omnivorous jack-of-all-trades, pilfers kibble from the bowls of tethered fidos. Phoebes also habitually dart to the ground to pluck insect prey, and Black Phoebe snaps insects off the surface of standing water, including swimming pools. The ingenuity and preponderance of the New World's largest bird family has filled the ecological niches of several Old World families through convergent evolution, including Old World Flycatchers, Old World Warblers, and shrikes.

In North America, the greatest diversity of tyrant flycatchers occurs in the desert and scrub habitat of the American West, where more than one species often occupies the same habitat. Conversely, the monotypic boreal forests of Canada show the least diversity.

Members of the family in North America fall between the 0.25-ounce Northern Beardless-Tyrannulet and the 2-ounce Great Kiskadee. While diversity of prey ranging from lizards to moths has given rise to a tailored diversity in bill shape and size, most members have slightly hooked triangular-shaped bills that are broad at the base and furnished with bristles. Many tyrant flycatchers have partially to fully concealed red or yellow crown patches that are raised when birds are excited, and some pump their tails when perched. Plumages range from drab to eye-popping, with most falling into the cryptic category.

Tyrant flycatcher pairs defend an established territory while the female assumes the duty of nest building. The name "tyrant" is well deserved (particularly among the kingbirds), and many species are vigorous defenders of their territories, as many a transgressing crow has learned, to its consternation. A few species secure their mostly cuplike nests to man-made structures, and some cavity-nesting species use nest boxes.

While not ranked among the planet's great vocalists (the syrinx of the family is of simple design), few bird groups have derived more names from their vocal utterances, including Eastern *Pewee*, Eastern *Phoebe*, and Great *Kiskadee*. Early risers, tyrant flycatchers are among the first birds to greet the new day. They also rank among the most itinerant of bird families, with nearly one-third engaged in some movement between breeding and nonbreeding areas. Several North American species head for winter quarters in Central and South America in August and September, soon after young have fledged.

The Myiarchus flycatchers (top) are mostly forest- and brush-loving birds that nest in cavities. From left: Great Crested, Ash-throated, and Brown-crested Flycatchers. The lower panel is a (non-Myiarchus) flycatcher sampler, including Scissor-tailed Flycatcher (left), Greater Pewee (center), and Willow Flycatcher (right).

ROSE-THROATED BECARD
Pachyramphus aglaiae

This chunky arboreal gleaner that plucks fruit and insect prey by sallying and sometimes hovering is our sole representative of this New World genus. Master builders, becards weave bulky gourd-shaped nests out of grass and bark, which they place near the end of branches, with the entrance hole situated near the bottom of the mass. They occur in the canopy of various subtropical forest types throughout Mexico and Central America, with a particular fondness for forest edges. Rose-throated reaches the northern limit of its range in southern Arizona and extreme southern Texas, where it mostly occurs in riparian woodlands. Unlike most tyrant flycatchers, the male's plumage differs greatly from the female's.

NORTHERN BEARDLESS-TYRANNULET
Camptostoma imberbe

With a name almost longer than the bird itself, this small drab flycatcher makes its presence known by a series of high, shrill, piping, whistled notes. It typically vocalizes from the top of thorn scrub or open branches as it interrupts its perch-to-perch hunt for insects and spiders near the tips of dense bushes and deciduous trees (most notably sycamore and mesquite). Often found near water, this subtropical gleaner is common and widespread in Mexico and Central America but reaches the northern limit of its range in the riparian woodlands of southern Texas and the arid scrubland of southeast Arizona.

DUSKY-CAPPED FLYCATCHER
Myiarchus tuberculifer

This common tropical and subtropical forest flycatcher reaches the northern limit of its extensive New World range in the shady canyon forests of southeastern Arizona, where its dawn song begins before sunrise and its plaintive, descending *wheeer* call emanates all day. Smaller and nimbler than other North American *Myiarchus*, it thrives in tight vegetative confines. Ranging north from Amazonia, where they are

mostly resident, Arizona birds retreat south in winter.

ASH-THROATED FLYCATCHER
Myiarchus cinerascens

A somewhat sun-bleached western *Myiarchus,* Ash-throated breeds widely in the western United States. It shows a temperature and habitat tolerance that ranges from the below-sea-level furnace that is Death Valley to the temperate woodlands of Washington and southern Idaho. Largely vacating its extensive North American breeding range in winter, it shows a pervasive pattern of vagrancy, with fall and winter records in many states east of the Mississippi. It is now regular in southern Florida in small numbers in winter. Many North American breeders retreat deeper into Mexico, where they occur mostly along Mexico's Pacific Slope south to Honduras.

GREAT CRESTED FLYCATCHER
Myiarchus crinitus

This large, brightly plumaged *Myiarchus* is common and widespread in woodlands of the eastern half of the United States and southern Canada. Loud and conspicuous, it seems ever out of sorts, filling woodland glens with an ongoing harangue that includes many whistled, rising *wheep* notes. Nesting in cavities, this species has a curious habit of garnishing its nest with a shed snakeskin, although clear or opaque plastic is a welcome substitute. Perch hunting around some forest clearings or edges, it changes perches frequently as it sallies out and snaps insect prey out of the air, near the ground, or from adjacent branches. Great Crested winters in southern Florida (where a resident population exists), southern Mexico, and Central and South America.

BROWN-CRESTED FLYCATCHER
Myiarchus tyrannulus

Our largest *Myiarchus,* Brown-crested has a bulky body structure with a heavy bill. It is a flycatcher of tropical deciduous forest and lowland scrub and reaches the northern limits of its range in the southwestern United States, ranging from southeastern California to southwestern New Mexico and southern Texas. It breeds in riparian woodlands before retreating south into Mexico for the winter.

GREAT KISKADEE *Pitangus sulphuratus*

This large, boisterous, kingfisher-like flycatcher is widespread in a variety of tropical and subtropical habitats and has made itself at home in urban and suburban areas in Texas. With an omnivorous diet including insects, fish, lizards, fruit, and small mammals, this perch hunter may drop to the ground or pluck prey from the water, which it seems never far from. In recent years it expanded its range northward and now occurs near Houston, Texas.

SULPHUR-BELLIED FLYCATCHER
Myiodynastes luteiventris

A large-headed and long-billed forest marauder, Sulphur-bellied is more often heard than seen. This streak-breasted flycatcher maneuvers through tropical deciduous and temperate montane forests searching for insect prey and fruit that it plucks by hover-gleaning. It occurs from southeastern Arizona to South America, with Arizona breeders retreating south in winter.

TROPICAL KINGBIRD
Tyrannus melancholicus

This common, large-billed denizen of second-growth forest and forest edge is common in residential areas with trees from southeastern Arizona and southeastern Texas south to South America. Kevin found the second record in Texas in 1988 (the first was 1916), and now a growing resident population occurs in Texas as far north as Corpus Christi. Tropical Kingbird is affectionately known to bird-tour guides as "TK," and the shorthand label is a tribute to the omnipresent nature of the bird in the Neotropics.

Kingbirds are open-country specialists that sally out from perches to snap insect prey out of the air. Woe to any crow or small raptor that intrudes into the breeding territory of these aggressive tyrants, as some kingbirds fly above and ride on the upper back of the intruder while pecking at its neck and head until it retreats. Clockwise from upper left: Gray Kingbird, Cassin's Kingbird, Eastern Kingbird, Eastern Kingbird in flight, Tropical Kingbird, Couch's Kingbird.

COUCH'S KINGBIRD *Tyrannus couchii*

While similar to Tropical Kingbird, Couch's has a much more abbreviated range, extending from south Texas to southern Mexico. Found in forest edge and open woodlands, most Texas breeders migrate south, with small numbers overwintering. Couch's has a rounder head and shorter, stockier bill on average compared to Tropical.

CASSIN'S KINGBIRD
Tyrannus vociferans

Fairly common and moderately widespread, this western flycatcher of open areas with trees breeds locally from South Dakota south into Mexico, with a strong concentration in the Four Corners states. A separate population occurs in California, where it represents the only kingbird that winters in the United States. A dusky gray hood with white throat and yellow belly are classic identification features of Cassin's.

THICK-BILLED KINGBIRD
Tyrannus crassirostris

This big, burly, shy, subtropical canopy specialist reaches the northern limit of its mostly Mexican range in the riparian woodlands of southeast Arizona. Favoring stands of mature sycamores and cottonwoods near water in otherwise arid landscapes, Thick-billed Kingbird is a recent immigrant to the United States. It was first found breeding in Arizona's Guadalupe Canyon in 1958.

WESTERN KINGBIRD *Tyrannus verticalis*

This widespread western flycatcher breeds in an array of open (often arid) habitats west of the Mississippi from southern Canada to northern Mexico. In winter, it migrates to southern Mexico and Central America, with a now established winter population in southern Florida. In fall, it shows a pervasive pattern of vagrancy to the Eastern Seaboard. Western is somewhat petite compared to

most other kingbirds, with a small bill and slender torso.

EASTERN KINGBIRD *Tyrannus tyrannus*

Common and widespread and (now) by no means "eastern," this tyrant returns to breeding areas in North America already open-mouthed and in a stuttering rage: *P'jeer, p'jeer, p'jeer, jer, jer, jer . . .* Prime territories are woodland edge abutting open areas, and vegetation abutting ponds, marshes, or rivers. Woe to any rival or transgressing crow that enters Eastern Kingbird airspace. They land on and peck the necks and upper backs of crows and hawks that make the mistake of entering their territory, thus exacting a tribute of feathers.

In summer, Eastern Kingbird feeds mostly on insects, but switches over to a fruit diet in fall and continues to consume fruit and insects on winter territories in South America. In North America, this once eastern breeder has expanded its range west to western Washington and across Canada from the Maritimes to British Columbia and Northwest Territories.

GRAY KINGBIRD *Tyrannus dominicensis*

This large, long-billed kingbird of tropical and subtropical regions is resident in northern South America and the Caribbean, reaching the northern limit of its breeding range in North Carolina. It breeds commonly along both Florida coastlines and less so in the Panhandle to Mississippi. It is common at the edge of dry, coastal forest habitat, farmlands, and cities, and frequently perches in the open on utility lines and old TV antennas. In winter, birds vacate the United States.

SCISSOR-TAILED FLYCATCHER
Tyrannus forficatus

An elegant, streamer-tailed flycatcher of dry, open habitats, Scissor-tailed is common in a number of the south-central United States from Nebraska south through Texas. Often seen perched on the top strands of barbed wire fences bordering pastures, they sally out and capture mostly insect prey, often after a spirited chase. During migration to wintering areas in Mexico and Central America, they often travel in small to very large groups. Kevin once saw 20,000 Scissor-taileds in one hour after dawn in early October 2001 in Veracruz, Mexico, which is normal. Small numbers also winter in southern Florida.

OLIVE-SIDED FLYCATCHER
Contopus cooperi

Olive-sided is a medium-large, burly, peak-headed, short-tailed flycatcher that announces itself with the loud, whistled demand, *"Quick three beers."* It breeds in mostly boreal forests from Alaska east across Canada, in the Rocky Mountains and western states, and in the Appalachian Mountains from Maine to Tennessee. This perch-hunting flycatcher typically takes the highest (often dead) snag and sallies out to snap up insects before returning to the same perch. Wintering in southern Mexico and Central and South America, it is among North America's latest spring migrants.

GREATER PEWEE *Contopus pertinax*

This crested, treetop perch hunter breeds in montane pine and pine-oak forests of Mexico and Central America. It reaches the northern limit of its range in the sky islands of southeastern Arizona, where its clear, whistled invitation, *"Oh say Maria,"* emanates from the tops of the tallest pines.

WESTERN WOOD-PEWEE
Contopus sordidulus

An industrious perch hunter of western forests and forest edges, this flycatcher sallies out from a dead snag to snatch insects out of pine-scented air, most notably wasps, beetles, flies, and ants. Birds intermix sallies with bouts of song, which are sung off and on during the day. The song is more hurried and burrier than Eastern's, but similar in pattern. Breeding in a variety of semi-open

coniferous and mixed forests from Alaska to Central America, the bird inhabits forested mountains from Colombia to Peru in winter.

EASTERN WOOD-PEWEE
Contopus virens

This small, gray-backed flycatcher of forest edge and forest clearings would easily go unnoticed except for the near-incessant renderings of its namesake song, *Pee-er-wee Pee-ur*. Late in the breeding season, it sometimes forgoes the punctuating phrase, leaving listeners holding their breath. Breeding in an assortment of mostly mature forest types across the eastern United States and southeastern Canada, the birds move to winter quarters in Central and forested South America by September. They establish a winter territory as well, where they sing their familiar song.

YELLOW-BELLIED FLYCATCHER
Empidonax flaviventris

Yellow-bellied nests in wet portions of boreal forests from Newfoundland and Labrador to the Yukon, and south to Wisconsin and New York. Despite the arboreal predilection of flycatchers, this one chooses to locate its nest and 4 or 5 white eggs in thick moss or a stump. In winter, it occupies dense vegetation from southern Mexico to Panama and is quite common in Honduras. Changing perches frequently, it may descend to the ground to capture prey.

ACADIAN FLYCATCHER
Empidonax virescens

This compact forest flycatcher breeds in mature deciduous and coniferous forests across most of the eastern United States from southern New England to northern Florida and west to the edge of the Great Plains. It favors ravines and streamside habitats, where it belts out its loud *we-seet* or *peet-see* call from an exposed perch, often before sunrise. In winter, it occurs in lowland forests

and plantations in Central America to western Panama.

ALDER FLYCATCHER
Empidonax alnorum

Lanky and olive shaded, our northernmost *Empidonax* breeds in wet, brushy (often alder) habitats from Alaska widely across Canada south to West Virginia. Similar to the more southerly breeding Willow Flycatcher, Alder winters exclusively in South America.

WILLOW FLYCATCHER *Empidonax traillii*

This small, drab flycatcher breeds coast to coast, across a good portion of the United States and southern Canada in brushy habitats, often near water. Where ranges overlap with Alder, Willow often chooses drier locations, but the two flycatchers are most easily distinguished by song—a wheezy, two-note sneeze, *fitz-bew,* for Willow, and a burry, three-noted snarl for Alder, *fee-be-o.* Willow Flycatcher winters in thickets and forest edges from southwestern Mexico south to northern South America.

LEAST FLYCATCHER
Empidonax minimus

Living up to its name, our smallest *Empidonax* with its small head and short tail is common and widespread across the northern United States and subarctic Canada in open mature or recovering mixed forests with a closed canopy. Wintering mostly in Central America north to northern Mexico, it uses the same forest-edge habitats that it favors in migration. Some also winter in southern Florida.

HAMMOND'S FLYCATCHER
Empidonax hammondii

This small gray flycatcher is often found high in tall conifers in cool mature coniferous and mixed forests from Alaska to central California and northern New Mexico. In the southern portion of its range, Hammond's may nest at altitudes above 10,000 feet. It occurs

Flycatchers are the largest family group in the New World. This sampler of North American flycatchers includes the following species, clockwise from upper left: Black Phoebe, Eastern Phoebe, Say's Phoebe, Western Wood-Pewee, Great Kiskadee, and adult male Vermilion Flycatcher. Sexes are similar in all but the Vermilion Flycatcher.

in tropical deciduous forest and forest edges in winter in Central America north to southeastern Arizona. Hammond's is quite similar to Least Flycatcher in physical structure and plumage.

GRAY FLYCATCHER *Empidonax wrightii*

This pale western flycatcher thrives in sagebrush and other arid brushy habitats. Breeding from southern British Columbia to New Mexico, with an isolated population in the Davis Mountains of western Texas, it has a distinctive tail-dipping behavior. It winters from southern Arizona south to central Mexico, where it favors riparian woodlands and mesquite.

DUSKY FLYCATCHER
Empidonax oberholseri

Small and olive-gray, this western flycatcher breeds west of the Rocky Mountains from the southern Yukon to central California and northern New Mexico. Similar in appearance to conifer forest–dwelling Hammond's Flycatcher, Dusky favors chaparral and brushy scrub on mountainsides and pine forests

with dense understory. In winter, Dusky prefers similar habitats from southern Arizona and southwestern New Mexico south to Guatemala.

PACIFIC-SLOPE FLYCATCHER
Empidonax difficilis

A flycatcher of dense, cool, humid (mostly coastal) pine-oak forests, Pacific-slope breeds from southeastern Alaska to southwestern California. It winters in montane evergreen forest from Baja to southern Mexico. It is virtually identical in appearance to Cordilleran Flycatcher, with which it was formerly grouped as a single species, Western Flycatcher.

CORDILLERAN FLYCATCHER
Empidonax occidentalis

Breeding widely throughout the Rocky Mountains from west-central Alberta south to southern Mexico, this denizen of dry, mid- to high-elevation pine-oak and coniferous forests is often found near streams or forest openings. Migrants winter with residents in montane pine-oak forests of Mexico. Cor-

dilleran and Pacific-slope Flycatchers share yellowish underparts and a bold rear eye crescent.

BLACK PHOEBE Sayornis nigricans

This dapper, black-cowled flycatcher of open woodlands usually occurs near water (including swimming pools), where it sallies out and plucks insects from the water's surface. A resident throughout its very extensive range extending from southeastern Oregon to South America, it is well acclimated to people. It often nests in the eaves of buildings and under bridges, as well as on natural cliffs.

EASTERN PHOEBE Sayornis phoebe

Arriving even as snow continues to fall, the aptly named Eastern Phoebe is often the first songbird to return to northern breeding areas in spring, having wintered mostly from the southeastern United States south into Mexico. Breeding from Northwest Territories to New Brunswick, and across much of the eastern United States except the far south, its burry, whistled chant *pheebee, phoebe* signals winter's end. Often affixing their grass nest under manmade structures, especially porches and bridges over streams, these industrious birds prepare for a busy nesting season that may involve a second brood, facilitated by the birds' early arrival.

SAY'S PHOEBE Sayonoris saya

Handsome and salmon bellied, this jack-of-all-flycatchers sallies, hovers, and perch hunts, as well as sometimes from the ground, in its quest for bees, wasps, ants, and grasshoppers. Breeding from Alaska to southern Mexico in two disconnected populations, Say's favors dry, mostly open habitats, including sagebrush, prairie, and subtropical scrub. Northern birds winter from coastal California and Texas south into Mexico, while many are resident in these same areas. Say's is partial to agricultural lands, including vineyards. Unlike other phoebes, it is a landlubber and mostly indifferent to water.

VERMILION FLYCATCHER Pyrocephalus rubinus

This small but stunning tropical and subtropical flycatcher occurs mostly in open arid habitats. It breeds in cactus and brush-studded grasslands from southeastern California to west Texas, which is the northern limit of its extensive New World breeding range. Often found near water, this perch hunter is so tenacious in its pursuit of insect prey that it may chase them to the ground. Many United States breeders winter south of the border, but some occur from southern California east to Florida's Gulf Coast.

Laniidae: Shrikes

Gram for gram, there are few predators tougher in the clinches than these predatory songbirds. While targeting mostly insects, shrikes may also kill vertebrate prey of their own size or larger, including small rattlesnakes and adult Mourning Doves. Thirty-one species range from the Arctic to the Equator and occur in Asia, Europe, Africa, and North America, but curiously not in Australia or South America.

Shrikes are medium-sized songbirds with mostly muted plumage. Gray, black, brown, and reddish brown shades predominate. Our Loggerhead Shrike is 10 inches long and 2.3 ounces, which is the same length as American Robin but half an ounce lighter. All but the black Magpie Shrike of Africa have a black mask across their face to reduce reflected light striking their eyes. Shrikes often face into the sun when hunting so that their advancing shadow does not alert prey.

The most celebrated trait of shrikes is their heavy, hooked, tomial tooth–equipped bill, which in combination with the bird's short, muscular neck serves to decapitate larger prey. This same notched bill arrangement

is also found on falcons, who likewise decapitate their prey.

Unlike most raptors, the tarsus (lower leg) of shrikes is short and the feet are weak, but the claws are curved and sharp. This anatomical shortcoming has given rise to a unique shrike adaptation. The "butcher birds" ingeniously impale prey on thorns or barbed wire, from which they then rend edible components. They carry smaller prey in the bill, medium-sized prey with the bill and feet, and larger prey with the feet.

Shrikes are visual perch hunters that fly to secure prey, which they kill with repeated strikes to the head or by grasping prey by the neck and whipping it back and forth until dead. Large insects are the favored prey of shrikes, but small birds and mammals may dominate the diet in winter. Like hawks and owls, shrikes regurgitate pellets containing packaged indigestible portions of prey. Most shrikes favor open or edge habitats that offer a surplus of strategic perches such as barbed wire fences, utility lines, isolated trees, and shelterbelts.

Shrikes are monogamous and territorial. Their rather large and messy nests are often built in the protective confines of a thorn tree. Many shrikes are migratory, including some Northern and Loggerhead Shrikes. Unlike other migratory passerines, shrikes do not accumulate fat reserves prior to migration, as they will doubtless find a bounty of exhausted passerines and large insects en route. Not accounted among the planet's great vocalists, the name "shrike" is thought to have come from the root word "shriek," an apt description of the bird's call.

Shrikes are colorfully known as "butcher birds," owing to their habit of impaling prey on thorns and barbed wire as they rend it with hooked bills. Northern Shrike (top) is slightly larger and often targets small songbirds for its meals, while Loggerhead (center and bottom) is a more southerly species that prefers large insects, lizards, and small snakes for food, but it will also take small birds if the opportunity arises.

LOGGERHEAD SHRIKE
Lanius ludovicianus

Loggerhead is the smaller of our two shrike species. While widespread across much of the United States and south-central Canada, it has a patchy distribution. The species is still relatively common in the South and West, but the upper and middle populations in the East have virtually disappeared, with habitat loss and pesticide use probable culprits. Loggerhead Shrikes are found in open habitats with short vegetation dotted with trees and shrubs. Northern birds migrate in late summer, while southern birds are year-round residents.

NORTHERN SHRIKE *Lanius borealis*

The arch-shrike is circumpolar in distribution, breeding in northern boreal forests and tundra interfaces, although some North American birds breed in mature willow stands. They mostly move to more temperate regions in winter, including southern Canada and the northern tier of the United States, as well as coastal Alaska and the Atlantic Maritimes. Hunting in a variety of open and semi-open habitats, Northern Shrikes target mostly birds and small mammals for food. Northern Shrikes are opportunistic, tenacious predators of small birds, pursuing them branch to branch in the confines of stunted spruces.

Vireonidae: Vireos

Vireos, some of which are also called greenlets (the Latin *vireo* translates as "I am green"), are small, mostly plain, leaf-gleaning specialists that excel in plucking insects from leaves and branches. Found only in the New World, most vireos occur in the tropics, with only 13 of 52 species spending part or all of their lives in North America. Ranging from the tropics to temperate regions, they choose habitats that have at least a brush component, although most occupy a variety of woodlands.

Most species in this family have greenish or olive upperparts that help conceal them in leaf cover, where they move deliberately from branch to branch and glean insects from the undersides of leaves, with a particular focus on caterpillars and leaf rollers. This is why you often see them momentarily sitting still with their heads turned sideways, after which they hover or leap upward as they pluck prey from underleaves.

Similar in many respects to warblers, vireos are plainer overall, and further distinguished by their short, hook-tipped bills; short, sturdy legs; and more deliberate manner of feeding. All vireos have pale underparts, and many have touches of yellow on the head, flanks, or breast. Some are capped or goggled, and some have whitish or yellowish wing bars, but the plumage is never streaked, barred, or spotted. Many are persistent vocalists, with males singing their monotonous incantations even into the midday heat.

Most North American vireos are migratory, and several species breed in the boreal regions of Canada. Vireo's messy, basketlike nests are bound by spider silk and are typically seated at the end of horizontal, forked branches. Nest parasitism by cowbirds is acute among several North American species. Fortunately, most vireo species are common and have stable populations.

BLACK-CAPPED VIREO *Vireo atricapilla*

Possibly our handsomest and most distinctive vireo, Black-capped is also the rarest, and a federally endangered species since 2018. More distinctly patterned than most vireos, it has greenish upperparts, which many vireos share. It is also the only noticeable sexually dimorphic vireo, with females having grayish, not blackish heads. A handful of other vireos have males that are more brightly plumaged than females. It breeds

Vireos are mostly arboreal, short-range shrikes. Their feeding style differs from the fast-paced motion of warblers by their slow, deliberate foraging technique whereby they perch on a branch and survey the undersides of leaves. After spotting worms or other prey, they may hover in place while plucking their meal from the leaves. Note the hook-tipped bills on these vireos. Clockwise from upper left: Warbling Vireo, Blue-headed Vireo, Cassin's Vireo, Bell's Vireo, eastern form, husky Yellow-throated Vireo, Philadelphia Vireo.

from Oklahoma to north-central Mexico, and winters in western Mexico. Black-capped is a persistent singer with a husky, chattering rant. The run-on ensemble of squeaky and whistled phrases typically emanates from a low bush and persists even into the heat of the day.

WHITE-EYED VIREO *Vireo griseus*

A common breeder in brushy understory and edge habitat of the eastern United States, this goggle-eyed, brush-loving vireo has a rapid nasal call that begins and ends with an emphatic note, and a song that often incorporates the calls of other birds. They are resident from coastal Virginia to Florida and Texas, and south to eastern Mexico. Others migrate to these areas, or as far as southeastern Mexico, Belize, and Guatemala.

BELL'S VIREO *Vireo bellii*

This plain, brush-loving, long-tailed vireo of the central and southwest United States is partial to willow and mesquite thickets. When perched, it raises and flicks its tail.

Eastern birds are greenish and resemble male Tennessee Warblers, while western birds are mostly grayish. Bell's migrates in winter to western Mexico and south to Honduras.

GRAY VIREO *Vireo vicinior*

Long tailed and shrikelike, this vireo breeds on hillsides in hot, arid, thorn-scrub habitats, as well as chaparral and piñon-juniper woodlands. It breeds locally in the Southwest and winters from southern Arizona south to northern Mexico and the Big Bend region of Texas. Feeding mostly on insects, this species may cross valleys to secure prey it has sighted. The birds have a habit of flicking their tail often.

HUTTON'S VIREO *Vireo huttoni*

This tiny vireo has two populations—one in coastal pine-oak woodlands from British Columbia to southern California; the other in Mexico, with birds reaching Arizona, New Mexico, and west Texas. Both populations are resident. Hutton's resembles Ruby-

crowned Kinglet, but with a larger, heavier bill, and commonly forages with other small birds in a variety of forested habitats.

YELLOW-THROATED VIREO
Vireo flavifrons

This large, sluggish, yellow-hooded and yellow-spectacled vireo is a common breeder in mature deciduous and mixed forests of the eastern United States. In winter, it occurs in various forest types from central Mexico to South America and the West Indies. Unlike many Neotropic songbird migrants, its population increased 62 percent from 1960 to 2014 (Partners in Flight).

CASSIN'S VIREO   *Vireo cassinii*

This large, gray-headed, greenish-backed vireo is a common breeder in western coniferous and mixed woodlands from southern British Columbia to southern California. In winter, it occurs from southwest Arizona to central Mexico in a variety of forest types.

BLUE-HEADED VIREO   *Vireo solitarius*

Similar to Cassin's Vireo, with whom it was once joined and labeled "Solitary Vireo," Blue-headed breeds in mixed forests widely across Canada and south through the Appalachians to northern Georgia. Partial to tall oaks and pines, it occurs in winter from Virginia to Texas and south to Costa Rica. This strikingly patterned vireo with a gray hood, white spectacles, and crisp white underparts with yellow sides is a favorite of birders everywhere.

PLUMBEOUS VIREO   *Vireo plumbeus*

This "middle member" of the Solitary Vireo complex is a large, common, mostly gray, white-spectacled vireo of open pine forests. Plumbeous breeds from Montana south through western Mexico to Honduras. It occurs in winter from southern Arizona south through western Mexico, with resident populations in Mexico, Guatemala, and Honduras.

Three species of vireos, including the very widespread Red-eyed Vireo (top); the geographically restricted Black-whiskered Vireo (center); and the goggle-eyed, federally endangered Black-capped Vireo (bottom).

PHILADELPHIA VIREO
Vireo philadelphicus

Similar to Warbling Vireo but more restricted in range, Philadelphia breeds widely in young deciduous forests across southern Canada to

Newfoundland and Labrador and northern New England. It is the farthest north-breeding vireo and migrates mostly east of the prairies to and from southern Mexico and Central America, where it occurs in open forests, gardens, and coffee plantations. The underparts of brighter adults are washed with yellow. It differs from Warbling Vireo with its dark lores, yellower underparts, and greener back.

WARBLING VIREO *Vireo gilvus*

The plainest of our vireos is also the most common and widespread, breeding or occurring across much of North America at some time of the year, except the Southeast. Look for this pale, grayish bird in the canopy of mature deciduous trees, especially near water. The male's hurried song seems like a taunt hurled at its mostly caterpillar prey: *"If I see it, I can seize it, and I'll squeeze it till it squirrrts."*

RED-EYED VIREO *Vireo olivaceus*

Red-eyed is a near-incessant vocalist and common widespread breeder in eastern and northern deciduous forests. The bill is uncommonly long for a vireo, and its sharply defined gray cap and dark eye line help distinguish it. In poor light, the red eye is difficult to discern. In winter the entire population migrates to the Amazon Basin.

BLACK-WHISKERED VIREO
Vireo altiloquus

This Caribbean foliage gleaner is mostly restricted to mangroves and coppice habitats along Florida's southern coastal areas. It also breeds in the West Indies and the Antilles, with a resident population in Jamaica. Winter range is South America, especially the Amazon Basin. It resembles Red-eyed Vireo and has a somewhat similar song, but Black-whiskered has a whisper-thin black whisker on the sides of its throat. This field mark and its restricted United States range help distinguish it.

Corvidae: Crows, Magpies, and Jays

This large cosmopolitan family (123 species) is represented everywhere except Antarctica and a handful of oceanic islands. In its ranks are some of the bird world's most intelligent representatives, including some that mimic human speech. They have also been known to use and even fashion tools to secure food. Corvids are highly social, vocally complex, and have exceptional memory and boundless curiosity. These qualities have endeared corvids to us for thousands of years, and it is a rare human culture that does not include corvids in its myths, religions, and lore.

Corvids are medium to large passerines. Common Raven is the largest perching bird on earth and one of the most widespread bird species in the Northern Hemisphere. Ravens are resourceful enough to survive in harsh Arctic environments, even through dark winter months.

While bills of corvids are variable, all are straight, sturdy, and fairly long, and used to secure food, often in ingenious ways. Long tarsi (lower legs) and round-tipped wings are also corvid traits, as are the spring-loaded legs that propel them. Crows and ravens are generally black, although some are black and gray or black and white. Occurring in mostly open habitats, black crows and ravens stand out. It is the more arboreal jays and magpies that don brighter plumage, with some of these having showy crests or elaborate tails. None have the streaked plumage patterns common in so many other passerines. Corvids molt completely once a year and females tend to be smaller.

Corvids have large brains, which accounts in part for their linguistic complexity. While varied, their vocalizations do not enjoy the intricacies of songs that are nearly universal among many other passerines, or songbirds. Common Raven can produce 80 distinct calls, but nothing that passes for a song.

Corvids are mostly omnivorous, but some are seed specialists, like Clark's Nutcracker and Pinyon Jay, who gather and store conifer seeds in autumn. It is perhaps in the quest for food that corvids show the extent of their intellect. Some species use tools to secure hidden food, and several advertise food to needy members of the flock via their communal roosting strategy, if resources are bountiful enough. Ravens and wolves have even developed a commensal relationship, with ravens guiding wolves to frozen carcasses beyond the leveraging reach of the corvid's bill. Once the wolf opens the carcass with its strong jaws, ravens feed on the scraps.

CANADA JAY *Perisoreus canadensis*

This small, compact, winsome, dark-capped resident of boreal forests is insatiably curious, and hardy beyond imagination. Ranging from Alaska east to Newfoundland and Labrador, and south to the Rockies and Pacific Northwest, this hardy jay will even breed and raise chicks in winter. In Eurasia, the closely related Siberian Jay occupies a similar

niche. Found in mostly coniferous (primarily spruce) forests, this opportunistic omnivore feeds on almost any nut, fruit, or flesh, including food left unattended around campsites. Its penchant for pilfering has earned the bird the nickname "camp robber."

BROWN JAY *Psilorhinus morio*

This very large jay is a common, vocal resident of tropical regions, ranging from the Rio Grande Valley of Texas (very uncommon) to northwestern Panama. It is mostly dark brown with a pale belly and dark bill (yellow in immature). Its loud call is similar to Red-shouldered Hawk's. They are highly social and travel in small flocks. They also breed cooperatively, with "helper" birds contributing to the fledging success of juveniles.

GREEN JAY *Cyanocorax yncas*

A brilliantly clad but furtive bird of tropical and subtropical forests, Green Jay is resident from southern Texas to South America. Traveling in family groups, these noisy jays are omnivores, feeding on insects, small

Jays are social and vocal, and apportioned across all of North America. Known for their intelligence, curiosity, and cunning, jays are among the favorites of birders and nonbirders alike. Clockwise from upper left: Green Jay, Steller's Jay, Blue Jay, Florida Scrub-Jay, Clark's Nutcracker, Canada Jay.

invertebrates, seeds, and fruit. While partial to forest edges, they generally avoid crossing open areas. The plumage of this jay is one of the most stunning in the world, and its personality is just as engaging.

PINYON JAY
Gymnorhinus cyanocephalus

This compact, straight-billed, pale blue jay spends much of the year traveling in flocks through piñon-juniper woodlands of the intermountain West in search of pine nuts, the species' staple food resource. Found mostly in the United States, the bird is resident from Oregon and Montana south to California and New Mexico. When piñon pines don't produce ample nuts, the birds wander in search of food.

STELLER'S JAY *Cyanocitta stelleri*

A large, dark blue, crested jay, Steller's occurs in assorted western forest types ranging from southern Alaska to the mountains of Mexico and Central America. Found mostly in pairs or family groups, Steller's feeds primarily on fruits, seeds, and berries, but its diet also includes insects and small vertebrates, including nestlings and eggs. It is common at backyard feeding stations.

BLUE JAY *Cyanocitta cristata*

Flashy is a good description of this common jay of eastern woodlands that has extended its range westward to the foothills of the Rockies and western British Columbia. Traveling in small, noisy groups, the birds thrive on acorns and are credited for proliferating the pin oak, whose jay-sized acorns they bury for later retrieval. While technically a permanent resident, Blue Jays regularly migrate south from northern breeding areas in search of adequate acorn crops, sometimes in very large flocks. They also prey on baby birds and eggs. Expert mimics, the birds are especially adept at imitating raptors, which they often do to clear out feeding stations.

FLORIDA SCRUB-JAY
Aphelocoma coerulescens

This Florida endemic is a resident of interior oak-scrub habitats sustained by frequent fires. With a population of only about 4,000 birds surviving in fragmented and geographically restricted locations (Partners in Flight), the bird is federally listed as threatened. It was split from Scrub-Jay in 1987.

ISLAND SCRUB-JAY
Aphelocoma insularis

Found only on Santa Cruz Island off the California Coast, Island Scrub-Jay is slightly larger but otherwise similar to California Scrub-Jay. Its preferred habitat is chaparral, dominated by low-growing oak. As is the case for many jays, acorns figure prominently in the diet of the roughly 2,300 birds in this population.

CALIFORNIA SCRUB-JAY
Aphelocoma californica

This slaty blue, crestless jay is the common "blue jay" from southern British Columbia south to Baja. Resident in a variety of woodland habitats, it mostly favors oaks and is common in suburban neighborhoods with oaks. Both this and Woodhouse's Scrub-Jay were recently deemed separate species in a two for one split from Western Scrub-Jay.

WOODHOUSE'S SCRUB-JAY
Aphelocoma woodhouseii

This paler western "blue jay" is fairly common but retiring in dry lowlands from Nevada south to Mexico and more widespread than California Scrub-Jay. It favors piñon-juniper and piñon-oak forests and frequents backyard feeders. It is very similar to California Scrub-Jay, but slightly paler and lacking a necklace.

MEXICAN JAY *Aphelocoma wollweberi*

Nearly endemic to Mexico, this large-billed, crestless, azure-colored jay of montane pine-oak and pine forests of Mexico ranges north

to eastern Arizona and western New Mexico, and just barely to a small area in western Texas. Found in small to large groups, they cache acorns and pine nuts.

CLARK'S NUTCRACKER
Nucifraga columbiana

A conifer specialist named after George Rogers Clark of Lewis and Clark fame, Clark's has many crowlike peculiarities, including a straight bill, short tail, and tendency to walk. Jays hop. In fact, when presented with the specimen, Alexander Wilson named the new species "Clark's Crow." Even the harsh call, *kraah,* is somewhat crowlike.

Frequently found above the tree line in parking areas where tourists gather, Clark's Nutcrackers often turn their corvid ingenuity toward panhandling instead of foraging for the conifer seeds that constitute their primary food source. Found at high eleva-

tions from British Columbia south to central California and New Mexico, they typically gather in small, loose flocks that descend to lower elevations both in winter and when cone crops fail.

BLACK-BILLED MAGPIE *Pica hudsonia*

A large, black-and-white, flamboyantly tailed jay, Black-billed prefers open-country habitats dotted with trees. It occurs from southern Alaska south to the central western states and east to the prairies. Found in small groups for most of the year, the birds make themselves at home near human habitation and have colonized city parks where, in winter, they augment their omnivorous diet by knocking back frozen dog feces.

YELLOW-BILLED MAGPIE *Pica nuttalli*

Except for its bright yellow bill, this California endemic differs little in plumage, voice,

Crows are known for their intelligence, and they exploit a range of opportunities, from robbing songbird nests of eggs and chicks to stealing food or trinkets from your car or picnic table. Top, from left: Northwestern Crow; Fish Crow; and American Crow, which is one of the most widespread species in North America. Magpies are flamboyantly tailed corvids of open and lightly vegetated western locations, including suburban areas. Black-billed Magpie (lower left) occurs across much of the West, while Yellow-billed Magpie (lower right) is endemic to California.

and mannerisms from its more widespread cousin, the Black-billed Magpie. Having taken a liking to suburban lawns, especially those astride riparian corridors, it is resident in the Sacramento and San Joaquin Valleys, and more coastally from San Francisco to Santa Barbara County.

AMERICAN CROW
Corvus brachyrhynchos

This most widespread and familiar crow occurs across most of North America south of the tundra, but it generally avoids the arid Southwest and much of southern and west Texas, where other large corvids reign supreme. It is celebrated for its intelligence, and Henry Ward Beecher's eloquent observation is fitting: "If men had wings and bore black feathers, few of them would be clever enough to be crows."

Permanent residents across much of their range, birds from much of Canada are migratory. Foraging mainly on the ground, American Crows are adapted to a variety of habitats, from woodlands and agricultural fields to urban centers. Their well-known deep *caw-caw* call is the best way to separate them from Northwestern Crow where their ranges overlap.

NORTHWESTERN CROW
Corvus caurinus

Smaller than American Crow, these small-ish crows of beaches and rocky coasts are never far from the marine environments from which they glean crabs, shellfish, and carrion. They gather at landfills in winter and occur from Alaska to Washington State. Their nasal *caw-caw* call is higher-pitched than American Crow's. Interbreeding occurs where ranges overlap with American Crow.

TAMAULIPAS CROW *Corvus imparatus*

This small, glossy, Mexican crow of scrubby lowlands, agricultural lands, and towns and villages is an irregular visitor and very rare breeder in the lower Rio Grande Valley in

Ravens are hawk-sized corvids whose uncommon intelligence and social proclivities allow them to thrive in a variety of habitats. Chihuahuan Raven (top) is an arid grassland specialist, while Common Raven occurs from the Arctic to the Saharan desert, and across much of North America.

summer, where it occasionally visits the Brownsville Landfill.

FISH CROW *Corvus ossifragus*

With a smaller size and shorter neck and legs than American Crow, this crow of beaches, forests, and shopping mall parking lots occurs from eastern Texas north to coastal New England and southern Illinois, but is curiously absent from much of the interior East. Almost never far from water, including major river systems, Fish Crow rarely mixes with American Crow. Its call is very different from that of other crows, with a nasal *eh-eh* vocalization.

CHIHUAHUAN RAVEN
Corvus cryptoleucus

A mostly sedentary raven of very dry areas and desert grasslands, Chihuahuan is larger than American Crow but smaller than Common Raven. It ranges north from central Mexico to western Kansas, and west to southeastern Arizona. In nonbreeding season, it often forages in large flocks in agricultural fields and landfills. Grayish nape feathers, best seen when wind blows them upward, distinguish Chihuahuan from Common Raven.

COMMON RAVEN *Corvus corax*

This large iconic bird of legend and lore is widespread across the landmasses of the Northern Hemisphere, except for much of the United States east of the Rockies. It shows an amazing degree of temperature tolerance, occuring from Arctic Greenland to the deserts of North Africa. In North America, this knife-billed corvid is mostly associated with wilderness areas, particularly Arctic and mountain habitats, where it shares a close relationship with large predators, whose kills the ravens pilfer. This opportunistic omnivore will consume just about anything edible and is associated with garbage dumps and landfills in winter in Arctic areas.

Alaudidae: Larks

What is small, furtive, dirt colored, and celebrated by poets and ornithologists alike? Try "larks." Ninety-six lark species have a worldwide distribution but are represented by only a single species each in Australia, Madagascar, and North America. Occurring mostly in dry, open, grassy or sparsely vegetated habitats, these ground-foraging, seed- and insect-eating birds walk or run across some of the world's most impoverished landscapes, relying on their natural earth-colored plumage to defeat hunting eyes. It is precisely this lack of feathered adornment that may have given rise (literally) to the signature trait of most larks: towering courtship flights, during which they are brought to song in order to catch a lady's eye. As captured in verse:

> Hail to thee blithe Spirit! . . .
> From the earth thou springest . . .
> And singing still dost soar, and soaring ever singest.
> —*Percy Bysshe Shelley,*
> *"To a Skylark"*

The skylark is certainly not alone in its aerial invocations. Our own Horned Lark also carries its voice and ardor aloft, filling the air with an outpouring of breathy chirps and high, clear, ascending tinkling notes. These displays may go on for many minutes and carry the birds to the limits of the unaided eye. Yet, despite larks' lusty singing, their syrinx is structurally simple.

Their small size, a peculiar flattened hind tarsus, and long legs with short toes and a long, straight hind claw physically unite larks. While larks prefer to run from danger, their wings are well developed, with ten primaries and extra-long tertials that cover the primaries on a folded wing, protecting them from wear in the harsh, sun-bleached environments that many larks call home.

Larks' bills range from stout and conical to long and pointy, with stout-billed species preferring a diet of grain, while pointy-billed species enjoy insects. The insect eaters also tend to have longer legs. While grains and invertebrates constitute the diet of most larks, the Greater Hoopoe-Lark of Cape Verde includes small reptiles in its diet. No matter the diet, larks typically take a break from foraging at midday and seek shelter in whatever shade is available.

Larks lead a terrestrial existence, laying their eggs and even roosting on the ground. Outside the breeding season, larks form single- or mixed-species flocks.

These ground-foraging birds feed in shortgrass and habitats so vegetatively impoverished that even a Savannah Sparrow might starve. Horned Lark (all three photos) is our native lark and, while it is aptly named, the "horns" do not always show. There are numerous subspecies of Horned Larks in North America, many of which are nonmigratory, and their appearance varies in many locations.

EURASIAN SKYLARK *Alauda arvensis*

The size of Horned Lark (7.25 inches), this streak-breasted, modestly crested, brown-backed bird of farmland, heath, and dunes generally avoids wooded habitats. On St. Matthew Island, Alaska, Pete once observed a male whose towering courtship display went on for many minutes. While North America has only one widespread native lark species, Horned Lark, Eurasian Skylark has a small and declining introduced population on Vancouver Island that may now number fewer than 100 individuals. It commonly occurs in Europe and Asia and is a regular visitor to the islands off Alaska, where it may have bred.

HORNED LARK *Eremophila alpestris*

This common, widespread, rakishly tufted New and Old World breeder ranks among the most numerous birds on the planet, favoring mostly barren terrain with scant vegetation. Its more than 40 subspecies attest to Horned Lark's extensive geographic range, and it occurs everywhere in Canada, the United States, and into Mexico, except for much of Florida and southwestern Louisiana. Most United States breeders are resident. Horned Lark is the only lark to penetrate Arctic regions and one of the first species to recolonize prairies denuded by fire. In winter, it often occurs in small to large flocks on plowed fields, beaches, and plowed roadsides, where it may mingle with Snow Buntings and longspurs.

Hirundinidae: Swallows

South of the Arctic, no airspace in North America is deprived of the shimmering elegance of these nimble aerial prey interceptors. Bad news for flying insects, but good news for millions of human admirers on every continent except insect-impoverished

Antarctica and Greenland. While martins carry a different last name, they are still included in the ranks of swallows.

Swallows are small to medium-sized scimitar-winged birds, with our largest swallow, Purple Martin, weighing in at a modest 2 ounces. While their streamlined bodies and wings assist them with speed, it is their tails that give swallows the agility to grab insect prey in flight. This specialization separates the planet's 83 swallow species from the ranks of other passerines and has given rise to such anatomical modifications as short necks, short legs, streamlined bodies, and long, tapered wings well suited for acceleration and gliding. The all-important tails, many of which have elongated and splayed outer feathers, can be spread, raised, lowered, and twisted, giving birds added lift and the ability to micromanage maneuverability, acceleration, and rate of climb.

Swallows have short, flat, wide bills and powerful jaw muscles to facilitate the capture of prey in flight. The scooping bill structure also aids some swallows in gathering and carrying mud for those species that build their own adobe nesting cavities as opposed to adopting a natural one in a tree, cliff, bank, or nest box.

Most swallows have dark upperparts and pale to whitish underparts, and some have iridescent upperparts (with blues and greens predominating). A few have rufous or pale foreheads, rumps, and/or throats. Habitats include farmland, mangroves, forested rivers, mountain cliffs, and urban areas. Some are solitary nesters, but many breed in colonies, building nests close to neighbors. In migration, large numbers may concentrate over insect-rich tidal marshes, and many breed near open water that provides insects during cool weather.

Swallows feed mainly in open country, from ground level to beyond the sight of the unaided human eye. It all depends on where the prey is. Swallows are fussy about their prey, generally targeting species ranging

In the eastern United States, these largest of swallows are wholly dependent on artificial Martin nest boxes for breeding. In the western United States, some nest in natural cavities, including old woodpecker holes in saguaro cactus. Unlike other swallows (except Tree and Violet-green), male (top) and female (bottom) don't appear similar. Martins undertake one of the longest migrations of any songbird, traveling to and from South America each year.

Swallows are nimble aerial interceptors, and many show touches of iridescence in their plumage. While insects make up the bulk of their diet, Tree Swallow also consumes dried fruit and berries, which allows it to remain in cold climates much longer in fall than other species. Clockwise from upper left: Barn Swallow, Cliff Swallow, Northern Rough-winged Swallow, male Violet-green Swallow, Cave Swallow, male Tree Swallow.

from ants to dragonflies. They mostly avoid stinging insects such as wasps, and some species, most notably Tree Swallow, include vegetable matter in their diet, consuming berries during migration and in winter.

As utilitarian as the bills of swallows are, the one application where they fall short is song. Twittering, chortles, chirps, snarls, and gurgled trills make up their vocal range, although Purple Martins have a distinct dawn song, often given aloft before first light.

Swallows have adapted well to humans, adopting our structures for their nests and reaping the harvest of insects stirred by farm equipment and animals. Swimming pools in arid climates provide swallows with water that they gather in flight. Their penchant for perching shoulder to shoulder on utility lines makes one wonder what they did before the invention of the telegraph.

PURPLE MARTIN *Progne subis*

Our largest swallow is widespread east of the Rockies, but breeding populations also occur in the desert Southwest, where birds nest in abandoned woodpecker holes in saguaro cactus, and locally from British Columbia to Baja, where they may also use natural cavities. In the eastern United States, they are virtually dependent on multichambered Purple Martin "apartments" or hollow gourds, a design that harks back to Native Americans.

While many Purple Martins return to North America from wintering grounds in Amazonia as early as mid-January (southern Florida), some far northern breeders may not return until late April. Ink-colored males and gray-breasted females enliven the summer skies of cities and towns fortunate enough to host a Purple Martin colony. In August, with young on the wing, the birds relocate to insect-rich marshes to fatten up for the long migration ahead (dragonflies and flying beetles are especially prized prey). Aggregations of over a million martins are possible, and they are gone by October.

TREE SWALLOW *Tachycineta bicolor*

Compact and snowy breasted, this blue-green–backed beauty is a widespread breeder, migrant, or winter visitor to most of open-forested North America, except far southern areas. Much of the population winters from Mexico south to Costa Rica, with

some remaining in Florida and southern Texas. They nest in old woodpecker holes and bird boxes designed for bluebirds that are placed in open areas. Tree Swallows gather in large postbreeding aggregations from midsummer to fall in marshes and coastal areas, with concentrations of over a million birds possible. Unlike most swallows, they augment their insect diet with berries (most notably bayberries), whose waxy cuticle sustains the birds even when temperatures fall below freezing.

VIOLET-GREEN SWALLOW
Tachycineta thalassina

This emerald-backed beauty is the western counterpart of Tree Swallow and occurs mostly in montane regions from Alaska to southern Mexico. It prefers open deciduous or coniferous forests, where it finds cavities for nesting. Somewhat social, large numbers may nest in relative proximity, although isolated pairs are also common. They often forage with other swallows and swifts. In winter, they occur from Baja and central Mexico (where resident populations occur) south to Honduras.

NORTHERN ROUGH-WINGED
SWALLOW *Stelgidopteryx serripennis*

A somewhat dowdy, brown-backed bird, this long-winged swallow is something of a loner, preferring to breed in isolated pairs in cavities near or over watercourses. This proclivity has led many a Rough-wing to build nests in ill-fitted seams of metal bridges. Widespread across the United States and southern Canada, most birds winter in Central America, although some winter along the Gulf Coast and extreme southern United States. In migration, they often occur with other swallows.

BANK SWALLOW *Riparia riparia*

Nimble and widespread, this highly social, brown-backed swallow with a neat, dark breast band (known elsewhere as Sand Martin) excavates cavities in sand banks, often adjacent to rivers or lakes. Colonies of over 1,000 pairs have been documented in Europe, but those in North America are typically more modest, involving scores to several hundred pairs. Bank Swallows occur as breeders or migrants across most of forested North America. Migrating soon after the breeding season (as early as late July), most winter in South America, but some also winter in western Mexico.

CLIFF SWALLOW
Petrochelidon pyrrhonota

This compact, hardy North American breeder affixes its gourd-shaped adobe nests to cliff faces and human structures. Highly social, with colonies from a handful to hundreds of pairs, they breed across much of North America, except for southeastern and some coastal mid-Atlantic states. In winter, birds range from Paraguay to central Argentina.

CAVE SWALLOW *Petrochelidon fulva*

Somewhat resembling a washed-out Cliff Swallow but with a rich buff throat rather than a dark one, this troglodyte among New World swallows has two breeding populations—one in the Southwest from Texas and southeastern New Mexico south to central Mexico, and the other in the islands of the West Indies, and southern Florida. Historically limited to using natural cave walls to secure their adobe nests, they have been increasingly drawn in recent years to buildings and highway overpasses. In winter, western birds withdraw into northern Mexico, while all but the southern Florida birds are resident in the West Indies.

BARN SWALLOW *Hirundo rustica*

This common, tine-tailed speedster nests across Eurasia and North America, where, as a common summer breeder, it is seen hunting low over pastures, yards, marshes, and open water. Its cup-shaped mud-and-

stick nest may be affixed to a vertical face beneath a sheltered overhang, or on a protected horizontal surface. The support beams of barns are ideal not only from a structural standpoint, but for dietary reasons as well. Livestock attract flies, and grazing livestock kick up flying insects—all grist for this nimble aerialist. Breeding across all of North America south of the Arctic, Barn Swallows winter from Mexico to South America, with a resident population in western Mexico, where they likewise favor open country. In winter and migration, Barn Swallows commonly roost in reed beds.

Paridae: Tits, Chickadees, and Titmice

This smallish family (56 species) of active, acrobatic, mostly woodland birds is widespread across the Northern Hemisphere and Africa, where they occupy a range of habitats. They are celebrated for their social proclivities and complex vocal repertoire. While a degree of uncertainty reigns regarding interfamily taxonomy, parids have one of the most cohesive physical makeups.

All are large-headed, plump-bodied, small to medium-sized birds (.18 to 1.7 ounces) equipped with short, strong, dark bills; strong legs and feet; and fairly long, narrow tails. Their soft plumage varies greatly, with some species exhibiting yellows, greens, and blues, while others are black, white, and gray. Colors are arranged in bold patterns without streaks or spotting typical of other passerines. Some species are acutely crested, while others are not. As befits sedentary forest birds, wings are generally rounded.

All parids nest in holes. Outside the breeding season, they form single-species flocks with a distinct social hierarchy. This group may then become the nucleus of a mixed-species flock that forages widely in search of food. During the breeding sea-son, they consume a variety of insects and larvae that they actively search for among leaves, while in winter they exhume insect larvae to supplement their seasonal focus on small seeds. While most parids are mostly sedentary, some engage in periodic irruptive flights related to food shortages.

Parids are generally confiding birds and are easily attracted to imitated scolding calls. Along with their active vocal nature, this makes them favorites among backyard bird feeding enthusiasts. Almost never silent, they may give contact calls when seemingly alone. Observers may be alerted to the presence of mixed feeding flocks by being attentive to parid vocalizations, most notably the widely used *chicka-dee-dee-dee* call that is the root of the chickadee's name.

CAROLINA CHICKADEE
Poecile carolinensis

Small and black bibbed, this beady-eyed leader of the pack is the common "black-capped" chickadee of the southern United States from Texas to Illinois and southern New Jersey. Common in deciduous, mixed, and pine woodlands, it concedes the higher elevations of the Appalachians to the Georgia border to Black-capped Chickadee. This smaller version of Black-capped sings a faster song with a few extra notes and gives the familiar *chicka-dee-dee-dee* call more quickly.

BLACK-CAPPED CHICKADEE
Poecile atricapillus

Our most widespread parid ranges across northern North America from coast to coast, with a geographic extension down the spine of the Appalachians to northern Georgia. At home in almost every forest type (with a partiality for birch), this hardy bird is resident to the south slope of the Brooks Range in Alaska, where bitter cold and limited daylight may prompt birds to enter an energy-conserving state of torpor. They are also irruptive, periodically deserting northern breeding areas when seed crops fail. Like

all chickadees, they are nimble and acrobatic, capable of hanging upside down and even hovering to reach food.

MOUNTAIN CHICKADEE *Poecile gambeli*

This rakish western chickadee is distinguished by a bold black eye line but is otherwise similar in appearance and habits to Black-capped and Carolina. Found mostly in montane habitat from southern Yukon south to California, Arizona, and New Mexico, it favors coniferous habitats. In winter, it may descend to lower elevations, where it occupies a range of woodland and suburban habitats.

MEXICAN CHICKADEE *Poecile sclateri*

Mexican is a mountain chickadee that reaches the northern limits of its mostly Mexican range in the sky island forests of southeast Arizona and southwestern New Mexico. Foraging in coniferous and pine-oak forests, it descends to lower elevations in winter, where it prefers oaks and their worm-infested galls and acorns. Its *chickadee* call is hurried and slurred. It resembles Black-capped but has a more extensive black throat, and lacks the buff tones found on other chickadees.

CHESTNUT-BACKED CHICKADEE
Poecile rufescens

A handsome tricolored chickadee of humid coniferous and mixed deciduous-coniferous forests, this species is resident from southeastern Alaska through the coastal ranges to central California.

BOREAL CHICKADEE
Poecile hudsonicus

This large (5.5 inches), brownish chickadee of northern coniferous forests occurs mostly in Canada and Alaska to the northern limits of forested terrain. It is the only chickadee with a brown cap and is mostly sedentary. In the United States, it occurs only in a few far northern locations.

GRAY-HEADED CHICKADEE
Poecile cinctus

Ultrahardy, this mostly Old World chickadee has a small, isolated, remote North American population extending from northern Alaska to the Yukon. It breeds mostly in mature riverside willow and aspen thickets, but also occurs in winter around human settlements, where it forages for scraps.

These winsome woodland birds often serve as the foundation of foraging flocks and are a favorite at backyard bird feeding stations thanks to their cheerful nature and tame behavior. Clockwise from upper left: Black-capped Chickadee, Carolina Chickadee, Mountain Chickadee, Oak Titmouse, Black-crested Titmouse, Tufted Titmouse.

Boreal Chickadee (top) is a hardy species that lives in far northern forests, far from the normal haunts of birders. Chestnut-backed Chickadee (bottom) is the only member of this family with bright color in its plumage. Bridled Titmouse (center) occurs only in the foothills and mountain canyons of Arizona and southwest New Mexico.

BRIDLED TITMOUSE
Baeolophus wollweberi

This rakishly crested titmouse of montane oak and mixed oak-pine-juniper woodlands occurs mostly in Mexico and reaches the northern limits of its range in central Arizona. As a resident species, birds show some altitudinal shift to lower elevations after the breeding season. It is the most strikingly marked of the chickadees and titmice.

OAK TITMOUSE *Baeolophus inornatus*

Formerly "Plain Titmouse," this nondescript, mostly gray oak and pine-oak specialist occurs from southwestern Oregon to Baja. It also occurs in well-wooded suburban areas.

JUNIPER TITMOUSE
Baeolophus ridgwayi

The other half of the now separated "Plain Titmouse" duo occurs mainly in dry, open piñon-juniper woodlands of the Great Basin (Nevada) and Upper Sonoran Zone (New Mexico). Its plain appearance is enhanced by a feisty tuft of feathers on its head and a boisterous attitude.

TUFTED TITMOUSE *Baeolophus bicolor*

This common, sassy woodland titmouse of mostly deciduous forests is widespread in the eastern United States. It typically forages singly or in pairs, but may join mixed-species flocks, where it often takes the lead. Its strong crest and large eyes set in a blank face give it a distinctive, endearing appearance.

BLACK-CRESTED TITMOUSE
Baeolophus atricristatus

Very similar to Tufted Titmouse, with which it freely interbreeds, this titmouse of Texas, southwestern Oklahoma, and northeast Mexico was once considered a subspecies of Tufted. A resident of oak woods and towns, it often joins mixed flocks with warblers and kinglets in winter.

Verdin is a tiny (4.5 inches) desert tit that is often the only bird found in the arid scrub habitats that it calls home. Typically found singly or paired, it builds a large cylindrical grass nest with an opening at one side, often situated in a thorny bush or cactus for protection from predators.

Remizidae: Penduline Tits and Verdin

Once considered a subfamily within the Paridae, this small family (13 species) of tiny, active, acrobatic, tweezer-billed, brush- and reed-loving birds behave like chickadees. Family members occur mostly in Europe, Asia, and Africa, and the tiny Verdin is the sole representative in North America. In addition to their sharp, pointy, conical bills, the members of this somewhat disparate group have fairly strong legs and feet, which allows them to cling to vertical perches and hang upside down for close inspection of leaves that may conceal their largely invertebrate prey. Their bills are ideally suited for exploring tight confines and opening gaps in insect-bearing reeds. Their nests are large and elaborate with hidden or tunneled openings, and those of Verdin are outfitted with a defensive armor of thorny twigs to deter predators.

VERDIN *Auriparus flaviceps*

At 4.5 inches, this tiny, brush-hugging bird occurs throughout arid habitats rich in cac-tus and thorny scrub. Usually solitary or paired, Verdins feed mostly on insects and spiders, but supplement their diets with fruit and nectar, sometimes from hummingbird feeders. The yellow head and chestnut shoulder patch contrast with a mostly gray and white plumage. They also have a surprisingly loud, shrill three-note whistle that carries in the dry desert air.

Aegithalidae: Long-tailed Tits

This small family of nimble, flocking birds ranges mostly across Europe and Asia. In North America, it is represented by a single western species, Bushtit.

The long-tailed tits (LTT) are tiny, long-tailed, petite-billed, chickadee-like birds that travel in cohesive small to large flocks and forage together, except during breeding season. For most of the twentieth century, they were grouped among the Paridae, sharing with the tits a small size, fluffy plumage, and short, rounded wings.

LTTs are mostly forest birds that favor a

Bushtits are active, nimble western tits commonly found in flocks that move around like a hungry cloud from bush to bush. The female (top) of the Pacific race has a pale eye, while Pacific males (bottom) have dark eyes.

lush understory, and are particularly partial to forest edge, riparian habitats, and clearings. They are also partial to parks, wooded cemeteries, and suburban habitats with trees. Usually in motion, the birds glean mostly insect prey from twigs and leaves, from the shrub layer to the canopy. To reach prey, they will hang upside down, hover, and even flycatch.

Clad for the most part in muted tones, if the birds were solitary and quiescent, which they almost never are, they would be virtually impossible to locate. However, LTTs are flocking birds, with small to large flocks moving through bushes like an animate cloud, taking short hops or flights from branch to branch. As befits highly social birds, LTTs are very vocal, with flock members emitting a near-constant stream of soft calls and muted sputterings and trills that do not carry far. They are tame, almost to the point of indifference. While they are permanent residents that typically defend territories, birds from higher altitudes may descend in winter and become seminomadic.

BUSHTIT *Psaltriparus minimus*

"Minimus" aptly describes this tiny, neckless, smoke-colored, nub-billed, wisp of a bird. Long tail included, Bushtit measures in at a diminutive 4.5 inches. Occurring widely across the West from southwestern British Columbia to Baja and south and east to central Texas, Bushtits occupy a variety of habitats, including chaparral and oak, piñon-juniper, and pine-oak woodlands, as well as well-vegetated suburban habitats. In winter, they favor riparian woodlands. Interior birds are pale and gray, while coastal birds are browner with brown caps.

Sittidae: Nuthatches

These sturdy, chunky, gravity-nullifying, mostly forest birds occur throughout much of the Northern Hemisphere. Twenty-seven species are physically similar and supremely adapted for clambering up and down tree trunks. While several bird families specialize in filling a similar niche, nuthatches have mastered the art of crawling down trunks headfirst, along with Black and White Warbler. Members of the family are typically smallish with long, straight, sturdy, pointed bills that can be as long as their neckless heads. All have compact bodies with short tails that are not used to prop them up, unlike other bark gleaners such as woodpeckers and creepers. Nuthatch legs are short with strong feet and long claws, and when moving along trunks, nuthatches place one foot ahead of the other. Their plumage is conservative and fundamentally similar. They have monochromatic (mostly bluish gray) upperparts, pale or rufous underparts, and a black to grayish bill. Some have black or brownish caps and/or black eye lines.

When moving up or down tree trunks, nuthatches move in a zigzag pattern, one foot grasping the trunk and bearing their weight while the other is moving. Some species hang upside down from horizontal branches, and many forage on the ground. Feeding on large nuts as well as insects, nuthatches do not anchor nuts with their feet, but instead wedge them into crevices and hammer their way in with their sturdy bills. Many cache seeds and nuts and are thus able to maintain year-round territories. Most are solitary or seen in pairs, but some join mixed-species flocks, and a few are true pack animals, foraging and roosting in small groups.

All nuthatches are vocal, but their vocalizations are simple and often limited to repeated one- or two-note utterances, with the exception of some spring songs.

Nuthatches live mostly in forest habitats and feed largely on insects during warm months, but seeds and nuts figure prominently in their winter diet. While many maintain year-round territories, some have separate breeding and nonbreeding territories. Several species are irruptive when food is scarce.

RED-BREASTED NUTHATCH
Sitta canadensis

Occupying primarily temperate coniferous or deciduous forests (eastern populations), this tiny nuthatch with a bright orange breast is a favorite among birders everywhere, especially at backyard feeders. They are resident from Alaska across Canada and south to California and New Mexico, and in the East from Wisconsin to Pennsylvania and south along the Appalachians. Some birds migrate or irrupt on an irregular basis to winter in most of the United States, except southern parts of Florida, Texas, and the desert Southwest. They often use standing dead trees for nesting. Males have bolder plumage and darker caps than females.

WHITE-BREASTED NUTHATCH
Sitta carolinensis

This distinctive and common resident species occurs across most of the United States and southern Canada, delighting homeowners with its gravity-defying movements. While the birds are partial to mature deciduous trees, they also occur in riparian and coniferous woodlands. They regularly visit backyard feeding stations, where sunflower seeds, suet, and peanuts are favored treats. While typically solitary, some join mixed feeding flocks in winter.

PYGMY NUTHATCH *Sitta pygmaea*

This western nuthatch typically occurs in pines, where vocal flocks give high, squeaky calls in sequence. Small even by nuthatch standards, Pygmy Nuthatches are tiny bundles of hyperactive energy, and they breed

Nuthatches are nimble acrobats capable of clambering up and down limbs, the true tree-huggers of the bird world. All four North American species appear here. Clockwise from top left: White-breasted, Red-breasted, Pygmy, and Brown-headed Nuthatches.

in large, extended-family groups. They are resident in scattered montane locations from southern British Columbia south into Mexico. In winter, birds may descend to lower altitudes and join mixed-species flocks.

BROWN-HEADED NUTHATCH
Sitta pusilla

Small, social, and vocal, Brown-headed Nuthatches swarm about the canopy of long-needle pine forests in the southeastern United States. They feed mostly on insects and spiders, and in winter, pine nuts figure prominently in their diet. They may use small sticks to help extract prey, making them among the few birds that use tools. In winter, they often join feeding flocks, but remain faithful to their forest habitat.

Certhiidae: Treecreepers

This small family (10 species) of bark-colored gleaners ranges widely across Europe and Asia but is represented by a single species in North America: Brown Creeper.

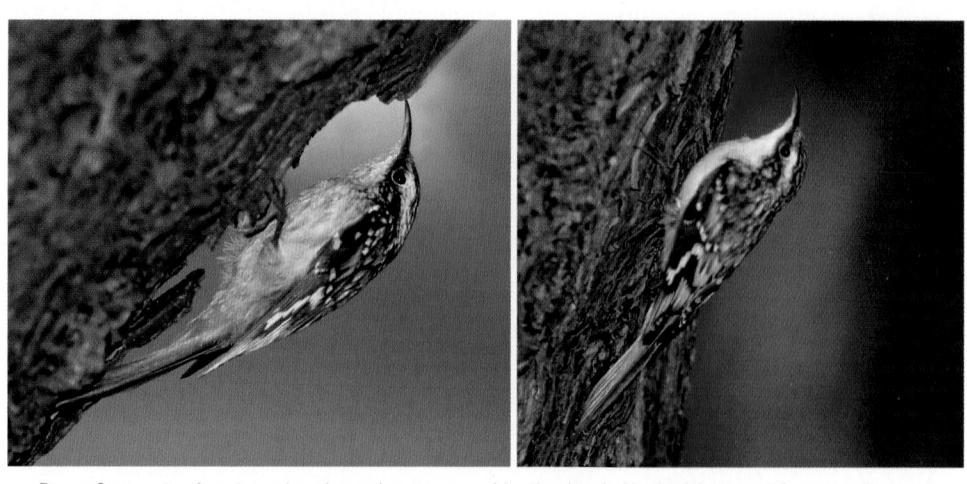

Brown Creeper is a forest species whose plumage resembles the dappled bark of the trees it forages in. It always starts its circular tree-trunk feeding motion from the bottom and works its way upward. After reaching its upper limit, Brown Creeper flies to the bottom of another tree, where it uses its stiff tail as a balancing prop.

Creepers are small, slightly built birds with slender, pointy, decurved, nutpicklike bills that are fitted with long, bristly-tipped tongues. Their legs are short with long toes and sharp claws, with the hind toe being particularly long. Especially long tails with 12 pointy-tipped feathers are stiff like those of woodpeckers and serve as anchoring props. All treecreepers look remarkably alike and, like woodpeckers, they maneuver only *up* tree trunks, not down. When they run out of tree, they flutter/fly to the base of the next tree on short, round wings. In flight, they resemble a falling leaf. The cryptic plumage is soft and intricately marked, giving upperparts the appearance of sun-dappled bark.

Creepers feed exclusively on insects and larvae that they extract from under tree bark; such specialized behavior mandates their living in woodland habitats. While mostly solitary, some join mixed-species flocks in winter, where their highly specialized feeding behavior outdistances the competition. When foraging, the birds move in short hops up and around tree trunks, with legs held to each side of the body, and insert their bills into promising cracks and crevices. Ants and spiders figure prominently in their diet.

Creepers build their hammock-shaped nests behind loose slabs of bark and deposit their 3 to 6 finely flecked white eggs into a cradle of fine bark, moss, plant down, and (sometimes) feathers.

BROWN CREEPER *Certhia americana*

This tiny, feathered nutpick frequents mature deciduous and coniferous forests, breeding in forested habitats in eastern and western North American locations. Its camouflaged plumage blends in perfectly with tree bark. In North America it is absent as a breeder in much of the central and southeastern United States, but it does winter in these locations. In the West, it is primarily a bird of montane forest. Only Canadian and central Alaskan populations are migratory.

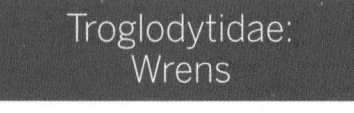

Troglodytidae: Wrens

These small, furtive birds with big voices thrive in low, brushy tangles. While represented in the Old and New Worlds, all but one of the family's 85 species occur exclusively in the New World, with most species

Almost always in motion, wrens use their narrow heads and nutpick bills to pry into nooks and crannies in search of insect prey. Most wrens cock their tails upward and sometimes do push-ups with their legs. Although they are skulkers, often in dense vegetation, their ringing songs give their location away. Clockwise from upper left: Carolina, Bewick's, Winter, Sedge, Marsh, and House Wrens.

occurring in tropical and subtropical regions. Only Winter Wren (*Troglodytes troglodytes*) colonized the Old World (where it is known simply as "Wren").

Wrens are mostly small with cryptic plumage, with browns and rufous dominating, though many have bold, often black-and-white patterning about the head and chest, and all have barred or banded tails. Tail lengths differ markedly among species, but the wings of wrens are short and rounded, as befits birds specialized to thrive in tight vegetative confines. Bills tend to be long, pointy, and slightly or markedly decurved, and the legs and feet of wrens are relatively large, which suits birds that spend much time foraging on or close to the ground. Wrens are adapted to occupy diverse ecological niches, from rain forests and temperate forests to deserts and open moorlands.

Most wrens roost and nest in cavities, and some roost in family groups. Some species destroy the eggs and young of other birds in prospective nest cavities, a behavioral trait

that, while not unique to wrens, does not endear House Wren to bluebird landlords.

Wrens rank among the planet's great vocalists, with some pairs engaging in duets. Some songs (like Carolina Wren's) are loud and repetitive, while others (like Winter Wren's) are elaborately complex. Invertebrates and their larvae are the primary food of wrens, although larger species are capable of subduing small vertebrates, and some species ingest small amounts of vegetable matter.

Most wrens are sedentary and solitary, but several North American species are migratory. Some tropical wrens join flocks attending ant swarms.

ROCK WREN *Salpinctes obsoletus*
This large, pale wren occurs widely as a resident or migratory species throughout arid western North America south to Honduras. Northern populations are migratory. At home in barren, boulder-strewn slopes, their fondness for bric-a-brac is well known, and they usually build a walkway of stones and

pebbles leading to their nests in tight crevices. They are remarkable singers and may have a repertoire of over 100 song types.

CANYON WREN *Catherpes mexicanus*

The canyons of the American West would seem empty without the voice of this large, ruddy wren to fill them. Found in mostly montane habitats west of the prairies, they are resident from British Columbia south to southern Baja and Texas, and deep into Mexico. Canyon Wrens thrive in steep-sided canyons amid piles of boulders, most commonly in arid locations, where they use their long, decurved bill to pry invertebrates out of rock crevices.

HOUSE WREN *Troglodytes aedon*

Breeding across much of the United States (except southern regions) and southern Canada, this ruddy brown to grayish wren is at home in a variety of semi-open habitats. It finds in suburbia a perfect mix of trees, shrubs, and garden insects, and nooks and crannies for cavity nesting, while many homeowners provide them with fancy nest boxes. Celebrated for their lusty singing and sometimes persecuted for their removal of eggs and chicks of other cavity-nesting birds, House Wrens winter across the southern United States into Mexico, where they skulk away the winter in low vegetation and overgrown abandoned structures.

PACIFIC WREN *Troglodytes pacificus*

This tiny, dark, West Coast wren is mostly a permanent resident from the Aleutians to southern California. Recently split from Winter Wren, it shares with that species a love of cool, damp, mostly old-growth forests, but in the Aleutians occupies tundra habitat, much as Winter Wren does in the moorlands of Scotland.

WINTER WREN *Troglodytes hiemalis*

A tiny nub-tailed ball with feathers, Winter Wren is the only wren to span the entire Northern Hemisphere. Its loud, prolonged song is heard from moist forests to well-vegetated parks, rocky sea cliffs, and taiga habitats. In North America, this mostly northern breeder favors damp coniferous forests from the Yukon east to Newfoundland and Labrador and south along the Appalachians to western North Carolina. Wooded ravines with streams are particularly favored breeding sites. Vacating northern breeding areas in winter, this hardy wren relocates to woodlands across the central and eastern United States. It prefers wet woodlands with stumps and fallen logs in winter.

SEDGE WREN *Cistothorus platensis*

Small and secretive, these buffy, streak-backed wrens are partial to tall, moist grass with scattered shrubs. Breeding mostly from central Canada to the central United States, they winter from southern New Jersey to Florida and west to Texas and northern Mexico, where they occur in marshes and fields. Isolated resident populations occur from Mexico to Costa Rica. This nomadic species may be abundant in a location one year, and absent the next. They are usually located by their sharp, dry chip notes.

MARSH WREN *Cistothorus palustris*

This widespread wren occurs in much of the United States and western Canada as a breeder, migrant, or resident species. Aptly named because it lives in tall reeds, it sometimes takes its sewing-machine song aloft. Nimble and acrobatic, the birds festoon their territory with multiple "dummy" nests. They are polygamous: males routinely mate with two or more females.

CAROLINA WREN
Thryothorus ludovicianus

Large and formerly southern in range, this wren with buff underparts occupies the understory of mostly deciduous woodlands from the Northeast to Texas and south into northern Mexico. A separate population

occurs on the Yucatán Peninsula in Mexico. Much at home in well-vegetated suburban environments, where their loud *tea kettle, tea kettle, tea kettle* song resonates, they have been known to roost in Christmas wreaths and nest in drainpipes, potted plants, and old boots. While invertebrates are their primary food, they enjoy suet and will consume seeds in a pinch. Carolina Wren has expanded its northern range greatly in the last 50 years to New England and southeastern Canada.

BEWICK'S WREN *Thryomanes bewickii*

This long-tailed, nervous, tail-flicking, brush-loving wren is now mostly relegated to the West, where it occurs from British Columbia to Baja and east to Nebraska and eastern Texas, and south to southern Mexico. Once breeding across much of the eastern United States, the bird was largely extirpated before the middle of the twentieth century, possibly because of competition with House Wren, which often sneaks into other birds' nests in its territory and pierces or removes eggs.

CACTUS WREN
Campylorhynchus brunneicapillus

A large Gray Catbird–sized wren of cactus-studded western deserts and arid scrub, Cactus Wren is resident from southern California to central Texas and south to central Mexico. Large nests placed in spiny cactus are pouchlike affairs woven of grass, sometimes incorporating feathers and trash. The song is a loud chatter that recalls a car that will not start.

Cactus Wren (top) is the largest North American wren at 8 inches long. It lives in arid habitats in the Southwest and Mexico. Canyon Wren (center) inhabits western canyons with steep rock walls, and sings one of the sweetest, most bubbly songs of all songbirds. Rock Wren (bottom) is a pale gray wren of arid rocky habitats throughout western North America.

Polioptilidae: Gnatcatchers

The members of this New World family of 17 small, long-tailed, mostly gray foliage gleaners have long, slender, slightly decurved bills and mostly short, rounded wings. Their presence in tropical and temperate forests

is often heralded by their vapor-thin voices or near-incessant sideways swishing of their tails. Each species of this generally arboreal family is partial to a certain plant community.

Typically found in pairs, gnatcatchers are active birds and rarely still as they search among leaves for invertebrate prey, usually arthropods. While some species move through the canopy, others spend their entire lives close to the ground. Their small, cuplike nests are shaded and concealed; constructed of plant fiber cemented with spider web or caterpillar silk, they are designed to stretch as young mature.

Only Blue-gray Gnatcatcher is truly migratory, vacating much of its North American breeding range in winter.

Earlier, we asserted that it is *not* correct to say of vireos "if you've seen one vireo, you've seen them all." Frankly and practically, this same level of discrimination does *not* apply to gnatcatchers. Essentially, to be familiar with one North American gnatcatcher is to know them all, at least as a member of this family.

BLUE-GRAY GNATCATCHER
Polioptila caerulea

Our most widespread gnatcatcher often occurs high in the canopy during breeding season. They use a wide variety of habitats and breed widely across the eastern United States and the southern half of the western states. They occur as residents along southern coastal areas and in far southern portions of the United States south through Mexico to Belize and Guatemala, where winter migrants join them. These active feeders often swish their tails sideways when foraging.

CALIFORNIA GNATCATCHER
Polioptila californica

This small, dark-capped California endemic occurs in coastal sage-scrub and is resident from Los Angeles to southern Baja. While the California subspecies is a federally

Gnatcatchers are small, active New World songbirds with thin bodies, small heads, and long tails. Blue-gray Gnatcatchers are some of the first Neotropical migrant songbirds to return in early spring. From top to bottom, all Blue-gray Gnatcatchers: western male, eastern male, eastern female.

Black-tailed Gnatcatcher (top and center) is a common bird in arid western habitats, where it forages low in bushes and small trees. California Gnatcatcher (bottom) is uncommon in its limited range of southern California, but fairly common in Baja.

endangered species, the bird is somewhat common in Baja, Mexico.

BLACK-TAILED GNATCATCHER
Polioptila melanura

Similar to California Gnatcatcher but more widespread, this high-strung bird of vegetated desert washes and montane scrub is a resident of the southwestern United States and northern Mexico. One of our smallest songbirds, it weighs as much as a nickel, and gets most of the water it needs from the insects it eats.

BLACK-CAPPED GNATCATCHER
Polioptila nigriceps

This wisp of a bird is resident in subtropical dry forests and frequents mesquite thickets in desert riparian flood plains. It reaches the northern limit of its mostly Mexican range in extreme southeast Arizona, where it is rare. Females and nonbreeders appear very similar to Blue-Gray Gnatcatcher.

Cinclidae: Dippers

If not comprising the most remarkable of all bird families, the world's five dipper species are at the very least a living tribute to the adaptiveness of birds. Not only are these stocky, thrushlike birds able to walk underwater, they are able to walk (and fly) in swift-moving waters. In fact, swift, clear, prey-bearing, rock-strewn water is requisite habitat for all dippers. In practical terms, this means dippers are found mostly in mountain streams.

These medium-sized passerines with short-cocked tails and straight, hook-tipped bills come equipped with long legs, strong feet, and sharp claws that allow birds to anchor themselves to streambeds. Their short, broad wings provide underwater propulsion that enables birds to "fly" underwa-

ter. Nostrils are narrow and equipped with a nasal flap as a further refinement to their aquatic lifestyle, and the oil gland at the base of the tail is large.

Three of the world's dippers are mono-chromatic gray or brown, while the other two have touches of white. Dippers also possess more body feathers than other passerines of comparable size, which protect an underlying layer of thick down.

The primary food of dippers is insect larvae, which they secure by wading, leaf turning, probing among pebbles, and diving. A good deal of the bird's daily time budget is spent foraging. The name "dipper" derives from the bird's habit of body-bobbing, one it shares with several other stream-foraging species. Where water remains open year-round, dippers tend to be permanent residents. Those breeding at higher altitudes descend to lower elevations in winter, remaining mostly in the same watershed.

AMERICAN DIPPER *Cinclus mexicanus*

Our sole representative of this family occurs from Alaska and the Yukon south through the western mountains to Central America. In classic dipper fashion, they occupy swift-flowing montane streams during the breeding season. Some relocate to mountain lakes and even rocky seacoasts in winter. Their body shape resembles a big gray tennis ball with legs.

Pycnonotidae: Bulbuls

This large family (138 species) of tropical forests and forest edges is widespread in Africa, Southeast Asia, and island groups of the Indian Ocean, with two species introduced to North America. Bulbuls are medium-sized, slender-bodied passerines with short necks; long tails; wide, rounded wings; and small, weak feet. Bill length varies, but most

As North America's sole representative of this remarkable aquatic family, American Dipper is often seen flying over the winding contours of swift-flowing western mountain streams, where it plunges into the cold waters and swims upstream to grab aquatic invertebrates. Lower bird is a juvenile.

Bulbuls are a family of mostly forest-dwelling birds native to Africa, Asia, and the Middle East. North America's two bulbul species are introduced, and this Red-whiskered Bulbul is fairly common in the suburbs of Miami, Florida.

are short to medium-long, and slender and down-curved near the tip. Some species are brightly colored, but most are more subdued, with dull browns, greens, grays, and yellows predominating. Some have brightly colored vents or rumps.

Bulbuls tend to be social, foraging in family groups. Many occur in clearings and forest edges, thus making them at home in vegetated human habitats. They are vocal,

although many are more noisy than musical. A number of species vocalize all day, commanding a prominent presence in the soundscape of tropical forests. Those in the genus *Pycnonotus,* which includes our two introduced species, sing from conspicuous perches (mockingbird fashion), and their songs are generally pleasing.

While bulbuls eat a range of food, most are mainly fruit eaters that augment their

diet with insects, small vertebrate, carrion, and even beeswax.

RED-WHISKERED BULBUL
Pycnonotus jocosus

This resident of Southeast Asia has established itself in suburban habitats in southern Florida (Dade County), where its conspicuously crested form is often seen perched on utility lines and old TV antennas. It generally avoids large forested tracts, preferring to forage for mostly fruit in bushes and trees.

RED-VENTED BULBUL *Pycnonotus cafer*

This resident of deciduous second-growth forests in India, Pakistan, and the Himalayas is established in broadleaf trees around Houston, Texas, where it is generally uncommon. Escapees are occasionally seen in southern California and southern Florida.

Regulidae:
Kinglets and Firecrests

The six species in this family of Northern Hemisphere forest birds are mostly similar in structure and behavior. They are tiny (0.2 to 0.3 ounces) and have plump bodies; short, notched tails; petite, needlelike bills; and a nervous habit of flicking their wings. All have a bland grayish to yellowish green color, subtle wing bars, and colorful erectile crests.

Hyperactive, they are by necessity usually foraging for food that they glean by balancing on the tips of twigs or pine needles or by hovering and plucking. They are specialized to prey upon the smallest of invertebrates, including aphids, spiders and their larvae, and eggs. While they glean much of this prey in bushes and trees, they may forage for cold-numbed insects on the ground in cold weather. Most are prone to forage in coniferous forests, but Ruby-crowned is equally at home in deciduous brush and weeds and is adept at snatching prey out of the air.

Kinglets are tiny, hyperactive foliage gleaners that flit through the canopy or low bushes in search of insects. The colored crown patches of male Ruby-crowned (top and center) and Golden-crowned (bottom) are often hidden unless birds are excited.

Kinglets are vocal when foraging, but their high and squeaky or low and sputtering sounds are subtle and easily missed by the human ear. They are migratory, and in winter they join mixed flocks with other birds.

GOLDEN-CROWNED KINGLET
Regulus satrapa

This tiny (4-inch), effervescent conifer specialist breeds widely in montane habitats across North America. It is boldly marked with a black eyebrow stripe and a flashy yellow crest. Barely larger than hummingbirds, these hardy songbirds can withstand frigid conditions to –40 degrees Fahrenheit. They occur in a variety of habitats in winter, where their thin, wispy song alerts you to their presence.

RUBY-CROWNED KINGLET
Regulus calendula

Breeding widely from Alaska to Maine, and in the Rockies and Cascades, this hardy mite winters across the lower half of the United States south to Guatemala. The male's namesake erectile crown is typically hidden, but raised when the bird is agitated. The male's long, loud song seems out of place for such a small bird.

Phylloscopidae: Leaf Warblers

This mostly Old World family, with only a single species found in North America, is perhaps best characterized by the sheer absence of unifying characteristics. All that might be said for the group as a whole is that they are small to medium passerines with a generally slender shape, pointy bills with bristles at the base, and wings with ten primaries (New World warblers have nine) that are short and rounded in the nonmigratory species that make up about half the family. Most have plain, inconspicuous plumage and are shy birds that occur close to the ground

The members of this mostly drab, Old World family make their presence known with songs that are often loud, staccato, and, generously speaking, monotonous. In North America, Arctic Warbler's run-on chatter song is an example of this. Arctic Warbler occurs only in subarctic Alaska, where it frequents willow thickets near streams.

The Sylviidae are a somewhat eclectic confederation of brush- and reed-loving, mostly Old World birds, of which Wrentit, North America's sole representative, is a case in point. Wrentit frequents coastal scrub habitats along the Pacific Coast, and it is the only member of its genus, *Chamaea*. It is most closely related to the parrotbills, which are sometimes regarded as a distinct family, the Paradoxornithidae. The name says it all.

in dense vegetation. Many make their presence known with monotonous songs that are generally complex but range from weak and thin to loud and staccato. The rapid, run-on chatter of our own Arctic Warbler is a classic example.

ARCTIC WARBLER *Phylloscopus borealis*

Breeding in subarctic willow thickets in western Alaska, this small, drab Old World warbler is fairly common in proper habitat. In fact, it is a rare stand of willows that does not host a breeding pair. Occurring from northern Asia and Europe to Scandinavia, Arctic Warblers winter in Southeast Asia, including the Philippines and Indonesia.

Sylviidae: Old World Warblers

This eclectic family of mostly brush- and reed-loving birds found in Eurasia, Africa, and the West Coast of the United States and Baja includes Old World warblers, parrotbills, and a number of birds formerly considered Old World babblers. DNA analysis, however, has given the group enough distinction to warrant the separate family status honored here. The parrotbills, which Wrentit most closely resembles, occur mostly in China.

Wrentit, once considered a babbler, remains something of a taxonomic paradox, but it shares with other members of the parrotbills a long tail, small neckless body, and penchant for dense cover. While most of the parrotbills ensconce themselves in bamboo thickets, Wrentit snugs itself in coastal chaparral, where it can be damnably difficult to find because of its skulking habits and cryptic plumage.

WRENTIT *Chamaea fasciata*

Our only Sylviidae member is virtually a California endemic, ranging in coastal sage-scrub from northwestern Oregon to western Baja. It also occurs in the interior of northern and central California in second growth, oak woodland, suburban yards, and urban parks. It deserves its description as the most sedentary species in North America, as young disperse only short distances from

the nest and even breed within their natal territory.

Wrentit's two-part vocalization begins with several emphatic chips followed by a squirrel-like trill, which, while distinctive, shies away from being labeled a "song." Wrentits are agile in their vegetated fortress, moving in quick hops from branch to branch while gleaning prey from bark and branches, and giving frequent contact calls with mates. Both males and females defend their territory and sing year-round. Their mostly grayish brown plumage includes a faint pink blush on the underparts.

Muscicapidae: Old World Flycatchers

This family strains the current craze for grouping and ordering birds based on their microscopic affinities. These two tundra-breeding North American representatives have little in common with the other 116 members of this largely arboreal Old World family beyond a shared insect diet and the preference for wintering in the Old World.

Anomalies aside, this large, mostly Old World family is widespread across Europe, Africa, and Asia, but these recent acquisitions from the family Turdidae (the thrushes) place our two somewhat disparate New World species, Northern Wheatear and Bluethroat, in the ranks of this bird group.

In the broadest sense, the Old World flycatchers (Bluethroat and Wheatear included) are small to very small passerines with wide-based, hook-tipped bills ideally suited for the capture of insect prey (often in flight). Their plumage is generally soft and typically dull, with browns and grays predominating, although some Asian species are quite colorful. The members of this family are mostly arboreal, using vegetative perches to sally out for prey. Not accounted among the planet's great vocalists, Old World flycatchers

Named for its white rump (in Old English "wheatear" approximates "white arse"), Northern Wheatear is an active perch-hunting bird of open, rocky country. Wintering in sub-Saharan Africa, Northern Wheatear has one of the longest migrations of any North American passerine. From top: adult female, immature Greenland race, breeding adult male.

Bluethroat is a stunning Old World chatlike songbird that breeds in Arctic Alaska and winters in northern Africa. Only the male has this colorful plumage, which it replaces in winter with drab brownish feathers.

are generally quiet and unobtrusive, though many species are given to wing flicking and tail jerking.

Insects constitute the bulk of the family's diet, though the manner of acquisition varies. Most species forage singly or in pairs. All the flycatchers that breed in the Palearctic are long-distance migrants, wintering in Asia and Africa, as do Bluethroats and Northern Wheatears that breed in North America. This biannual trek puts the "long" in long-distance migrant.

BLUETHROAT *Cyanecula svecica*

Until recently ranked with the thrushes (Turdidae), this pert, active tundra breeder has much in common with a group of small, ground-foraging Old World birds collectively called "chats." Breeding across Arctic regions from Scandinavia to northern Alaska, this New World breeder maintains its ties to the Old World by wintering in Southeast Asia, the Middle East, and Africa, where it frequents a diversity of semi-aquatic habitats, riverine thickets, reed beds, and tidal fringes. Breeding mostly in low, dense Arctic willow and birch thickets near water and

surrounded by open tundra, Bluethroats find a bounty of insect prey that they glean from the ground or from low vegetation during the 24-hour sunlit Arctic summer. Mostly dull brown above, the birds are named for the male's brilliant blue and chestnut throat patch.

NORTHERN WHEATEAR
Oenanthe oenanthe

Highly insectivorous, this ground-foraging chatlike bird uses boulders as vantage points, then sallies out to secure prey. Breeding in open, rocky tundra across the Holarctic region, it occurs in North America from northern Alaska south to the Kenai Peninsula, as well as Baffin and Ellesmere Islands, northern Quebec, and Newfoundland and Labrador. It winters (as befits an Old World flycatcher) mostly in Africa, where it forages for prey on the ground in open, rocky, arid steppe. Northern Wheatear's affinity for boulders even extends to habitat selection during migration. In the absence of natural stone, the birds adopt concrete rubble or construction site debris. Its 10,000-mile migration makes it a true migratory champion.

Turdidae: Thrushes

This very large family (336 species) enjoys a worldwide distribution, absenting itself only from Antarctica. As befits such a geographically dominant family, there is much ground for evolutionary divergence. Therefore, this highly evolved, numerically imposing family is subdivided into three subfamilies: Myadestinae (solitaires, bluebirds); Turdinae (typical or true thrushes, of which our American Robin is one); and Saxicolinae (the largest subfamily, which includes European robins and chats). Some authorities consider the chats to be part of the Old World Flycatchers.

The success of this family can be traced in part to their ability to exploit both a terrestrial and arboreal existence. Here they utilize food riches of the forest floor and also find safety, food, and nest locations in trees. While many thrushes target terrestrial invertebrate prey in the summer, they switch over to mainly fruits and berries in fall and winter. While the family appears to have evolved in tropical forests, they have colonized temperate forests, arctic tundra, harsh deserts, high altitudes, and remote islands. The only habitat they have not mastered is the aquatic one, although several species exploit streamsides, and American Robin routinely roosts in tidal marshes. Their terrestrial proclivities have also allowed thrushes to exploit habitats modified for humans, as any farmer or suburbanite can attest.

Thrushes are mostly medium-sized passerines with plumpish bodies and sturdy bills that are used for probing and moving leaf litter in search of primarily invertebrate prey. Plumage varies widely from gray, black, and brown to the most vivid of colors. Females are sometimes paler or more cryptic, and all young in this family have spotted underparts.

Most are solitary sight hunters that employ a scan-and-pursue strategy. Bluebirds are birds of open country and dedicated perch hunters. Some forest species flip leaf litter to expose food, or flush prey with a quivering foot before grabbing it, while others, like American Robin, detect prey (such as hidden earthworms) by sound, or by feeling an earthworm's vibrations through their feet. Some species roost communally outside the breeding season, and most are migratory, either short or long distance, or altitudinal.

If asked to name the family's most endearing quality, from poet to ornithologist, few would fail to say "their song." The thrushes rank among the planet's most accomplished vocalists, whether the applied standard is richness, complexity, or sheer beauty. This vocal superiority is shared by all, with the more solitary species (like the solitaires) upstaging more gregarious ones.

EASTERN BLUEBIRD *Sialia sialis*

Observed John Burroughs of this pretty little thrush of orchards and open country, "He carries sky on his back and the earth on his breast." Upon seeing this bird, most delight in the radiance of the male's colors, which, though shared by the female, are muted on her. Originally birds of fire-maintained savannah, Eastern Bluebirds quickly colonized pastures and orchards kept by European settlers, finding there the open habitats and nesting cavities the birds require. With their territory now augmented by nest boxes erected by an army of bluebird landlords, Eastern Bluebirds thrive across most of the eastern United States and southern Canada, generally east of the Great Plains, but also south into Mexico and northern Nicaragua. A disparate resident population exists in southern Arizona south along the Sierra Madres in Mexico. In winter, they vacate Canada and northern breeding areas, retreating into southern portions of the breeding range.

WESTERN BLUEBIRD *Sialia mexicana*

As handsome and beloved as Eastern Bluebird, which it somewhat resembles in plum-

age and mannerisms, this western counter-part breeds from southern British Columbia and western Montana south to Baja and southern Mexico. Breeding in open pine and piñon-juniper forest and other wooded habitats, it winters south to Arizona and western Texas, and south into Mexico, where it inhabits a variety of open and semi-open habitats, most notably vineyards and agricultural lands.

MOUNTAIN BLUEBIRD
Sialia currucoides

Breeding from Alaska south to California and New Mexico, this bird of open montane forests, aspens, subalpine meadows, sagebrush, montane grasslands, and piñon-junipers is a delight to the eyes. The male's cerulean blue plumage rivals a summer sky. In winter, it retreats from northern breeding areas and higher altitudes to open habitats from Oregon and South Dakota south into Mexico, where it forages in small homogeneous flocks, sometimes mixing with Western Bluebirds.

TOWNSEND'S SOLITAIRE
Myadestes townsendi

This elongated, wide-eyed songbird of western mountain forests breeds from Alaska south to the Mexican Plateau. It migrates from northern breeding areas and higher elevations to winter locally from southern British Columbia south into Mexico, particularly where juniper berries are abundant. This elegant thrush has a mostly gray plumage, but beautiful buffy wing patches and a bold eye-ring lift its appearance.

VEERY *Catharus fuscescens*

Named after its descending, spiraling song, *vee, veer, veer, verr,* this most faintly spotted of the four spot-breasted thrushes favors willow thickets and dense understory in damp deciduous woodlands. It breeds across much of southern Canada and east of the Rockies in the United States. Migrating mostly east of

Bluebirds are petite members of the thrush family that inhabit open areas, often with nearby woodlands. These three New World species occur throughout much of North America, except for far northern central and eastern regions. From top, all males: Eastern Bluebird, Mountain Bluebird, Western Bluebird.

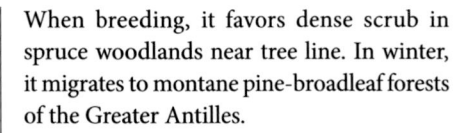

When breeding, it favors dense scrub in spruce woodlands near tree line. In winter, it migrates to montane pine-broadleaf forests of the Greater Antilles.

SWAINSON'S THRUSH
Catharus ustulatus

Like Gray-cheeked, Swainson's is a northern breeder, and one whose breeding range also extends south into the Rockies and coastal ranges. It breeds in streamside alder and willow thickets, while in migration it often forages in fruiting bushes and on open ground beneath a canopy. In winter, Swainson's occurs from central Mexico to northern South America in broadleaf forests, where birds forage mostly on the forest floor. The Pacific population has reddish plumage tones and a slightly different song. Swainson's buffy "spectacles" are helpful ID field marks.

HERMIT THRUSH *Catharus guttatus*

This small, richly spotted thrush breeds in the dense understory of open coniferous and mixed coniferous forests from Alaska east to Newfoundland and Labrador, south to New Jersey and down the Appalachians, as well as in numerous western locations. It is the only spot-breasted thrush that winters in North America, where it occupies a variety of woodland habitats from southern New Jersey south to Florida and west to Arizona, and from southwestern British Columbia south to southern Baja and most of Mexico. In winter, it favors berry-rich understory. Several subspecies exist, with the eastern race having a redder tail and buffy flanks. It often raises its tail and lowers its wings between steps.

WOOD THRUSH *Hylocichla mustelina*
Large and portly, this spot-breasted thrush with rich brownish red upperparts is celebrated for its enchanting, flutelike song. A bird of mature eastern deciduous forests, Wood Thrush winters mostly in the interior of broadleaf forests from eastern Mexico south through Central America. At all sea-

Townsend's Solitaire is a slender thrush with a small head and bill that conveys a subtle beauty and mystique to all who view it. It inhabits mountain canyons and foothills in the western United States.

the Rockies, it winters in forest understory in South America.

GRAY-CHEEKED THRUSH
Catharus minimus

Nesting in mostly stunted taiga forest, this northern thrush breeds from Newfoundland and Labrador to western Alaska, north to the limits of taiga forests. In winter, it occupies the understory of mature forest and secondary woodlands in South America. While somewhat similar to Swainson's Thrush, Gray-cheeked has overall colder plumage tones and only a thin, broken, whitish eyering.

BICKNELL'S THRUSH *Catharus bicknelli*
While similar to Gray-cheeked, Bicknell's is smaller and has a yellower bill and reddish tones to its wings and tail. It also nests and winters in entirely separate regions, breeding at higher elevations from southern Quebec and the Maritimes to New England.

These six spotted thrushes inhabit shady woods with leafy understories, where they feed mostly on the ground. Their foraging style is similar to American Robin's, with a start, stop, tilt motion. Clockwise from upper left: Veery (Eastern subspecies), Swainson's Thrush, Gray-cheeked Thrush, Wood Thrush, Bicknell's Thrush, Hermit Thrush.

American Robin (left) is probably the most well-known and recognized bird in North America, and is the inspiration for countless songs, poems, and stories. It inhabits just about every habitat in North America that has trees or bushes for nesting. Clay-colored Thrush (center) is a tropical species very similar to American Robin in structure and behavior, but it occurs only in extreme south Texas in the United States. Varied Thrush (right) is a bird of far west coniferous forests whose song resembles an off-pitch tuning fork.

sons, and in migration, it forages mostly in leaf litter for invertebrate prey.

CLAY-COLORED THRUSH (ROBIN)
Turdus grayi

This aptly named thrush does indeed resemble a drab, pale brown robin, with only the greenish bill adding a touch of color to this ground-loving thrush of tropical and sub-tropical deciduous forest. A resident species in tropical regions from Mexico to northern South America, it reaches the northern limits of its range in the brushy woodlands of the lower Rio Grande Valley of Texas.

AMERICAN ROBIN *Turdus migratorius*

An iconic North American bird, American Robin breeds wherever trees and bushes are

found throughout North America and the Sierra Madre of Mexico, except for much of Florida, southern Louisiana, southern Texas, and the arid Southwest. It would be difficult to find a North American resident who could not identify this species at a glance. Foraging mostly on open ground near trees, they build their stick, grass, and mud nests in bushes and trees. Pete once found a nest on the interior of a sod outhouse serving an abandoned whaling station 50 feet from the Arctic Sea and 100 miles from the nearest stunted tree. Males have blacker heads and richer orange underparts than females.

VARIED THRUSH *Ixoreus naevius*

This boldly patterned arboreal thrush flourishes in humid coastal and montane coniferous forests with lush understory, from western Alaska and the northern Yukon south to northwestern California. Varied Thrush's reedy ventriloquial song sounds like an off-key tuning fork and adds a haunting quality to the mature conifer forests where it breeds. Northern and interior breeders winter from coastal British Columbia south to Mexico, where they occupy a variety of woodlands.

Mimidae: Mockingbirds and Thrashers

This small, physically similar family of 34 New World species somewhat resembles thrushes, but its members are overall larger and lankier. All species range between 8 and 12 inches long and have little to no sexual dimorphism (differences) in size or plumage. Ranging from southern Canada to the southern tip of South America, most mimids have long, decurved bills suited for plucking fruit or digging for invertebrates, both of which comprise most of their food. Uniformly bland in their typical brown or gray plumage, many thrashers sport spotted and/or streaked breasts. Iris colors are often distinctive, ranging from orange or yellow to white, with many young birds sporting darkish eyes.

The group generally favors low, scrubby habitats or desert scrub. Thrashers are mostly skulkers, except when revealing their presence by loud vocalizations. Highly terrestrial, many thrashers elect to run rather than fly from danger. Strongly territorial, birds define their territorial perimeter largely by song, and many species are resident. Songs include a succession of repeated phrases and whistles, and some species are great mimics, incorporating the songs of other species and other noises into their repertoire.

Mimids are omnivorous, and up to half of their diet may consist of fruit. Interestingly, mockingbirds were among the bird groups that Charles Darwin studied that led to his theory of evolution.

Of the four species that breed as far north as Canada, only Northern Mockingbird is resident. The remaining three—Gray Catbird, Brown Thrasher, and Sage Thrasher—vacate much of their northern breeding range in winter.

GRAY CATBIRD *Dumetella carolinensis*

Small (8.5 inches) and slate colored, this mimid with a lot of character breeds in and haunts the brushy understory of deciduous forests from British Columbia to New Brunswick, and from Oregon east to northern Florida. It winters from southern New England to Florida, west to Texas, and south to Panama and the West Indies. Its name is derived from its catlike mewing call. It also mimics calls of other birds and strings them along to create its own song.

CURVE-BILLED THRASHER *Toxostoma curvirostre*

This overall gray-brown thrasher of open habitats dotted with shrubs announces its presence with its loud *wit-WEET* call and is common from southwestern Nebraska

and Texas to western Arizona, including suburban locations. Underparts are variably spotted on this bird who readily adapts to backyard bird habitats.

BROWN THRASHER *Toxostoma rufum*

Large, long tailed, and rufous backed, this brush-hugging skulker breeds across most of central and eastern United States to southern Canada. Foraging mostly on the ground, where they pick through leaf litter for invertebrates, most northern birds retreat in winter to southern breeding areas from southern New Jersey south to Florida and west to east Texas, where they feed mostly on berries and seeds. It mimics other bird songs, which it typically repeats in duplicate fashion.

LONG-BILLED THRASHER
Toxostoma longirostre

While similar to Brown Thrasher in size and structure, Long-billed is brownish, lacking the rich reddish upperparts of Brown Thrasher, and has a longer, thinner, more decurved bill. This south Texas and eastern Mexico resident is common in riparian woodlands and brushlands. Long-billed adjusts its territory in winter to take advantage of seasonal food opportunities, but is mostly resident.

BENDIRE'S THRASHER
Toxostoma bendirei

Straight billed and lightly spotted, this thrasher of the desert Southwest and northwestern Mexico has declined almost 90 percent since 1960 (Partners in Flight). Its range overlaps with the larger, longer-billed Curve-billed Thrasher, which also occurs in desert scrub.

CALIFORNIA THRASHER
Toxostoma redivivum

Large and mostly brownish, California Thrasher has a long, decurved bill and rust undertail and is virtually a California

Northern Mockingbird (top and center) and Gray Catbird (bottom) are two of the three mimid songbirds that incorporate songs and calls of other birds into their vocal repertoire. Brown Thrasher is the third mimid. Northern Mockingbird is the king of mimicry, with some birds able to perfectly reproduce sounds of up to 100 other birds in triplet fashion. Gray Catbird is a subtly beautiful bird with a lot of character. It inhabits hedgerows, thickets, and forest edges.

Thrashers are large, strongly terrestrial songbirds with long tails and slightly to strongly decurved bills. They are skulkers by trade, but often sing or sit on exposed perches, where you can easily view them. From left: Long-billed Thrasher, Bendire's Thrasher, Brown Thrasher.

These three western thrashers reside in very different habitats, with Sage Thrasher (center) found in the vast sagebrush flats of the western United States, while California Thrasher (right) frequents chaparral and suburban locations from northern California to Baja. Curve-billed Thrasher (left) enjoys dry, arid locations from Texas to California.

endemic, found year-round from northern California to northern Baja. It is very hard to see in chaparral, but in suburban settings it will often wander onto lawns and driveways, and even glean insects off car bumpers. It is often found in pairs searching for insects in leaf litter.

LECONTE'S THRASHER
Toxostoma lecontei

Named after John Lawrence LeConte (1825–1883), this large, pallid desert thrasher with a long, thin, decurved bill and orangish undertail thrives in sparsely vegetated arid deserts dotted with creosote bush, from California and Nevada south into Mexico. Usually solitary, it runs from bush to bush, where it digs in the leaf litter for insects.

CRISSAL THRASHER *Toxostoma crissale*

Large and grayish overall, this thrasher with a long decurved bill, reddish undertail, and very long tail occurs in desert washes and riparian thickets of the American Southwest and central Mexico. It is less common and more secretive than Curve-billed Thrasher, which occupies similar habitats. Crissal rarely mimics other species.

SAGE THRASHER
Oreoscoptes montanus

These smallish, grayish brown, heavily spotted mimids of western sagebrush steppe have a fairly short, straight bill and upright stance. Breeding north in the Great Basin to southern Canada, they winter from southern California to central Texas, and south into central

Mexico. They appear more like small, spotted mockingbirds than their thrasher kin.

NORTHERN MOCKINGBIRD
Mimus polyglottos

These dapper gray mimids of open and semi-open habitats range coast to coast across most of the United States, save for the upper central and western states and upper New England. They also occur in the West Indies and Mexico. Permanent residents in much of their range, males famously hitch themselves on a conspicuous perch and define their territories with song. Ideally suited for suburban habitats and urban parks, they may sing up to 100 perfect songs of other birds, usually in triplets and often during nighttime hours, much to the consternation of some human neighbors. They also aggressively attack cats and other predators that stray into their breeding territories. These are truly birds with a lot of spunk and character that endlessly entertain humans fortunate enough to have a pair in their yard.

Sturnidae: Starlings and Mynas

Many who are familiar with the introduced European Starling, *Sturnus vulgaris,* are surprised to learn that it is but one of 112 worldwide starling species, most of which occur in Africa and Asia, but which also have branched out to Australia and some Pacific islands. This highly successful group of mostly compact, medium-sized passerines evolved to exploit a wide array of habitats, including forests, savannah, cities, and towns (in fact, many species thrive in habitats modified by human activity).

Starlings consume a variety of wild and cultivated grains and fruit, but also invertebrates, so the terms "omnivorous" and "opportunistic" are labels best applied to this group. European Starling seems particularly adept at exploiting whatever food resources other birds are consuming. In the spirit of "anything you can do, I can do better," these birds fly-catch, probe mudflats shoulder to shoulder with sandpipers, and draw grubs from lawns with a finesse that would make American Robin proud to be an understudy. Some species have learned to peck the eggs of other species, and a few ride oxpecker-like on the backs of large mammals to pluck ticks and other parasites.

Many species have iridescent plumage, and for many species bathing is particularly important. However, the two most noteworthy traits are their ability to maneuver in tightly packed flying flocks (murmurations) and their vocal repertoire. Some African and Asian groups gather in "choirs" and sing for extended periods (sometimes during the heat of midday), and some species are particularly vocal at roost sites. It is precisely European Starling's skill at mimicry that is responsible for the birds' presence in North America.

In 1890, a Shakespeare zealot introduced 60 European Starlings into Central Park, New York. Several weeks later, the joyous news was celebrated: a pair was nesting under the eaves of the American Museum of Natural History. The line of text that prompted the release comes from William Shakespeare's *Henry IV, Part 1*: said Hotspur, "I'll have a starling shall be taught to speak nothing but 'Mortimer.'" These fateful words let loose the plague of starlings that infests North America today. Many starlings are cavity nesters that are capable of evicting (even killing) birds the size of Red-headed Woodpecker to acquire nest sites. This murderous proclivity has not endeared starlings to bluebird or Purple Martin landlords.

In addition to European Starling, North America has three introduced myna species with limited distributions.

EUROPEAN STARLING *Sturnus vulgaris*

Commonly found almost everywhere humans exist, the only habitats this versatile

bird seems unable to exploit are open tundra and open oceans, although starlings do feed on beaches. They are particularly prevalent in orchards, feedlots, and landfills, and very common in urban areas where nooks and crannies of buildings offer nest sites, and discarded doughnuts and pizza crusts are substitutes for grain. Often found in large flocks numbering hundreds of birds, they have even spread to Alaska and central Mexico.

COMMON MYNA *Acridotheres tristis*

Brown bodied and yellow billed, this Asian native is thriving in the suburbs of southern Florida. Vocalizations include harsh chatter and musical phrases.

CRESTED MYNA
Acridotheres cristatellus

This bushy-crested Chinese native has a small but declining population around Vancouver, British Columbia. Vocalizations include harsh chattering and musical phrases.

COMMON HILL MYNA *Gracula religiosa*

Mostly black with an orange bill, this native of India and Southeast Asia occurs in small numbers in suburban habitats of southern Florida. It is an expert mimic, and its vocal renditions include whistles, squawks, and chirps.

Bombycillidae: Waxwings

Common Myna (top and center) is an Asian species introduced to south Florida many years ago. It thrives among human habitation, where it often nests in holes in man-made structures, such as traffic lights and light poles. European Starling (bottom) is a cosmopolitan species introduced to the United States in 1890, and it has spread widely across North America, where it thrives around human habitations. This species has caused major problems with a number of our native cavity-nesting songbirds owing to its aggressive nature and habit of evicting native species from their cavities, resulting in nest failure.

Consisting of only three species, the waxwing family managed to infiltrate most of the Northern Hemisphere, where its members occur across Asia, Europe, and all of North America. In winter, they also occur in Mexico and Central America. Named for the waxlike red teardrops that adorn the tips of their tertials, the entire bird seems cast from caramel-colored wax. Add a black mask and a red- or yellow-trimmed tail, and what you

Waxwings are named for the colorful waxlike tips on their wing feathers. They are truly flocking birds away from nest sites and are nomadic outside the breeding season, where they hone in on fruit-bearing trees. From left: Cedar Waxwing; Bohemian (top) and Cedar Waxwings in tree; Bohemian Waxwing. Note Bohemian's larger size and rust undertail in the center photo.

have is one of the planet's most beautiful birds.

Starling sized but thinner, these songbirds brandish short tails, sweptback crests, and an upright stance that would seem haughty on a less endearing bird. Bills are short but wide and ideally suited for plucking the berries that constitute up to 90 percent of waxwings' diet. They occur in forested habitats, where they eat an ample supply of berries, cherries, mountain ash, mistletoe, and especially cedar and juniper berries. Waxwings are highly social outside the breeding season, often joining robins in winter in apple orchards with trees bearing fruit. In spring, when fruit stocks are depleted, they may turn to eating flowers, including apple blossoms.

While many waxwings migrate annually, the birds are also irruptive and somewhat nomadic in winter, shifting to places of greater food abundance. The birds' short, strong legs permit them to reach down for fruit and even dangle upside down. Even though their wings are short, waxwings may travel great distances daily in search of food, and they rank among the world's greatest agents of seed dispersal.

Waxwings are usually seen more than heard, with their high, vapor-thin, lisping calls skipping close to the upper range of human hearing. Insofar as males and females stay in loosely managed flocks and territories, there is no need to advertise with emphatic songs, as is the case with most passerines. Waxwings have no true song.

BOHEMIAN WAXWING
Bombycilla garrulus

At 8.5 inches, this portly, northern waxwing is more than an inch longer than Cedar Waxwing and noticeably bulkier. Adding cinnamon undertail coverts to its arsenal of winsome attributes, this waxwing of northern forests ranges across boreal Asia, Europe, Canada, and Alaska. Breeding from Alaska east to Hudson Bay, and south to British Columbia, they irregularly wander east and south in winter, staging irruptions during years when food crops (especially mountain ash) are diminished. Their winter range includes much of southern Canada and the northern United States south to central Colorado, where they team up with Cedar Waxwings or starlings.

Waxwings flock to fruit trees in winter to feast on the old fruit, with the result occasionally being a slightly drunken state due to fermented fruit and berries. On the right is a typical tight flock of Cedar Waxwings, which can range from a handful to hundreds of birds. Note the large number of juvenile birds in this early fall flock, attesting to the nest success of this species. Juveniles have pale, spotted bellies and grayish hoods and lack the strong dark mask of adults.

CEDAR WAXWING *Bombycilla cedrorum*

Combine the visual smoothness of their plumage with a black mask and shiny feather bling, and you have one of the most elegant and beautiful birds in North America. Breeding across most of the lower half of Canada and the upper half of the United States, they retreat from Canada to the entire lower 48 states and south to Panama in winter, giving Cedar Waxwing the distinction of being the only waxwing to penetrate the tropics. As the name suggests, this species is especially partial to cedar and juniper berries.

Ptiliogonatidae: Silky-flycatchers

This small (four species), enigmatic, and geographically restricted family is found only from the southwestern United States to Panama. The members of this group were formerly included with the waxwings, which share with them crested heads and a mostly fruit diet. Silky-flycatchers are slender, long tailed, mostly (montane) woodland birds with crests that can be raised and lowered. The plumage is soft and glossy and ranges from black and gray to olive green and bright yellow. All members are sexually dimorphic, with males having longer tails and brighter plumage. Bills of silky-flycatchers are small but admirably suited to plucking and swallowing berries, which constitute the bulk of their diet. The birds also consume insects during the breeding season, capturing them on the wing.

Silky-flycatchers are social and travel in small groups. Males and females pair off during the period of peak abundance of fruiting trees and insects, which designates the breeding season. Ornithologists suspect that Phainopepla has an unusual breeding strategy that involves two distinct and separate breeding habitats in the same year, though it is unknown whether the same individuals breed in both habitats. For example, Phainopeplas spend the winter months in the desert, where they forage on mistletoe and breed, and then relocate in spring to riparian woodlands for a second round of breeding to coincide with a seasonal abundance of red berries and insects. This second location

Phainopepla is the only member of this small New World family (four species) that ranges from the United States to Panama. These slender songbirds are social in nature and forage in groups on fruits and berries, which make up a major part of their diet.

may be over 100 miles from their desert territories.

PHAINOPEPLA *Phainopepla nitens*

Glossy black males and gray females are typically seen perched high atop trees in open woodlands or desert washes, or clustered in groups in fruiting trees. Their name comes from the Greek term for "shining robe," a fitting description of the male's plumage. Observers are usually alerted to the birds' presence by their distinctive, soft, rising, whistled call, or by their spirited and erratic pursuit of insect prey. Greatest densities for this species occur in the Sonoran Desert, but good numbers also occur in central California. Phainopeplas extend north to northern California, east to western Texas, and south to southern Baja and south-central Mexico.

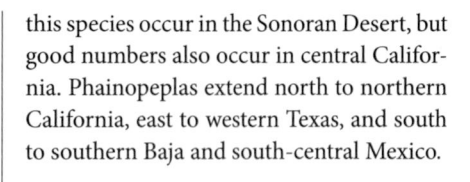

Peucedramidae: Olive Warbler

While outwardly similar to the Parulidae wood-warblers (p. 123), with which it was formerly grouped, Olive Warbler is a methodical feeder, eschewing the frenetic darting and chasing that typifies the Parulidae and instead foraging comfortably in the top of the same montane pine all day long. As the sole member of its family, Olive Warbler occurs in fir, pine, and pine-oak forests

Formerly a member of the New World warbler family, this species was recently split into its own family, Peucedramidae. Instead of the fast-paced feeding style typical of our warblers, Olive Warbler forages slowly and methodically in mixed montane forests from the southwestern United States to Nicaragua. Pictured here: male (top) and female (bottom).

from southeastern Arizona and southwestern New Mexico south through the Mexican highlands to northern Nicaragua. Mostly resident, it undergoes some altitudinal shift in winter, and may join flocks of Hermit and Townsend's Warblers, Mexican Chickadees, and Bridled Titmice.

OLIVE WARBLER
Peucedramus taeniatus

This medium-sized passerine with a long sturdy bill is often seen creeping along the inner branches of long-needled pines in the upper canopy searching for insect prey. It pauses to pry into needle clusters, sometimes hangs upside down, and occasionally engages in aerial sallies. The copper-colored hood worn by adult males is yellower in females and faint in immatures.

Passeridae: Old World Sparrows
(House Sparrow and Tree Sparrow)

Despite the shared names, Old World sparrows (a.k.a. weaver finches or passerine sparrows) and New World sparrows are not closely related. In fact, Old World sparrows are more closely related to the weavers of Southeast Asia and the waxbills of sub-Saharan Africa. Our two representatives of the Passeridae, House Sparrow and Eurasian Tree Sparrow, were introduced to the United States and quickly adapted to urban life in the New World, demonstrating a plasticity that underscores the family's close association with human habitation.

All 40 species herald from Africa, Europe, and Asia, and it is presumed that the family originated in semiarid grasslands, where their seed-eating habits were established.

Old World sparrows are mostly stocky, short-tailed birds with broad blunt wings and ten primaries, compared to the New World sparrows' nine. Legs are typically short and sturdy, as befits birds that spend a great deal of time foraging on the ground for grain. The palate, tongue, and lower bill are especially suited for husking seeds to separate wheat from chaff.

Members of this family are highly social, foraging and even breeding communally. Nests are large and often messy, but some species have exacting standards for roosting and nesting. House Sparrow prefers cavities and nooks and crannies in human structures, a proclivity that makes it a villain in the eyes of bluebird and Purple Martin landlords.

Pete's first experience with House Sparrows was a colony of 10 to 20 nests tucked into the wall of English ivy that covered the brick chimney of his neighbor's house. As they sat on her porch reviewing the day's bird sightings, they were serenaded by the burble and churps of the colony and mesmerized by the frantic comings and goings of adults. Knowing nothing about the bird's immigrant status, they treated House Sparrows with the same level of interest as any other species—maybe even more, though, since House Sparrows were easily studied, unlike the catbirds and cardinals that nested locally.

Forty years on, House Sparrows continue to engage Pete. In summer, in his postage-stamp backyard, House Sparrows forage in the grass, flushing and fly-catching small white moths that they ferry to open-mouthed young waiting in the warped eves of the nearby Methodist church.

Pete's experience with Eurasian Tree Sparrow was no less memorable, but more challenging. In the winter of 1994, en route from Texas to New Jersey, Pete and David Sibley made a detour to St. Louis, Missouri, which was the only place Eurasian Tree Sparrow occurred. Having no preliminary planning, they arrived in downtown St. Louis one bitterly cold January Sunday, presuming that Tree Sparrows would be as common as House Sparrows in their urban environment. However, Tree Sparrows are not called "tree"

House Sparrow (left) is possibly the most widespread bird in the world. Introduced to the United States in Brooklyn, New York, and other northeast locations in the mid-1800s, it has spread throughout North America and thrives wherever humans live, especially urban areas. It can be a pest species when it takes over nest boxes meant for bluebirds and swallows, as its aggressive nature prevents the native species from re-occupying its nest box. Eurasian Tree Sparrow (right) is a geographically restricted species introduced from the Old World in 1870 near St. Louis, Missouri. It has spread out in recent years but generally remains in that area.

sparrows without foundation. Not realizing that the birds favored a somewhat more vegetated environment, they missed the more suburbanized bird. It was years later, while working on another book (*Pete Dunne's Essential Field Guide Companion*), and now properly armed with directions, that Pete and his wife Linda were treated to a bevy of birds in the shrubbery of a quiet suburban side street.

HOUSE SPARROW *Passer domesticus*

Possibly the world's most widely distributed bird, this doughty weaver finch is native to Europe, the Mediterranean region, North Africa, and much of Asia. It has been introduced widely elsewhere, and it flourishes in human habitats, most notably and quite remarkably urban environments. However, you will not find them in forests, extensive woodlands, or grasslands.

In the Americas, the birds were initially introduced in Brooklyn in 1850 or 1851, with subsequent releases elsewhere in the Northeast through 1867. Finding in the urban environment a surplus of nooks and crannies in which to nest, they quickly discovered that the undigested grain lodged in the drop-pings of draft animals were a dependable source of nourishment. In the automotive age, this flexible granivore then discovered that processed grains housed in bread crusts, dropped doughnuts, and pizza crusts were a viable nutritional substitute. Following us into rural areas and suburbia, the birds are now established as permanent residents throughout much of North America, Mexico, and Central America, and are expanding rapidly south to much of South America. In short, they occur almost anywhere our food-wasteful species thrives. Habituated to people, they actively solicit handouts.

EURASIAN TREE SPARROW
Passer montanus

This handsome Old World native occurs from the United Kingdom and Scandinavia to Manchuria, Japan, and the Philippines. Twelve tree sparrows were introduced to St. Louis, Missouri, in 1870, and the species is now established in vegetated sections of the city and has spread into east-central Missouri and western Illinois. Similar in manner and appearance to House Sparrow, with which it associates, this social species prefers open areas with shrubs and trees.

Motacillidae: Pipits and Wagtails

This relatively small family of chiefly ground-hugging birds consists of 65 primarily Old World species. Only five species occur in North America, and three of these, barely. Found in mostly open habitats, especially grasslands, all members nest and forage on the ground. While a great deal of fundamental similarity exists within the species groups, a measure of uncertainty reigns regarding the status of species versus subspecies.

The members of this family are almost wholly insectivorous, and their thin, pointy, slightly curved bills are ideally suited for plucking or prying for prey. Insects and other invertebrates constitute the bulk of their diet, while some species supplement these with plant matter.

Other defining family traits include a smallish to medium size, short necks, long slender tails, and long pinkish legs and toes with long hind claws, a refinement common to ground-dwelling versus arboreal species. Leg structure permits them to run quickly and stand erect in search of prey. All have nine primaries and uncommonly long tertials, which cover the primaries on the folded wing, thus protecting them from sun bleaching in open habitats. Plumage is mostly cryptic, with browns and buff dominating. Sexes are similar.

While mostly birds of open country, members of this family also occupy an array of micro-habitats, including grasslands, tundra, cliff faces, seacoasts, rocky hillsides, and broadleaf or coniferous forests. Many species use open, dry, often denuded fields (particularly agricultural land) during migration and winter.

Tail wagging is a binding trait among many members of this family, although its function is uncertain. Their distinctive vocalizations are varied and far-reaching and, while not particularly musical, are generally pleasing. Calls are limited to one- or two-note utterances. Songs, often given in flight, are sometimes a hurried and prolonged series of spiraling notes.

EASTERN YELLOW WAGTAIL
Motacilla tschutschensis

Until 2004, this yellow-breasted Arctic breeder with an animate tail was one of 16 subspecies of Yellow Wagtail, *Motacilla flava*. The AOS split the subspecies breeding in Siberia and Alaska into the present species, relegating those breeding across northern Europe and much of Russia into Western

This slender, ground-hugging, long-tail-wagging songbird is the only member of this large Old World family that nests regularly in the Americas (Alaska). Yellow Wagtail nests in subarctic thickets near water and migrates to Africa, Asia, and the Middle East in winter. This subspecies may achieve full species designation in the future, though the AOS already considers it a full species in North America.

Yellow Wagtail (*M. Flava*). Eastern is distinguished by a grayish cap and narrow white eyeline. All Yellow Wagtails breed in wet habitats with low vegetation, with Eastern partial to wet meadows and shrubby tundra along streams. Breeding in near coastal northern and western Alaska, they winter mostly in Southeast Asia in open grasslands, cultivated fields, and bare ground, and the Philippines south to Indonesia.

WHITE WAGTAIL *Motacilla alba*

Strikingly patterned, this pied wagtail is a widespread, mostly Old World breeder, ranging from Iceland and Great Britain east to western Alaska. Foraging alone or in pairs on roadsides, pond edges, and beaches, White Wagtail typically nests among boulders and stone walls. In winter, birds migrate to North Africa, the Middle East, and southern Asia. In North America, it is a rare breeder in western Alaska and offshore islands. This species has a great deal of plumage variation across its extensive range, with some subspecies having black bibs, and others having collars. Some authorities consider the White Wagtail found in western Alaska, Nome, Attu, and the Aleutian Islands a distinct species, Black-backed Wagtail (*Motacilla lugens*).

RED-THROATED PIPIT *Anthus cervinus*

This fairly distinctive, mostly Old World Species ranks as one of the most common breeders in the subarctic willow thickets it calls home. Ranging from Scandinavia to Siberia, it breeds in North America in western Alaska and offshore islands. While it winters mainly in Southeast Asia, including the Philippines, some birds turn up irregularly along the Pacific Coast from British Columbia to Baja.

AMERICAN PIPIT *Anthus rubescens*

Also known as Buff-bellied Pipit, this Arctic and alpine tundra breeder is common in winter across North America from Washington State south to Arizona, and east to

American (top and center) and Sprague's (bottom) Pipits are the only two widespread members of this global family in North America. Sprague's is a shy bird of the western prairie regions, while American Pipit breeds in grassy and boulder-strewn tundra in most of Alaska and northern Canada and winters in much of the United States. Both species are mostly terrestrial by nature, foraging on the ground for insects and seeds.

Florida and Virginia, where it forages in small flocks on bare agricultural fields, beaches, and shortgrass. Nesting widely in grassy tundra meadows and boulder-strewn tundra across most of Alaska and northern Canada, the breeding population extends south through the Rockies to northern Arizona and other isolated montane locations. This species was formerly considered a subspecies of the European Water Pipit (*Anthus spinoletta*).

SPRAGUE'S PIPIT *Anthus spragueii*

Compact and bug-eyed, this pipit of dry, shortgrass prairies breeds (locally) from south-central Canada to northern Texas. Always solitary and secretive, it winters in grassy habitat from northwestern Alabama and Oklahoma to Arizona, and south through Mexico. A very shy skulker in its preferred grassy habitats, it often flushes before being seen, but then returns to almost the exact location after an extended spiraling flight.

Fringillidae: Finches

The finches (another family marked by reexamination and transition) consist of 130 to 145 small to medium-sized passerines (17 species in North America) with conical bills adapted to crush and husk a targeted seed. Females are slightly smaller than males. The tongues of finches are specialized to manipulate the kernel within the shell so that it alone is swallowed. Finches are found on every continent but weakly represented in the New World, and they occur in Australia only because of human introduction.

Finches are flocking birds, and their plumages are variable and often vibrant. A single dominant color, which may be yellow, orange, red, scarlet, purple, brown, black, or blue, defines many species. Others are brownish, olive, or gray on the upperparts and streaked below, and/or sport a distinctive white or yellow rump or have a touch of color on the crown, nape, forehead, or cheek. Some have wing bars or patches. Can you say "diverse"?

Bills range in size from large and swollen (grosbeaks) to small and pincerlike (goldfinches), but all are calibrated to gather and husk seeds, with larger-billed species able to consume a wider variety of seeds. The overlapping bills of crossbills are an extreme evolutionary adaptation suited to prying conifer seeds from the protective confines of the cone. The bills of many crossbills are also specialized for a specific tree species and its cones. A prime example is the Cassia Crossbill, *Loxia sinesciuris*, an endemic of southern Idaho (and a recent split from Red Crossbill), whose bill is calibrated to extract seeds of lodgepole pines. In addition to having strong, clinging feet, crossbills use their bills to maneuver while feeding, similar to parrots.

Finches have adapted to exploit a variety of habitats, especially those that offer a seasonal abundance of seeds. Consequently, most finches are somewhat nomadic, moving short to long distances from a depleted food resource to one of greater opportunity. Some species have an irruptive pattern, migrating south in greater numbers when key seed crops fail.

Highly social, many finches roost communally outside the breeding season, a social habit that may serve as a communication mechanism that conveys the location of food resources to be exploited by all. For some species, these roosts may number in the hundreds and thousands.

As might be expected of such a social species, finches have developed a complex repertoire of vocalizations, with Red Crossbill having about ten distinct contact calls. Attesting to the vocal capacity of finches, one of our most common caged birds, the canary, heralds from wild finch stock.

These three stunning medium to large finches are part of a much larger group of seed- and nut-eating birds. Pine Grosbeak (left) is a true "snowbird," as it breeds in far-northern coniferous forests (as well as some Rocky Mountain and Pacific locations) and does not migrate south unless seed crops are compromised. Brown-capped Rosy-Finch (center) is one of three rosy-finch species that inhabit high-elevation montane habitats but descend to lower elevations in winter to visit feeding stations in foothills. Evening Grosbeak (right) is a large finch with a massive bill that has experienced huge declines in population numbers over the last few decades, for incompletely known reasons.

EVENING GROSBEAK
Coccothraustes vespertinus

These large, stocky, bulbous-billed finches of northern coniferous forests are songbirds without a song, using instead sweet, piercing notes and burry chirps. They are ferocious seed-crackers, and in winter, flocks swarm to feeding trays that offer sunflower seed, emptying them in record time. In summer, Evening Grosbeaks eat insects such as spruce budworms, a serious forest pest. Most depart their northern and high-mountain breeding areas and disburse across many of the northern United States in winter. Their breeding range includes much of lower Canada, western and northwestern Pacific coniferous montane forests, and far north-central and northeast United States, where the population declined 97 percent from 1966 to 2015 (Partners in Flight). They are more common in the western portion of their breeding range, and nesting birds seek out mature conifer forests, primarily spruce and fir. In Mexico, they favor ponderosa pine.

PINE GROSBEAK *Pinicola enucleator*

Breeding in conifer forests across the entire Northern Hemisphere, this large, long-tailed, northern finch's range extends across much of upper Canada and coastal Alaska and British Columbia, and extends south to breed locally through the Rockies to New Mexico.

Feeding on seeds and buds of juniper, larch, spruce, pine, aspen, and birch, some wander south of breeding areas in winter, but rarely farther south than the far northern United States, except in irruption years, when food becomes scarce. The raspberry-colored male and electric yellow female make for a stunning couple, and birders everywhere particularly enjoy seeing these tame finches. A winter flock will typically stay near a fruiting tree until all the food is consumed.

GRAY-CROWNED ROSY-FINCH
Leucosticte tephrocotis

This most widespread of the montane finches forages even in summer on residual snow patches. These long-winged, rose-tinged birds with beautifully patterned gray and black heads occur in boulder-strewn tundra and scree slopes above the tree line from northern Alaska to Montana and Washington State. In winter, they occur from British Columbia south to California and New Mexico. A resident population exists on the

This group of small to medium-sized finches represents some of the most colorful birds in North America, which also have some of the sweetest songs. Many finch species form flocks away from the breeding season, and some are regular visitors at backyard feeding stations. Clockwise from upper left: (all males) Purple Finch, White-winged Crossbill, House Finch, Lawrence's Goldfinch, American Goldfinch, Common Redpoll.

Aleutians. Birds flock and move to lower elevations in winter, where they occur in fields, along roadsides, and around human habitations.

BLACK ROSY-FINCH *Leucosticte atrata*

Geographically exiled, these alpine finches breed in rocky alpine tundra, cliffs, and glaciers above tree line in the western United States. They seem oblivious to cold and snow, and nest in cliffs and crevices where few people go. A black upper body with white skull cap and pink lower body make for a truly dapper appearance. In winter, they occur from southern Montana to northern New Mexico east to far eastern California.

BROWN-CAPPED ROSY-FINCH
Leucosticte australis

A very restricted alpine finch, Brown-capped breeds above the timberline in alpine tundra in Colorado and north-central New Mexico. Pink underparts, a pale brownish upper body, and dark brown cap create a subtly beautiful appearance. It occurs in winter in open areas at lower elevations, including cropland, within its limited breeding range.

HOUSE FINCH
Haemorhous mexicanus

This one-time western species of arid scrub chaparral and open woodlands was inadvertently introduced into the eastern United States in the early 1950s, where it quickly established and expanded westward to be reunited with its native kin by the 1990s. It is now a common resident across much of the United States and most of Mexico. In the United States, it is absent in Alaska and much of Florida, and mostly absent from North Dakota to eastern Texas, but elsewhere is a common urban and suburban breeder. The reddish males and brownish-streaked females are common visitors to backyard bird feeding stations.

PURPLE FINCH *Haemorhous purpureus*

Hardly purple, this compact finch with a short, forked tail breeds widely across Canada and the upper eastern United States, with a segregated resident subspecies from British Columbia south to California. The raspberry-colored male lacks the heavy streaks found on House Finch, and the female's strong white eyebrow and mustache differ from the plain face of female House Finch. In winter, far northern Canadian breeders disburse south as far as the Gulf of Mexico and southern Arizona, where they occupy a range of open forest types and edges and readily visit feeders.

CASSIN'S FINCH *Haemorhous cassinii*

The rosy-tinged males with brown-streaked females are the characteristic finches in western mountains, where they breed mostly in coniferous forests from British Columbia south to California, northern Arizona, and New Mexico. They occur in winter in southern California, eastern Arizona, and New Mexico south into central Mexico, where they reside (often at lower elevations) in deciduous woodlands and second-growth scrub. Unlike Purple and House Finches, Cassin's does not favor suburban habitats.

COMMON REDPOLL *Acanthis flammea*

Plump and crop tailed, this treetop finch with crisp red cap and rose-tinged breast occurs in Arctic and boreal environs. It is typically seen feeding on birch and willow catkins, even though trees may be only a few inches high in some Arctic locations. Common Redpoll's range spans the entire global Arctic region, including Greenland. Breeding in open spruce-birch habitats as well as lowland tundra with dwarf birch and heath, northernmost breeders retreat south in winter across southern Canada to the northern United States. An irruptive species, Redpolls occasionally disburse to more southerly areas, sometimes in great numbers. In winter, birds forage in tight flocks that festoon catkin-bearing trees in a frenzy of streaky browns, patchy blacks, and rosy blushes. They also feed in weedy fields.

HOARY REDPOLL *Acanthis hornemanni*

While breeding ranges of this panboreal and generally more northerly breeding redpoll overlap with Common Redpoll, there is little evidence of interbreeding. In North America, this pale, ghostlike finch with a crisp red spot on its forecrown and a tiny, triangular yellow bill breeds along the upper tier of North America from Alaska to Hudson Bay, and north to Greenland. In winter, except in extreme northern areas, Hoary winters within its breeding range, but some are rare visitors to southern Canada and the upper eastern United States. During irruption years, a few birds accompany bands of Common Redpolls into the northern United States, where the adults' overall frostier appearance and limited pink wash on the breast are apparent in direct comparison.

RED CROSSBILL *Loxia curvirostra*

This compact, large-headed, northern and western montane finch takes bill calibration to an evolutionary crossroads, with overlapping bill tips designed to extract the seed riches secured within armored confines of pinecones—a surface largely impervious to all but crossbills and fire. The birds breed in boreal and montane forests of the Northern Hemisphere, and in North America range across the entirety of forested Canada to southeastern Alaska and northern New England. In the western United States, they are mostly resident in coniferous forests from Alaska south to Mexico and Nicaragua. Wintering throughout their breeding range, they are irruptive nomads. In times of cone failure, they range in small flocks across much of the United States south to the Carolinas and central Texas. Based on morphology and vocalizations, as many as nine Red Crossbill species may exist in North America, but thus

far only one has been teased out of this subtly heterogeneous assembly.

CASSIA CROSSBILL *Loxia sinesciuris*

While very similar to Red Crossbill, from which it was split in 2017, this Idaho endemic is resident in the Albion Mountains of Cassia County in southern Idaho, where it finds mature lodgepole pinecones that its large bill is calibrated to open. Its song differs from Red Crossbill, and is a good way to distinguish them.

WHITE-WINGED CROSSBILL
Loxia leucoptera

Breeding in dense coniferous northern forests in the New and Old Worlds, White-winged Crossbill breeds in North America across all forested Canada to western Alaska, and south through the Rockies to northern New Mexico. Wintering mostly within their breeding range, small flocks "invade" the United States in winters marked by cone shortages, where they feed in conifers as well as deciduous trees. They often hang upside down to access the edible parts of pinecones and use their crossed bill to pluck tasty morsels from the cone crevices. Raspberry-colored males with black wings adorned with white racing stripes are a favorite of birders everywhere, but the yellow-tinged female holds her own in his presence.

PINE SISKIN *Spinus pinus*

These spunky, streaky little finches of open coniferous and mixed forests occur widely across North America and central Mexico each year in response to seed crop availability. They generally nest in open coniferous or mixed forests, but also inhabit parks, cemeteries, and suburban woodlands. While preferring to feed in open forest canopies where cone seeds are abundant, they forage in a wide variety of habitats and flock in large numbers to backyard feeders. In winter, they may disperse through all the lower 48 states and Mexico.

Pine Siskin (top) and Hoary Redpoll (center) are two of our smallest finches. Pine Siskin occurs widely across North America as a breeder and irruptive winter visitor. Hoary Redpoll is a far-northern finch that rarely ventures across the Canadian border to the lower 48 United States. Red Crossbill (bottom) is a medium-sized finch whose strange bill configuration enables it to extract seeds from conifer cones.

LESSER GOLDFINCH *Spinus psaltria*

Tiny (4.5 inches), dark capped, and sometimes dark backed, this agile acrobat is widespread in the western United States from Washington State to Texas, and south through Mexico to Peru. Found in a variety of open woodlands and woodland edges, they feed primarily on seeds in the sunflower family and are a regular feature at backyard feeders. They are also common in vegetation around human habitation. Although they are mostly resident, interior and high-elevation breeders move to warmer locations in winter, where they forage on weed seeds and tree buds, and frequently visit backyard feeders.

LAWRENCE'S GOLDFINCH
Spinus lawrencei

A stunning little grass-loving finch, this species typically occurs in small monotypic groups in arid habitats, usually near water. Virtually a California-breeding endemic, it winters from southwestern California to northern Baja, southern Arizona, and southwestern New Mexico. Its preference for remote arid habitats of California and the desert Southwest makes it unfamiliar to most birders. Lawrence's Goldfinch may flock with American and Lesser Goldfinch and Dark-eyed Junco.

AMERICAN GOLDFINCH *Spinus tristis*

This energetic dollop of sunlight is a common breeder across much of the United States and southern Canada, where it is a fixture in weedy fields, dandelion-strewn lawns, and on thistles gone to seed. Cup-shaped nests lined with thistle down are placed in the fork of a sapling's branch or tucked into thistle stalks. The nest is so tightly bound that it holds water, sometimes to the detriment of nestlings. The striking yellow male with black cap and wings outshines the female, who is a shadow of his bright plumage. Nonbreeding birds are dull grayish overall with a splash of yellow about the head. Northern breeders disburse south in winter to all the lower United States and mostly northeastern Mexico.

Calcariidae: Buntings and Longspurs

This newly constituted family includes six sparrowlike species, including two that span the Northern Hemisphere. They are mostly stocky, ground-dwelling birds with conical bills and elongated hind claws. All breed in open habitats, and two of the four North American species nest in the Arctic. They have different breeding and nonbreeding plumages, with the longspurs sporting boldly patterned or brightly colored adornments that change to mostly brown in winter. Snow and McKay's Buntings have mostly white bodies in summer, which turn cryptically brownish in winter. All gather in sometimes large, often mixed flocks with other members of this family, as well as with larks. Diets consist mainly of insects in summer and seeds in winter. (The Calcariidae were formerly part of the Emberizidae—Buntings and New World Sparrows, now the Passerellidae).

LAPLAND LONGSPUR
Calcarius lapponicus

This smallish, spunky, Holarctic nester breeds in Arctic tundra across the entire Northern Hemisphere, where it is often the most obvious and commonly found bird. The male has a black face, neck, and crown with white underparts and a chestnut nape, while the female lacks the strong head pattern and is mostly brownish overall. In North America, it breeds from Alaska east to Hudson Bay and Newfoundland and Labrador. Its preferred breeding habitat is barren, moist Arctic tundra, or tundra with tussocks and shrubs. In winter, they forage in any open, sparsely vegetated habitat, where they often flock with other longspurs, Snow Buntings,

and Horned Larks. This most widespread of longspurs may occur throughout the lower United States in winter, except for the arid Southwest and Florida.

CHESTNUT-COLLARED LONGSPUR
Calcarius ornatus

Our smallest longspur is a shortgrass prairie and rangeland specialist, colonizing recently grazed or burned areas. Males are stunning with their black underparts and harlequin head pattern of black, white, and chestnut, while females are mostly brownish with a pale chestnut nape and black speckling on the breast. They breed east of the Rockies from south-central Canada south to northern Colorado. They place their cup-shaped grass nest on the ground in mixed prairie grasses, often near cattle droppings. In winter, they move to Arizona, east to southern Oklahoma and Texas, and south into central Mexico, where they gather in small to large flocks in grasslands and open cultivated fields.

SMITH'S LONGSPUR
Calcarius pictus

This striking, buff-orange longspur with a true harlequin head pattern nests on dry, grassy, hummocky tundra with stunted spruces. Nonbreeding birds are nondescript brownish with streaked, buff underparts. They breed narrowly from northern Alaska to western Hudson Bay, and locally from southeastern Alaska to northwestern Yukon. Winter range for this now tawny-colored bird is even smaller, from central Iowa to north-central Texas and northern Louisiana. In winter, it occurs in shortgrass fields and prairies.

Lapland Longspur (left) breeds in Arctic tundra regions of North America, where it nests on the ground. Snow Bunting (right) is a hardy bunting that also breeds in far-northern Arctic tundra and forms large flocks in winter that forage in wide-open spaces, including coastal beachfronts.

MCCOWN'S LONGSPUR
Rhynchophanes mccownii

Small and stocky, this shortgrass prairie specialist with a largish bill is the palest of the longspurs, as well as the most geographically restricted. The male has a white head and underparts with a black cap and mustache and a black upper breast patch, while the female is cryptically patterned brown. Breeding from southern Alberta and Saskatchewan south to northern Colorado, they winter in over-grazed prairies and pastures mainly from north and west Texas into north-central Mexico. In summer, they forage on the ground for insects, but sometimes pursue prey in the air, switching over to seeds and grains in winter.

SNOW BUNTING *Plectrophenax nivalis*

This common, widespread, Holarctic tundra breeder occurs in treeless tundra and rocky habitats and sea cliffs across the entire global Arctic region, breeding as far north as the absence of standing snow permits. Breeding males are pure white with black upperparts and tail, while females are a muted version of this with streaked upperparts. Nonbreeders have streaked brown upperparts and white underparts with a pale brown cap,

chestnut cheek patch, and thin collar. The nest of grass, moss, and feathers is typically tucked into a rocky crevice, but birds readily adopt human dwellings and refuse, including discarded cans, empty oil barrels, and even skulls. Adults and young eat mostly invertebrates in summer. Outside breeding season, they occur in small to very large flocks across much of lower Canada and the United States, except for more southern areas, including most of California. Winter habitats include wide-open spaces such as beaches, fields, and lakeshores, where they may mix with other species.

MCKAY'S BUNTING
Plectrophenax hyperboreus

During breeding season, these highly localized and mostly white tundra breeders occur on two remote islands in the Bering Sea (Hall and St. Matthew). The nest is in talus or rocky tundra slopes, or in the protective confines of driftwood or a whale's skull. In winter, birds withdraw to the west and southwestern coasts of Alaska, where they forage in small to medium flocks in coastal areas. The entire world population probably numbers fewer than 6,000 individuals (IUCN, 2016).

Passerellidae: New World Sparrows

The birds of this large and newly constituted family (138 species) were formerly part of a larger and more geographically expansive family, the Emberizidae (buntings and New World sparrows). In 2017, based mostly on DNA analysis, members of eight "well-defined" New World groups were teased out and united under the Passerellidae, a family purged of Old World affinities. These groups of conical-billed, seed-eating songbirds whose members span the latitudinal length of the New World include some Neotropic species not traditionally regarded as sparrows, such as ten species of brushfinches and Sooty-capped Bush-Tanager (or Chlorospingus). All members are small to medium-sized songbirds (5 to 9.5 inches), and many are cryptically clad in grays and browns.

North American sparrows are often divided into two groups: grassland species and those favoring open woodlands and edge habitats. They are a unique group of birds that have no comparable matches around the world, so we should appreciate them with extra enthusiasm, regardless of how hard it may be to get satisfying views of them. The famous birding term "LBJs," or "little brown jobs," has its origin with this family.

The conical bills of sparrows are ideally suited to masticating seeds and other vegetable matter, as well as the insect prey that figures in the diet of most species, particularly during breeding season. Sparrows forage on or near the ground, including species like Chipping Sparrow, which place their cup-shaped nests in trees. Sparrows either hop or run, and many prefer to run from danger rather than fly. Some New World sparrows have flight displays, and while vocalizations of many grassland species are subdued and insectlike, those of brush-loving sparrows may be loud and musical (*towhee! towhee!*). Some species, like the large *Zonotrichia* sparrows, sing their musical songs all year-round.

New World sparrows occur in a wide variety of habitats, including Arctic tundra, grasslands, coniferous forests, chaparral, forest edges, and cactus-studded deserts. Savannah Sparrow breeds in the Arctic, among other locations, and Harris's Sparrow nests in tundra-taiga ecotones. Fox Sparrow is at home in coniferous forests, while Bell's Sparrow thrives in chaparral. The ubiquitous Rufous-collared Sparrow is a lowland and mountain scrub specialist that lives near human habitation from Central America to the southern tip of South America.

After the breeding season, many gather in small to moderate-sized flocks, often with other sparrows, and most North American species are altitudinal or short-distance migrants. One exception to this is Lincoln's Sparrow, which breeds in far northern regions and migrates to the southern United States and south to southern Honduras in winter. In southern South America, some species undertake northward movements during the austral autumn.

OLIVE SPARROW
Arremonops rufivirgatus

This plain, shy, large-billed, brush-hugging sparrow occurs mostly in mesquite and ebony thickets, rarely wandering outside those thorny fortresses. Found along the east and west coasts of Mexico south to northern Guatemala, the birds reach the northern limit of their range in southern Texas, where they are resident. They have a greenish back, a striped head, and strong, sturdy legs.

GREEN-TAILED TOWHEE
Pipilo chlorurus

At 7 inches long, Green-tailed Towhee is small for a towhee but large for a sparrow. This handsome, rufous-capped sparrow of shrubby mountainsides and sagebrush expanses breeds west of the Rockies south of Canada, and winters from southern Cali-

fornia east to central Texas and south into Mexico. In winter, they occur in dense mesquite thickets along desert washes as well as well-vegetated habitats around human dwellings, where they may occur in small groups or mixed-species flocks. They derive their name from the chartreuse color in their wings and tail.

SPOTTED TOWHEE *Pipilo maculatus*

This large (8.5 inches), handsome, long-tailed western sparrow of dense brush and forest understory was formerly grouped with Eastern Towhee in a species called Rufous-sided Towhee. Its handsome plumage includes a black (male) or brown (female) hooded cowl, rufous flanks, white belly, and boldly white-spotted wings. It occurs widely in the western United States and southern Canada as both a resident species and migrant, and some disperse only a short distance into Mexico in winter. They retain their partiality to brushy habitats in winter, where they consume mostly seeds and berries.

EASTERN TOWHEE
Pipilo erythrophthalmus

A counterpart to Spotted Towhee, Eastern resembles its western cousin, minus the white wing spots. It seems that every sizable patch of brushy understory east of the Great Plains and south of southern Canada hosts this large, colorful, long-tailed sparrow, whose namesake call rings out even as birds remain hidden. They breed in the upper half of the eastern United States, barely reaching Canada, and are resident in virtually the entire Southeast to east Texas, where many of their northern kin join them in winter. Southeastern birds have whitish versus dark eyes.

RUFOUS-CROWNED SPARROW
Aimophila ruficeps

Common and widespread, this desert sparrow of arid rocky and brush-studded hillsides often occurs in pairs. They are locally

Towhees are large, somewhat shy sparrows that inhabit thickets and brushy habitats, where they scratch vigorously with their large rear toes in a backward, scraping motion for seeds and insects. Their loud, ringing songs brighten up the scene wherever they occur. From top: Eastern, Green-tailed, and Abert's Towhees.

resident from California to central Texas, and south into Mexico. These bulky, nondescript, long-tailed sparrows with rufous caps often forage beneath bushes and tall grasses and prefer to run from danger.

CANYON TOWHEE *Melozone fusca*

This large, clay-colored, brush-loving sparrow of the desert Southwest often occurs near water, especially in mesquite and riparian thickets, as well as near human dwellings. Resident from Arizona and Colorado south into Texas to central Mexico, pairs remain together and defend territories year-round.

CALIFORNIA TOWHEE
Melozone crissalis

Very similar to Canyon Towhee, with which it was once grouped as Brown Towhee, California occurs as a resident species from southwestern Oregon through western California to Baja. Here it prefers tangled chaparral and hot scrublands. In suburban habitats, it sometimes leaves its shrubby confines to forage on lawns and driveways.

ABERT'S TOWHEE *Melozone aberti*

Closely related to California and Canyon Towhees, this large, bulky, sandy-colored sparrow with a black-fronted face is a permanent resident of dense brush along rivers and streams in the desert Southwest. In all seasons, Abert's diet is mostly insects.

RUFOUS-WINGED SPARROW
Peucaea carpalis

This hardy, slender desert sparrow with a long tail, reddish cap, and rufous patch on the forewing occurs in grassy, lowland desert scrub. It occurs locally and is uncommon in the Sonoran Desert of Arizona and northern Mexico. Although shy, it readily responds to "pishing" or squeaking.

BOTTERI'S SPARROW *Peucaea botterii*

A mostly Mexican and Central American resident of mesquite- and cactus-studded arid grasslands, this sparrow reaches the northern limits of its range in extreme southeastern Arizona and southeastern Texas. Solitary and secretive, the word "flock" seems not to exist even as a concept in Botteri's mind. They are best seen during monsoon season in late summer, when they sit on exposed perches and sing for long periods.

CASSIN'S SPARROW *Peucaea cassinii*

This understatement of a sparrow that closely resembles Botteri's occurs in shrubby, arid grasslands from western Nebraska south to Arizona, Texas, and central Mexico. Only central U.S. breeders are migratory. What they lack in exciting plumage (they are mostly drab and nondescript) Cassin's Sparrows make up for with their sweet, melodious song that they sing while fluttering high above their territory.

BACHMAN'S SPARROW
Peucaea aestivalis

Large and heavy billed as well as solitary and secretive, this sparrow of mature pine forests with a grassy understory occurs mostly as a resident in the southeastern United States. Some interior breeders retreat to more southern and coastal portions of their range in winter. Like Botteri's, this is not a flocking bird. The best chance of seeing this shy, furtive species is in early spring, when males sit up and sing on low perches.

AMERICAN TREE SPARROW
Spizelloides arborea

Pert and pretty, this tundra breeder occurs from Alaska across upper Canada to Quebec and winters south to northern and central North America. Breeding in stands of willow, birch, and stunted spruce, Tree Sparrow consumes mostly insects and alder seeds. It occurs in a variety of mostly open weedy habitats in winter, usually in small single-species flocks. Its red cap, rusty back, and black stick pin make it a favorite of birders everywhere.

CHIPPING SPARROW *Spizella passerina*

One of our most common and widespread species, "Chippers" occur in most of North America as breeders, migrants, or wintering residents. Breeding virtually coast to coast, except for Florida and some arid southwestern regions, this pert, rusty-capped, suburbanized species nests in a variety of trees and bushes, but prefers evergreens. Chipping Sparrow occupies a variety of open habitats in winter and occurs across the entire southern United States into Mexico, where birds form loose flocks or mix with other sparrows. It is a regular component of a winter pine forest bird community, where flocks of Chipping Sparrows join Eastern Bluebirds and Yellow-rumped and Pine Warblers.

CLAY-COLORED SPARROW
Spizella pallida

Plain and streak backed, this long-tailed sparrow with a gray nape occurs in shrublands of the northern Prairies and Great Plains. Its winter range is Texas south into Mexico, where it forms small to large flocks, like Chipping Sparrow. The birds are also regular migrants well outside their central U.S. range.

BREWER'S SPARROW *Spizella breweri*

This patently plain, grayish brown sparrow with almost no distinctive field marks relies almost exclusively on the vast sagebrush steppe for breeding and is the most abundant bird in this habitat. While similar to Clay-colored Sparrow, it lacks the darkish cap with whitish central stripe and the grayish nape in winter. The winter range is from Arizona and Texas south into Mexico, where they gather in semiarid scrub, saltbush, and weedy fields. A subspecies, Timberline Sparrow (*S. b. taverneri*), breeds at higher-elevation timberline, mainly in northwestern Canada.

FIELD SPARROW *Spizella pusilla*

Plump and pinkish, these cherublike sparrows thrive in brushy fields and roadsides of the East and Midwest. They are mostly resident across their range from New England to northern Florida, and east to Texas, with only northern breeders migrating south in winter. Their bouncing-ball trill is a familiar sound in summer, and they occur in small groups in winter, often mixing with other sparrows. Their wide breeding range barely extends into southeastern Canada.

BLACK-CHINNED SPARROW
Spizella atrogularis

Seemingly a sparrow-junco hybrid in appearance, Black-chinned is exacting in its habitat requirements, breeding on recurrently burned arid foothills covered by extensive tracts of chaparral, sagebrush, arid scrub, and juniper. Its fragmented, localized breeding range extends from California east to New Mexico, and south into Mexico. In winter, U.S. breeders move to southern Arizona and New Mexico south into Mexico.

VESPER SPARROW
Pooecetes gramineus

This handsome, streaked sparrow with a rust shoulder patch and bold white orbital ring is named for the evening prayer service celebrated by Roman Catholic clergy. A sparrow of sparsely vegetated grasslands near trees and brushy second growth, it celebrates the beginning and end of the day with its clear, sweet song sung from an elevated perch—two long, low notes, followed by two higher ones and a rippling trill. It breeds widely across much of the northern United States and Canada and winters across much of the southern United States into Mexico, where birds form small flocks in open weedy habitats. When flushed, they often fly high into a tree and sit still.

LARK SPARROW
Chondestes grammacus

Large and harlequin headed, Lark Sparrow has a black spot on its chest and bold white tail edges. It occurs in grasslands and

shrubby borders in open country, where it often flies to bush tops or utility lines when disturbed. They breed in the Great Plains and much of the West to California, where they are resident. In winter, they disperse to southern Arizona, New Mexico, and all of Texas, where they are also resident, and south into Mexico, where birds concentrate in small, loose flocks on agricultural land, vineyards, grassy coastal plains, and semi-open, thorn-scrub habitats.

FIVE-STRIPED SPARROW
Amphispiza quinquestriata

This large, subtly handsome, and refreshingly distinctive desert sparrow has a large bill and bold, black moustachials. It has very specific habitat requirements: steep, rocky, sparsely vegetated hillsides with a smattering of grass and tall brush. Its narrow, mostly Mexican range barely extends to the Arizona border, where it is rare and local.

BLACK-THROATED SPARROW
Amphispiza bilineata

This dapper desert denizen is one of the smartest-looking sparrows, with its pale charcoal head sporting two white racing stripes and a large black bib. It occurs in semi-open habitats with scattered trees and shrubs, especially canyons, desert washes, and desert scrub. It breeds locally from Washington State south to southeastern California and central Texas, and south into central Mexico. Southern birds are residents and northern birds migrants.

SAGEBRUSH SPARROW
Artemisiospiza nevadensis

Formerly called Sage Sparrow, this aptly named species breeds in the extensive sage flats and desert scrub of the intermountain West. Northern breeders migrate to the Southwest and to extreme northern Mexico in winter, with a small resident population on the southern Utah-Colorado border. Sagebrush is a shy sparrow that is best seen

in early morning in breeding season, when males sing for attention on exposed perches. They forage on the ground for insect prey and run with tails cocked upward, roadrunner style.

BELL'S SPARROW *Artemisiospiza belli*

This handsome gray-headed sparrow of California and Baja's dense coastal chaparral communities and desert scrub was recently split from the Sagebrush Sparrow. While it is a mostly resident species, some birds disperse to southwestern Arizona in winter. They also occur in the Mojave Desert and San Clemente Island, where a federally threatened subspecies exists.

LARK BUNTING
Calamospiza melanocorys

A large and stocky sparrow with a big bill, this distinctive western sparrow is at home in arid shortgrass prairies and brushy areas, generally east of the Rockies in the High Plains from southern Alberta to northern Texas and western Oklahoma. Its winter range is mainly from northern Texas and southern Arizona south into Mexico, including Baja, where birds gather in large single-species flocks in dry, weedy fields and desert scrub. The male's jet-black breeding plumage with bold white wing patches differs greatly from the brown-streaked female, but he replaces the black plumage with one that is streaked brown in winter.

SAVANNAH SPARROW
Passerculus sandwichensis

Small, compact, and short tailed, this grassland sparrow with a yellow wash in front of the eye has a huge breeding range, encompassing much of northern and central North America, including Arctic tundra. These streak-breasted birds show a great deal of regional variation across their extensive range. Most vacate their northern breeding range in winter and disperse to an array of grassy habitats, including sandy beaches

The top three sparrows are part of the genus *Zonotrichia*, which includes some of the largest sparrows in North America. All sing at least part of their songs year-round. Top, from left: White-crowned, White-throated, and Golden-crowned Sparrows. The lower three sparrows are unique in their appearance and habitat preferences. Bottom, from left: Lark, Seaside, and American Tree Sparrows.

and weedy patches near water. They may join mixed-species flocks across the southern United States south to Honduras.

GRASSHOPPER SPARROW
Ammodramus savannarum

This short-tailed, feathered dumpling has a bull neck and large bill. A grassland specialist, it is small enough to perch on an individual stalk of grass. Grasshopper Sparrow breeds widely from southern Alberta east to southern Maine, and south to coastal Texas and central Georgia. It also has scattered, isolated breeding populations in some upper western states, coastal California, and southeastern Arizona, but is mostly absent as a breeder in most of the Southeast and Rocky Mountain West. It is also resident on Hispaniola and Jamaica. In the Kissimmee Prairie region of Florida, the Florida Grasshopper Sparrow (*A. s. floridanus*) is resident and a federally endangered subspecies. Northern birds withdraw from most of their breeding range to winter in the southeast United States through Texas south to Honduras and Cuba.

BAIRD'S SPARROW *Centronyx bairdii*

Thick necked and short tailed, Baird's is a prairie specialist that breeds in the northern Great Plains of the United States and southern Canada. Its habitat requirements are shortgrass prairies with lightly grazed native grasses and grass clumps several years recovered from a burn. Often likened to a "feathered mouse" because of its habit of running under grass when alarmed, it is truly one of the hardest sparrows to see in winter, as it rarely perches up when flushed. Baird's Sparrow's winter range is equally exacting and geographically prescribed, ranging from southeastern Arizona and southwestern Texas into northern Mexico, where it shows

These six small to medium-sized sparrows represent some of the most common and widespread members of this highly diverse family. Chipping and Swamp Sparrows have distinctly different breeding plumages, while the others appear similar throughout the year. Clockwise from upper left: Swamp, Song, Lincoln's, Brewer's, Chipping, and Savannah Sparrows.

a marked preference for undisturbed mixed grasses.

HENSLOW'S SPARROW
Centronyx henslowii

Large billed and flat headed, this grassland specialist breeds from New York State and western Pennsylvania west to Wisconsin and Nebraska and winters from central Texas east to North Carolina and Florida. Its habitat preferences at all seasons are thick, weedy grasslands; lowland prairies; and wetlands, though it often occurs in fire-maintained pine savannahs during winter. A striking facial pattern with buff and greenish cast and rust-tinged upperparts give this sparrow a unique appearance, and one worth appreciating. Henslow's does not readily leave the ground when disturbed, but when it does, it tends to perch for a good amount of time.

LECONTE'S SPARROW
Ammospiza leconteii

This pretty little grassland sparrow has an orange face and upper breast and a black racing stripe behind the eye. It breeds mainly from central Canada south to northern Min-

nesota, Wisconsin, and Illinois and winters from southern Illinois south to eastern Texas and the Florida Panhandle. Breeding in wet grasslands and grassy meadows, it is one of the more secretive sparrows and is often difficult to see well, except for singing birds that perch in the open when breeding. Once flushed in migration and winter, it often perches in low bushes for a good amount of time, as long as you don't approach it. It prefers grassy fields with tall grasses in winter.

SEASIDE SPARROW
Ammospiza maritima

Short tailed and bulbous billed, this gray lump of a sparrow has a single adornment: a splash of yellow above the eye. Found in tidal wetlands and favoring low marshes that are inundated daily, its nine subspecies range coastally from New England to Florida, and west to southern Texas. The federally endangered Cape Sable Seaside Sparrow (*A. m. mirabilis*) is a resident of brackish and freshwater habitats in extreme southern Florida. Seaside Sparrows retreat into phragmites stands in winter and at times of unusually high tides. Only the *A. m. maritima* subspe-

cies of New England and the mid-Atlantic is migratory, though some hardy birds remain each year.

NELSON'S SPARROW
Ammospiza nelsoni

Pretty and spiky tailed, this sparrow with a buff-orange face and breast occurs in wet, grassy marshes (tidal and fresh). There are three separate breeding populations: one along the southern shore of Hudson Bay; another in central Canada south to North Dakota and Minnesota; and the third in salt marshes from Quebec south to Maine, where it overlaps with the closely related Saltmarsh Sparrow (*Ammospiza caudacuta*). In winter, birds frequent salt or brackish marshes from the mid-Atlantic coast south to Florida and west along the Gulf Coast to south Texas. It is a secretive sparrow but readily responds to pishing.

SALTMARSH SPARROW
Ammospiza caudacuta

Once considered conspecific (the same species) with Nelson's Sparrow and called Sharp-tailed Sparrow, this small, pointy-faced sparrow with an orange face, gray cheek, and wide gray central crown stripe occurs in coastal wetlands. It prefers the higher, drier portions of marsh that support salt hay (*Spartina patens*), leaving wetter areas to Seaside Sparrow. Breeding coastally from Maine to North Carolina, most are residents, except for upper New England breeders, whose members winter as far south as Florida.

FOX SPARROW *Passerella iliaca*

These big, burly, richly patterned sparrows are a favorite of birders everywhere. They prefer thickets and dense shrubs, often near water, where they spray leaf litter "towhee-like" with a double-scratch foraging style in search of seeds, insects, and other invertebrates. A cold winter scene is quickly enhanced with the rich tones of this beautiful sparrow, and they often fill the air with their loud, sweet songs in late winter. At present there are four distinct subspecies occurring in North America, each with different plumage. These mostly northern breeders range from Alaska to Newfoundland and Labrador and south through western Canada to California and Colorado. Subspecies are Taiga (Red) Fox Sparrow of the North and East; Thick-billed Fox Sparrow of the Sierra Nevada's west slope; Sooty Fox Sparrow from coastal Alaska south to British Columbia and western California; and Slate-colored Fox Sparrow from central British Columbia south to western California and Colorado. In winter, Fox Sparrows' winter range is from southern Alaska south to Baja and from New England and Minnesota south and west to northern Florida and Arizona.

SONG SPARROW
Melospiza melodia

It's the sparrow next door. At some point in the year, this widespread, streak-breasted vocalist with a strong, dark, breast stickpin is residing in a thicket near you. They breed across Canada and the eastern and western United States, with only the central and southeastern United States missing this affecting sparrow as a breeder.

There are numerous subspecies of Song Sparrow, with some differing in plumage and others strongly different in physical appearance. The Aleutian form, which is resident along coastal southern Alaska, is very dark and almost as large as Red-winged Blackbird, and the southwestern subspecies is very pale. Everywhere it breeds, *M. melodia* is as advertised, a dedicated vocalist that may sing up to 300 times an hour. Henry David Thoreau rendered the jingle *"Maids, maids, maids! Hang up your teakettle-ettle-ettle."* However you may interpret it, the song of this versatile sparrow is part of the summer soundscape, especially near thickets, brambles, and shrubby areas.

In winter, small to large flocks occur along weedy edges, where they forage for

seeds and grit for their digestive mill. Their winter range includes most of the United States and northern Mexico, and southwestern Canada. When you flush this sparrow, it flies away while cocking its tail and pausing its wing flap, giving it a distinctive escape flight style.

LINCOLN'S SPARROW
Melospiza lincolnii

This handsome, gray-washed, brush-loving gremlin was discovered by Audubon in 1834 on a collecting trip to Quebec, and he named it for his young companion Thomas Lincoln of Maine. Its reddish-brown cap with thin pale stripe, gray face, tan mustache, and buffy upper breast with fine streaks give this delicate sparrow a soft, pleasing appearance. Breeding in willow thickets and brushy edges near streams or bogs, Lincoln's occurs across most of forested Canada and south-central Alaska and south along montane habitats to central California and central New Mexico. Vacating most of its breeding range in winter, it occurs from southwestern British Columbia to southern Baja, east across the southern United States to Florida, and south through Mexico to Honduras.

SWAMP SPARROW
Melospiza georgiana

Breeding in small to large wetlands with reeds, sedges, or similar vegetation, this all-dark sparrow sings day and night during summer months. In winter and in migration, Swamp Sparrow readily adapts to brushy habitats and weedy fields, even gardens, where it often joins other sparrows. Its breeding range extends from central Canada to the eastern United States, and it winters widely from Iowa and Massachusetts south to Florida and west to New Mexico. It also occurs along the entire Pacific Coast in winter, as well as eastern Colorado and southeastern Arizona. This small sparrow looks like a dark mouse with wings as it flies away after being flushed.

WHITE-THROATED SPARROW
Zonotrichia albicollis

One of our hardiest sparrows, able to withstand frigid winter conditions, this very large sparrow is a regular winter visitor to much of the United States, except for the intermountain West and Great Plains. Breeding across much of Canada and north-central and northeastern United States, this forest sparrow's whistled lament to *poor Sam Peabody, Peabody, Peabody* charms the people residing in those areas. During winter, almost every woodland edge south and east of a line drawn from New England to central Arizona south into northern Mexico has a flock of White-throats, including Pacific near-coastal areas. The birds' celebrated flocking tendencies are evidenced by the chorus of explosive chip notes the birds utter as they retire for the night.

HARRIS'S SPARROW
Zonotrichia querula

So geographically restricted is this brush- and edge-loving sparrow that active eastern and western birders may go their entire lives without seeing one of these big, burly, black-faced birds. This robust sparrow nests exclusively in Canada. It breeds along the boreal forest and tundra interface from northwestern Mackenzie River south and east to Hudson Bay, a region not heavily trafficked by birders. The entire population relocates to the central United States from South Dakota south to central Texas in winter, where they join with other *Zonotrichia* sparrows in hedges, brush, and riparian woodlands.

WHITE-CROWNED SPARROW
Zonotrichia leucophrys

This large, stunning sparrow has a crisp gray breast and black and white crown stripes that form a cross in the rear. It occurs throughout most of North America as a breeder, migrant, resident, or wintering species. The sweet, bubbly song of this trim, well-marked sparrow is nearly constant in summer and

The top three sparrows are not in the same genus but represent some of the most beautiful and strikingly plumaged sparrows in North America. Top, from left: LeConte's Sparrow, eastern Fox Sparrow, Henslow's Sparrow. The bottom three birds are part of the junco group, which are small sparrows with long tails and small bills, and which form small to large flocks in winter as they forage on the ground for seeds. Bottom, from left: Dark-eyed (Slate-colored subspecies), Yellow-eyed, and Oregon Juncos.

on warm winter days. Breeding in open or shrubby habitats, alpine meadows, and forest edges, it adopts more grassy habitats in winter but still prefers, in *Zonotrichia* fashion, a brushy edge component.

GOLDEN-CROWNED SPARROW
Zonotrichia atricapilla

Similar to White-crowned, but more geographically restricted, this Alaskan and western Canadian breeder of tundra and shrubby lowlands winters coastally from British Columbia to southern California. It gathers in small flocks in thick brush along creek beds, field edges, chaparral, and in gardens, where it sometimes mixes with White-crowned Sparrow. Its gray face and black cap with bold yellow forecrown give it a striking appearance.

DARK-EYED JUNCO
Junco hyemalis

Known to many North American residents as "the snowbird," this multipatterned forest sparrow breeds across most of forested Canada and occurs as a resident in much of the East and West. Its winter range includes most of the United States and northern Mexico, except much of Florida. Active, vocal, and social, juncos arrive with cold winds and enliven the winter landscape until tree buds pop. They typically forage and travel in small to large single-species flocks. Several subspecies of Dark-eyed Junco occur, and while they are physically similar, plumage varies greatly. The widespread Slate-colored Junco is mostly grayish to black with a white belly, while the western Oregon Junco has a black hood, reddish back, and rusty sides.

YELLOW-EYED JUNCO
Junco phaeonotus

This resident junco with its fiery eyes occurs from southeastern Arizona's sky islands south to Mexico and Guatemala, where it frequents montane pine and pine-oak forests. Its gray head, reddish back, and orange eye create a colorful appearance, and it is a regular at feeding stations. Some birds relocate to lower elevations in winter.

Icteriidae: Yellow-breasted Chat

YELLOW-BREASTED CHAT
Icteria virens

This large, vocal buffoon of the bird world is widespread in thickets and open brush-studded habitat across much of the United States and extreme southern Canada, absenting itself only from New England, much of Canada, the Upper Midwest, and southern Florida. Chats are given to exaggerated aerial displays, and birders are usually alerted to the male's presence by a series of whistled toots and flatulent utterances. Its versatile diet, which includes foraging on berries as well as insects, permits some individuals to remain in North America in winter north to New York, while others retreat deep into Mexico and Central America for the winter, where they occupy scrub habitat. It was removed from the ranks of New World warblers in 2019.

Icteridae: New World Blackbirds, Orioles, and Meadowlarks

No bird family is treated with more opposing human regard. Included in this group are orioles, which are celebrated for their entrancing plumage and engaging songs, but also blackbirds, which are disdained for their lack of colors, often-harsh utterances, and massed flocking practices that at times attain plague proportions. Few bird families surpass icterids in their diversity of nesting strategies, which range from energetically extensive (elaborate, pouch-shaped, hanging nests built by orioles and oropendolas) to building no nests at all (cowbirds). Breeding strategies range from solitary nesters (like meadowlarks) to communal efforts that may involve multiple pairs (like oropendolas) or thousands of birds (like Tricolored Blackbird).

This large (7.5 inches) former member of the New World warbler family was recently awarded its own family status, Icteriidae. Because of the ongoing uncertainty of where it truly belongs, be prepared for more changes in its taxonomic status in the future.

While most members of the family are resident, some undertake extensive migrations, like North American orioles that fly to Mexico and Central America in winter. Bobolink is the family's long-distance champion, navigating the distance between North American breeding grounds and Argentinian wintering grounds twice a year.

Limited to the New World, 111 icterids have colonized all of Central and South America. In North America, the only place icterids have been unable to colonize is the treeless Arctic, but one species, Rusty Blackbird, has pushed the blackbird beachhead to the Arctic's woody edge. Within the family, grackles and allies (the "Quiscaline blackbirds") are the most numerous and diverse subset, occurring from the tropics to the edge of the Arctic tundra and the Andean Plateau, while occupying forests, grasslands, marshes, and semidesert habitats. And while the greatest species diversity among icterids occurs in the central prairies of North America, Mexico houses the greatest number of oriole species.

Icterids range greatly in size (from 6 to 21 inches), and most are sexually dimorphic, with males larger than females and often having very different plumages. All members of the family have sharply pointed conical bills that may be short and finchlike, as with cowbirds, or long and slightly decurved. Some have elongated upper bills that cover part of the forehead, which is particularly exaggerated in oropendolas and caciques. The dominant plumage color among icterids (other than orioles) is black, with iridescent shades of purple, green, or blue. Colored shoulder patches occur in several genera. It is in the variability in iris color, however, that icterids exhibit strong diversity, with eyes ranging from brown, blue, and yellow to white and red.

Icterids are adapted to most habitat types and demonstrate a lack of habitat specificity. Wetlands, however, are important to many species, particularly grackles. Icterids generally have been successful in exploiting man-made environments, including orchards, grain fields, suburban environments, pastures, rice fields, and feed lots.

Many icterids are suited for terrestrial environments, where they walk or run, but arboreal species hop or jump. A good number are highly social and feed and roost together, often in huge numbers. Roosts are typically situated in dense vegetation, including marsh grass, palm trees, and tree groves.

Whether beautiful or harsh, few bird families rival icterids in the complexity of their vocalizations. The song of Eastern Meadowlark ranks among the most pleasing of bird sounds, while the call of Yellow-headed Blackbird ranks among the most uncouth of bird utterances.

Blackbirds feed mainly on grains and small animals, primarily arthropods. Some species, including orioles, feed on fruits and insects, as well as nectar. A few capture and consume vertebrate prey, including fish, lizards, and small birds.

ORCHARD ORIOLE *Icterus spurius*

Smallish and brick colored (male), this arboreal blackbird with a black hood, back, and tail shuns dense forest, but is truly at home in open woodlands with nearby fields, as well as orchards and riparian woodlands. It seems particularly attracted to trees bordering marshes, and often nests close to Eastern Kingbird, which may provide air cover against nest marauders. Breeding widely across the United States east of the Rockies and south into Mexico, the russet male and pale yellow female arrive early in spring and depart in late summer. They are mostly absent from Canada and northern New England. In winter, they retreat south from southern Mexico to northern South America.

HOODED ORIOLE *Icterus cucullatus*

Mostly tropical, this curve-billed, long-tailed, arboreal oriole of palm groves, riparian

woodlands, arid scrub, and native trees around human habitations breeds from northern California south to Baja, New Mexico, and lower Texas, and further south into Mexico. The orange male with black face and bib and black upperparts sporting white racing stripes contrasts sharply with the mostly dull yellowish female with a brownish gray back. The birds retreat in winter to western and eastern coastal Mexico, where a resident population exists south to the Yucatán.

BULLOCK'S ORIOLE *Icterus bullockii*

This slender orange oriole with a black bib, cap, and eye line and bold white wing patches occurs widely in open woodlands from extreme south-central Canada south to western Texas, California, and northern Mexico. In winter, it occurs from central Mexico south to Guatemala. The female is lemony yellow with a gray back and whitish belly. Bullock's was previously grouped with Baltimore Oriole as Northern Oriole.

SPOT-BREASTED ORIOLE
Icterus pectoralis

This large, stout-billed oriole occurs in arid scrub forests of tropical lowlands from Mexico to central Costa Rica. Introduced to southern Florida, it occurs in suburban neighborhoods north to Brevard County. It sometimes makes a nuisance of itself by savaging hibiscus flowers for their nectar. Sexes are similar, as they are with many tropical orioles.

ALTAMIRA ORIOLE *Icterus gularis*

A robust oriole of tropical deciduous forests of Mexico and Central America, Altamira occurs along the Caribbean slope from Nicaragua north to the Rio Grande Valley of Texas, where it is a resident of dry woodland scrub, often near water. This beautiful orange oriole with a black throat and orange and white wing bars builds huge basket nests of grass, which it suspends from horizontal limbs. Sexes are similar.

AUDUBON'S ORIOLE
Icterus graduacauda

This large and mostly Mexican oriole with deep yellow underparts and black hood, wings, and tail occurs from the Rio Grande Valley north to the King Ranch, where it is a common breeder in open scrub habitats. Sexes are similar.

BALTIMORE ORIOLE *Icterus galbula*

A common orange oriole with a sweet song and black hood and back (male), Baltimore breeds in eastern and western Canadian deciduous woodlands and bears the name of the colonial proprietors of Maryland, whose orange and black livery matched the male's plumage. In winter, most migrate to southern Mexico south to northern South America, but some winter in Florida and Hispaniola, and occasionally much farther north with the help of appropriate bird feeding stations. While males are brightly colored, females are mostly dull yellowish orange with brown backs.

SCOTT'S ORIOLE *Icterus parisorum*

Long tailed and lemon yellow, male Scott's has a black head, bib, and upperparts. Females are dull yellow with grayish upperparts, but they also have some black markings on the throat. Scott's breeds in assorted habitats of the arid Southwest north to southern Idaho, where it feeds on invertebrates, fruit, and nectar. It moves to Baja and central and western Mexico in winter, where it joins resident populations.

YELLOW-HEADED BLACKBIRD
Xanthocephalus xanthocephalus

Large and showy, this western blackbird sports a yellow hood (male) and breeds in well-vegetated freshwater marshes from central and western Canada south to northern Arizona and New Mexico. Found in loose colonies during the breeding season, birds emit liquid gurgles and harsh rattles that approach the level of a din as males flare their

Orioles are some of the most colorful songbirds in North America, and their sweet songs liven up the forest edges that they call home. Males and females of the migratory orioles appear very different, with females a mostly yellowish color, while tropical orioles appear similar by sex. Clockwise from upper left: Altamira Oriole (tropical species from southern Texas), male Baltimore Oriole, male Orchard Oriole, male Hooded Oriole.

white epaulets and writhe in sexual exaltation from elevated tule stalks. They typically flock to agricultural lands and grasslands in winter from northern California and the Southwest, south to southern Mexico. Birds roost in marshes at night, often with other blackbirds. Females are smaller and lack the full yellow hood.

BOBOLINK *Dolichonyx oryzivorus*

This small, handsome, saffron-naped blackbird of northern grasslands breeds across the upper tier of the United States and southern Canada. Its jet-black plumage with white and gold racing stripes on the upperparts and whitish gray lower back and rump make it one of the most attractive birds. Females are cryptically streaked brown and buff. In winter, this long-distance champion relocates to the pampas of Argentina, migrating in large straw-colored flocks whose conjoined *bink* flight calls recall the tinkle of ceramic wind chimes.

EASTERN MEADOWLARK
Sturnella magna

Portly, pointy faced, and V-bibbed, this yellow-breasted vocalist is a common component of grasslands from the eastern United States and southern Southwest south to northern South America and the West Indies. In winter, only far northern breeders

Eastern (top) and Western (center) Meadowlarks are mostly terrestrial members of the Icterid family group and are characterized by stocky bodies, short tails, and long, pointed bills. Their sweet songs carry over the open grassland habitats that they prefer. Bobolink is a smallish, delicate icterid that nests in grasslands and winters in South America. While meadowlarks are similar by sex, male Bobolink (bottom) has a flashy mix of black, white, and yellow in its striking plumage while the female has mostly muted, brownish plumage.

migrate south. Eastern Meadowlark occurs in a wide variety of grassy habitats, including pastures, fallow agricultural fields, and hayfields, and can be readily identified by its characteristic interrupted wing flap in flight.

WESTERN MEADOWLARK
Sturnella neglecta

This western counterpart to Eastern Meadowlark is similar in appearance, behavior, and habitat preferences but, where ranges overlap, generally chooses drier habitat. An exception is the southwestern United States, where Western often chooses moister grassland habitat than the "Lillian's" form of Eastern Meadowlark, which also occurs there. Its song is richer, slower, more variable, and more blackbirdlike than Eastern's. Western ranges across the western United States and southern Canada from the Great Plains north to central Alberta and south to central Mexico.

RED-WINGED BLACKBIRD
Agelaius phoeniceus

This handsome, histrionic blackbird is a resident in much of the lower 48 states, as well as the Bahamas and Haiti. It breeds across much of North America (except for most of Alaska) south through Mexico to Honduras. Typical breeding habitat includes cattail marshes, roadside ditches, and marsh edges. In winter, Red-wings retreat from most of Canada and join resident populations on farmlands, fields, and marshes, sometimes with other icterids. Red-wings are early breeders, and

males establish territories as early as January in North America, and court prospective females by flaring their red epaulets and calling loudly from exposed perches. Males set up harems of females, which they lord over with stern control. Winter flocks often segregate by sex, with young males often siding with females. Females are brownish streaked and resemble large sparrows, but differ with a pointed, conical bill.

TRICOLORED BLACKBIRD
Agelaius tricolor

Similar in most respects to Red-winged Blackbird, this highly social western marsh blackbird is as geographically restricted as Red-winged is not. Virtually a California endemic, Tricolored breeds in large, densely packed colonies in farm fields and marshes in California's Central Valley, but also in isolated locations from Oregon to Baja. Colonies of up to 200,000 nests have occurred, but Tricolored has experienced a decline in recent years due to habitat loss. It occupies agricultural lands within the breeding range in winter, where it often occurs with other blackbirds. Despite its impressive numbers, the population declined dramatically in the twentieth century, and Tricolored is listed as threatened by the state of California.

SHINY COWBIRD
Molothrus bonariensis

Smallish, slender, and glossy, this tropical blackbird of open environments is resident across much of South America and the West Indies and is well suited to exploit human habitation. It is a recent immigrant to North America, establishing itself in southern Florida in the 1980s, where it poses a threat to songbirds owing to its nest parasitism. Thankfully, it is not presently common in Florida.

BRONZED COWBIRD *Molothrus aeneus*
This large (nearly 9 inches), bull-necked, flat-headed cowbird of open dry habitats, parking lots, and second-growth scrub is resident in much of Mexico south to northern Colombia. It occurs as a resident and migrant from southern Mississippi to the American Southwest and Baja, and in winter across the southeastern United States. Blackish males with bluish wings and brownish gray females frequent fields, parking lots, and backyard feeders. Over 100 other bird species of all sizes have hosted the eggs of this nest parasite.

BROWN-HEADED COWBIRD
Molothrus ater

This smallish blackbird is widespread across North America south to central Mexico, with resident populations across about half of its range. Originally a prairie species, it spread widely as humans cleared forests and built towns, and it acclimated itself to a variety of open habitats and woodland edges. This species is a notorious nest parasite: females dump their eggs into the nests of unwitting host species, who raise the cowbird chick as their own. Males are black with brown hoods, and females are mostly grayish brown.

RUSTY BLACKBIRD *Euphagus carolinus*
Implications of the scientific name notwithstanding, this handsome, boreal forest blackbird breeds in wooded swamps from Alaska to Newfoundland and Labrador, with only small numbers reaching northern New England. In winter, most of the breeding population relocates to the central and southeastern United States, where they typically gather in small monotypic flocks in swampy woodlands with standing open water and leaf cover. Given a hard freeze or blanketing snow, Rusty Blackbirds may leave woodlands and join other blackbirds in open habitats or visit bird feeders. This species has declined by over 90 percent in the last 40 years, for reasons unknown (Partners in Flight). The iconic rusty plumage tones occur mostly in nonbreeding birds, with breeding males fully inky black.

Blackbirds, cowbirds, and grackles include some of the most abundant birds in North America, with many species forming huge flocks outside the breeding season. Some blackbirds form harems in marshy locations, where males oversee multiple females with an iron hand. Cowbirds lay their eggs in other songbird nests, and their larger young often outcompete the native chicks for food and survival. Grackles are large to very large icterids with long tails and heavy bills. Clockwise from upper left, all males: Red-winged Blackbird, Brown-headed Cowbird, Bronzed Cowbird, Boat-tailed Grackle, Great-tailed Grackle, Yellow-headed Blackbird.

BREWER'S BLACKBIRD
Euphagus cyanocephalus

This small, nimble, busy blackbird of mostly open western habitats resembles breeding Rusty Blackbirds but avoids deep woodlands in favor of forest openings, pastures, road-sides, lawns, and agricultural lands. They breed widely from the western Great Lakes west to British Columbia and south to Baja and New Mexico, with a large western resident population. Central and eastern breeders winter from Arizona, Nebraska, and the Panhandle south into Mexico. Males resemble mini–Common Grackles, with females mostly brownish gray.

COMMON GRACKLE *Quiscalus quiscula*

This large, blackish to bronze-bodied, pale-eyed blackbird with iridescent highlights is a widespread breeder of open forests and edges east of the Rockies across most of eastern North America. Vacating northern and far western breeding areas in winter, they concentrate in large flocks across open areas from southern Illinois and western Texas to southern New England and south to Florida. In winter and migration, large to huge flocks forage over suburban yards and agricultural lands, often with other icterids. They are generally unwelcome visitors to backyard feeders, where they bully other birds and quickly consume all the food.

BOAT-TAILED GRACKLE *Quiscalus major*

A large, passive grackle of Gulf Coast and Atlantic coastal environs and all of Florida, Boat-tailed is resident throughout its range. Breeding in small loose colonies in trees and bushes near water, they are known for their loud, gurgling calls and chatters and the male's theatrical displays. Males of the Atlantic population from Georgia north have pale eyes, while all others have dark ones. Females are a soft brown color with dark eyes and

blackish wings, rump, and tail. Coastal birds frequent marshes and parking lot dumpsters in winter, while in Florida birds occur everywhere, from parking lots to flooded ditches to more traditional grackle habitats.

GREAT-TAILED GRACKLE
Quiscalus mexicanus

This very large, aggressive grackle formerly of southwestern environs has spread east to Louisiana, much to the consternation of backyard bird feeders who dread seeing this bully in their yards. It is a common bird in residential tropical areas from Mexico to South America and occupies almost all habitats except unbroken forests. Males are glossy black with incredibly long segmented tails, pale eyes, and iridescent purple necks and heads, while females are brownish with dark eyes, wings, and tails. They are particularly fond of roosting at night in palm trees in parking lots, where tens of thousands create a din of loud clacks, whistles, and squawks.

Parulidae: New World Warblers

This large family (116 species) of New World passerines, sometimes referred to as woodwarblers, is arguably our most exciting bird group, if not the most strikingly plumaged. Subdivided into 25 genera, almost half of the species breed in temperate North America, and many winter in tropical regions. Warblers are small, active birds with pointy beaks, and all fall between 4 and 6 inches in length. The plumage of species that forage or nest on or close to the ground is cryptic. Arboreal species often have bright plumage, or at least patches of it. Numerous warblers have a colorful breeding plumage and muted nonbreeding plumage, and many females have more subdued plumage than adult males.

Warbler nests are mostly cup-shaped vessels constructed with grasses, bark, and leaves. Depending upon the species, these nests may be placed on the ground or in the tree canopy, or anywhere in between. One species, Ovenbird, builds a dome-shaped nest on the ground, and waterthrushes build balls of tightly packed moss with an entrance hole on the side. Waterthrush nests are sometimes fitted into a cleft in a streambank or in a hollow log. Lucy's and Prothonotary Warblers are cavity nesters, whereas the two parula warblers secure their nests in hanging moss.

These highly insectivorous birds are mostly diurnal, but many are nocturnal migrants whose migrations carry them out over large bodies of water, most notably the Gulf of Mexico. Warblers have a wide range of feeding techniques; some species are bark gleaners, and others are probers of leaf or needle clusters. Some sally out to catch insects on the wing, while others forage amid leaf litter. It is safe to say that every segment of a forest has a warbler suited to exploit its insect riches.

Many species, especially those breeding in vast boreal forests, rank among our most abundant warblers, but two very specialized species whose habitat needs are very specific, Kirtland's Warbler and Golden-cheeked Warbler, are federally endangered species.

As the name suggests, warblers are highly vocal, emitting a variety of conversational chips and songs. Vocalizations of breeding males, while not as rich as those of the thrushes, are generally short, pleasing phrases that lend themselves to mnemonic interpretation. Examples are Chestnut-sided's loud *pleased, pleased, pleased to meet-cha,* Black-and-White Warbler's monotonous boast *we-see, we-see, we-see, we-see,* and Black-throated Green's somnambulant chant *I am so LAY-zee.*

In spring and fall, migrating warblers join mixed-species flocks and may occur in almost any vegetative habitat, even on the ground, if that is where cold-numbed insects are located.

OVENBIRD *Seiurus aurocapilla*

A portly denizen of the forest floor, Ovenbird breeds in hardwood forests from the mid-Atlantic states to northeastern British Columbia. It often gives its loud, ringing *teacher, teacher, teacher* song from an elevated perch. Ovenbird is one of five warbler species that walk instead of hop, and their tail-cocked strut across the forest floor is full of attitude. Breeders east of the Appalachians winter in Florida and the Caribbean, while the rest migrate to Mexico and Central America.

WORM-EATING WARBLER
Helmitheros vermivorum

This caramel-colored warbler inhabits mature, eastern deciduous forests and moves nimbly through dense understory, where it pries into hanging leaf clusters in search of prey. It breeds locally in the eastern United States and winters in a variety of forest types from Mexico to Panama, and in the West Indies and the Antilles. This compact warbler works tree limbs and the ground for its favorite caterpillar prey.

LOUISIANA WATERTHRUSH
Parkesia motacilla

These bobbing birds of well-shaded, swift-flowing woodland streams and shaded ravines are widespread across much of the eastern United States south of Canada. During the breeding season they maintain linear territories along these watercourses, which are sources of much of their invertebrate prey. In winter, they occupy a variety of forest habitats, usually near fast-flowing water, in the Caribbean and from Mexico to Panama. Both waterthrushes walk rather than hop, which is helpful in their precarious streamside habitats.

NORTHERN WATERTHRUSH
Parkesia noveboracensis

Streak breasted and industrious, this rear-bobbing denizen of wooded swamps and bogs occurs near standing water, where it flips leaves in search of prey. Northern Waterthrush breeds widely from Alaska across much of forested Canada and from New England south to Virginia. They also breed south to Montana and Idaho and in a few scattered western locations. In winter, they occur from Mexico to northern South America, and throughout the Caribbean, where they mostly frequent mangrove wetlands and wooded swamps.

BACHMAN'S WARBLER
Vermivora bachmanii

Sorry. You missed this one. The last verifiable record of this eastern warbler was in 1962, near Charleston, South Carolina.

GOLDEN-WINGED WARBLER
Vermivora chrysoptera

Striking and boldly marked, this second-growth specialist is one of our most sought-after warblers. It has declined so much in the last several decades (68 percent from 1966 to 2014, according to North American Breeding Bird Survey) that Minnesota now hosts about 50 percent of the world population, but powerful conservation efforts are underway to reverse that trend. The birds breed in wet, shrubby tangles of the Upper Midwest and Appalachians, and winter from the southern Yucatán in Mexico through Central America. Hybrids occur where breeding ranges overlap with Blue-winged Warbler, and a few different plumages result, including Brewster's and Lawrence's Warblers.

BLUE-WINGED WARBLER
Vermivora cyanoptera

This mostly yellow warbler with bluish wings and tail and two strong whitish wing bars is a successional-growth specialist that thrives in second-growth shrubs and forest edges of northern portions of the eastern United States and extreme southern Canada. Males are brighter than females. Because of their edge habitat usage, they are especially susceptible to cowbird parasitism.

Kentucky Warbler (left) is a southern species that lives close to the ground, where it often forages in leaf litter on the forest floor for insects and their larvae. Northern Waterthrush (right) is one of only four warblers that walks rather than hops. The other three are Louisiana Waterthrush, Connecticut Warbler, and Ovenbird. Northern Waterthrush bobs its tail and teeters its body while foraging for food.

BLACK-AND-WHITE WARBLER
Mniotilta varia

Compact and zebra striped, this breeder of eastern and northern forests resembles nuthatches in shape and feeds like them, creeping up and along trunks and major tree limbs in search of insects and their larvae. They are among the earliest returning warblers in spring, and they build their nests in leaf litter on the ground. Breeding mostly east of the Great Plains from Texas to Newfoundland and Labrador and west to northeast British Columbia, they winter in the Southeast and Texas south through Mexico to South America and the Caribbean, where they occupy a variety of woodlands and scrub habitats, including plantations and mangroves.

PROTHONOTARY WARBLER
Protonotaria citrea

The "golden swamp warbler" is uncommon and limited by its particular habitat needs, breeding in cavities in dead timber surrounded by standing water. Cavities may be low and situated on stumps, but the element of standing water is necessary. Breeding across much of the Southeast from Texas to Florida and north to Minnesota and New Hampshire, they inhabit mangroves and wooded forests near water in winter from coastal Yucatán south to South America. The name derives from the yellow robes worn by papal clerks (prothonotaries) in the Roman Catholic Church. Its song is a loud *sweet, sweet, sweet,* which helps in finding the birds in wet woodlands.

SWAINSON'S WARBLER
Limnothlypis swainsonii

Shy and pointy faced, this dull brown understory specialist with a large bill and short tail maneuvers through lowland swamps and forested ravines of the Southeast west to Texas and north to eastern Kentucky and Maryland. Feeding mostly on the ground, and turning leaves in search of invertebrates and spiders, it is one of the earliest returning warblers in spring. In migration and winter, it occupies a variety of habitats with dense understory and rich leaf litter, similar to those on the breeding grounds. Its winter range is mainly Caribbean islands and the Yucatán Peninsula in southern Mexico.

TENNESSEE WARBLER
Leiothlypis peregrina

Dainty and greenish backed, this gray-capped warbler of Canadian boreal forests is a treetop specialist that breeds from the southeastern Yukon to Newfoundland and

Labrador and winters from southern Mexico to South America. It feasts on spruce budworms in Canada and is a nectar specialist in its tropical wintering range. In spring migration, it is especially attracted to insects associated with flowering oaks.

ORANGE-CROWNED WARBLER
Leiothlypis celata

Hardy but plain looking, Orange-crowned Warblers breed widely across Canada from central Newfoundland and Labrador to Alaska and south to northern California, Arizona, and New Mexico, where they nest on the ground in a variety of habitats. In winter, they occur from coastal Washington to southern Arizona and south to Honduras (western subspecies), and from North Carolina to Florida and Texas and south to Honduras. They favor open forests and brushy habitats, and often join feeding flocks with other wintering birds. The western subspecies is dull yellow below, while eastern birds are a drab olive and gray, but both have yellowish undertails.

COLIMA WARBLER *Leiothlypis crissalis*

Large and sluggish, this grayish brown warbler with bright yellowish vent and red crown spot occurs in oak-pine canyons of Mexico but reaches the northern limit of its breeding range in the Chisos Mountains of western Texas. In winter, it withdraws to similar habitat in Mexico. Many a birder has taken the long hike to Boot Canyon in Big Bend, Texas, to see this species for the first time.

LUCY'S WARBLER *Leiothlypis luciae*

A small gray sprite with a red crown patch, Lucy's is our tiniest warbler at about 4 inches long. It forages actively in dense mesquite and willows lining desert washes and riparian habitats of the Southwest and northwestern Mexico and winters in near-coastal western Mexico. Its plain gray and white plumage has no outstanding field marks. Young lack the red crown patch.

NASHVILLE WARBLER
Leiothlypis ruficapilla

Slight and attractive, this fairly tame warbler with yellow underparts, gray cap, greenish back, and bold eye-ring breeds in second-growth forests of north-central and northeastern North America. There is also an isolated population in the mountainous Pacific Northwest that was once considered a separate species called Calaveras Warbler. Nashville Warbler winters from extreme southern Texas through Mexico to central Honduras but also has a habit of remaining in northern areas into the winter months.

VIRGINIA'S WARBLER
Leiothlypis virginiae

Small and mostly gray, this western warbler with a big-eyed look is similar to Nashville Warbler, but lacks the extensive yellow on the underparts. It breeds in piñon pine and oak woodlands in the Southwest, and winters in southwestern Mexico. It wags its tail while foraging for insects, usually in the interior and middle level of trees.

CONNECTICUT WARBLER
Oporornis agilis

This large (nearly 6 inches) gray-hooded skulker with a bold white eye-ring, yellow underparts (adults), and a big bill breeds in spruce bogs, muskeg, and poplar forests across south-central Canada, northern Minnesota, and Wisconsin. Its shy behavior and ground-foraging habits make it one of the most difficult warblers to see in all seasons. It walks rather than hops, and occurs in winter in South America in a variety of habitats.

MACGILLIVRAY'S WARBLER
Geothlypis tolmiei

A western counterpart of Mourning Warbler, MacGillivray's breeds in disturbed areas of second growth in coniferous and mixed forests from northern British Columbia south to Arizona and New Mexico. In winter, it

occurs in dense scrub (moist or dry), often at forest edges, from Mexico south to western Panama. Its bold, white eye crescents are distinctive.

MOURNING WARBLER
Geothlypis philadelphia

A gray-bibbed skulker of brushy second-growth habitats, especially burns and clearcuts, Mourning Warbler breeds across much of Canada and north-central and northeastern United States to Maine. Its plumage is similar to Connecticut Warbler's, but adult males lack any eye-rings. In winter, it is found in dense (often damp) scrub and thickets from southern Costa Rica to northern South America.

KENTUCKY WARBLER
Geothlypis formosa

Large and rakishly masked, this eastern warbler with yellow underparts and olive upperparts breeds in mature deciduous forests from Wisconsin to eastern Texas and from New Jersey to the Texas Panhandle, where it forages and nests on the ground. It is generally uncommon and often difficult to see, but its loud, ringing song gives its location away. In winter, it occupies broadleaf forests with dense undergrowth from southern Mexico to northern South America. It has expanded its range northward in recent years because of a warming climate.

COMMON YELLOWTHROAT
Geothlypis trichas

This small (5 inches), furtive, yellow-breasted warbler with a bandit's mask adorned with a white fringe (males) is a widespread breeder across most of North America and is resident in the Southeast and southern California. It lives in thick, tangled vegetation in a wide variety of habitats. In winter, northern breeders move south to their United States resident range, or south through Mexico to Central America and the Caribbean. Although shy and fond of dense vegetation, they respond well to pishing and squeaking and usually offer good views to birders.

HOODED WARBLER *Setophaga citrina*
Large, striking, and active, this brush-loving warbler with a black hood (male) and yellow underparts, cheek, and forehead is a common breeder in the shady understory in mature deciduous woodlands across most of the eastern United States. Its loud song and tail-flicking behavior are distinctive, and it is not particularly shy. It occupies a wide variety of habitats in winter, including vegetated backyards, from Mexico and Central America to the Caribbean. A favorite of birders everywhere, Hooded has increased about 50 percent in numbers since 1970 (North American Breeding Bird Survey).

AMERICAN REDSTART
Setophaga ruticilla

Active, nimble, and boldly patterned, this warbler of second-growth forests with understory specializes in catching insects on the wing that it flushes by foraging frenetically amid the leaves, a technique for which its gape bristles and broad-based bill are well adapted. It breeds widely across North America, except for Alaska, the western United States, and the extreme Southeast. In winter, it uses a variety of woodland habitats from Mexico south to South America, and from southern Florida throughout the Caribbean. The male is colored for Halloween (black and orange), while the female is gray and brown with yellow flashes where the male has orange.

KIRTLAND'S WARBLER
Setophaga kirtlandii

Large, tame, and geographically restricted, Kirtland's breeds only in young, scrubby jack pine forests in Michigan and Wisconsin and relies on regular fires to keep its preferred habitat available. Kirtland's is a federally endangered species, with an estimated world population of only 3,600 birds (Partners in

These six warblers represent some of the most striking members of this very popular bird family. Clockwise from upper left: Black-throated Blue Warbler, Blackburnian Warbler, Townsend's Warbler, American Redstart, Magnolia Warbler, Painted Redstart. All have bolder-plumaged males except Painted Redstart, whose sexes are similar.

Flight), and it is especially susceptible to cowbird nest parasitism. It winters mostly in the Bahamas in low, dense scrub, but the exact distribution remains largely unknown.

CAPE MAY WARBLER *Setophaga tigrina*

Handsome but inappropriately named, Cape May breeds in remote spruce-fir forests across Canada and winters mostly in the Caribbean and a small coastal area near the Yucatán Peninsula. It occurs in Cape May, New Jersey, only during migration, when it is uncommon. Its greenish back, yellow breast with dark stripes, and chestnut cheek patch give it a unique, striking plumage.

CERULEAN WARBLER
Setophaga cerulea

A pretty little treetop warbler with feathers the color of a deep blue sky, Cerulean breeds in mature, deciduous eastern forests from extreme southern Canada south to Oklahoma and South Carolina and winters on the east slope of the northern Andes. The female is equally attractive but is dressed with unusual blue-green colors. This declin-

ing species (72 percent since 1970, according to Partners in Flight) is greatly prized by North American birders, and always attracts a crowd when seen in migration.

NORTHERN PARULA
Setophaga americana

This common, tiny, compact, multicolored warbler favors the canopy of eastern forests with Spanish moss or beard lichens, where it hides its nest. It breeds from southern Canada south to Texas and Florida, and winters from southern Texas south to Honduras and from southern Florida through the Caribbean. Its bold white eye-arcs, chestnut breast-band on bright yellow breast, and yellow-green patch on the back distinguish it from other warblers, and its tame behavior in migration and in winter affords great views for birders. The Northern Parula population has increased 62 percent since 1970 (Partners in Flight).

TROPICAL PARULA *Setophaga pitiayumi*

Aptly named, this tropical species breeds from South America to Mexico and reaches its northern limit in southern Texas, where

it is uncommon in mossy forests. Males differ from Northern Parula by their strong black mask and a lack of chestnut color on the breast.

MAGNOLIA WARBLER
Setophaga magnolia

Strikingly patterned with a yellow breast and bold, black necklace and flank streaks, this treetop beauty breeds in northern coniferous forests from Newfoundland and Labrador to New Jersey and Tennessee and west to British Columbia. Its winter range is from southern Mexico to Panama. This stunning warbler's numbers have increased over 50 percent since 1960 (Partners in Flight), much to the delight of birders everywhere.

BAY-BREASTED WARBLER
Setophaga castanea

This large, handsome warbler breeds in remote northern boreal forests across Canada to northern New England, where it relies on spruce budworms for food. Its chestnut, black, and buff plumage offers a unique, attractive appearance. This long-distance migrant winters from Costa Rica to northern South America, and its numbers have remained stable over the last 50 years.

BLACKBURNIAN WARBLER
Setophaga fusca

Smallish and flame throated, this beauty breeds in eastern mixed deciduous-coniferous forests from central to eastern Canada and across the northern tier of the eastern United States, south through the Appalachians to northern Georgia. A long-distance migrant, Blackburnian winters in South America. As Blackburnian is possibly our most stunning warbler, sightings usually result in a few gasps or exclamations of disbelief.

YELLOW WARBLER *Setophaga petechia*

This brilliant all-yellow warbler with red racing stripes on its breast (male) is North America's most widespread warbler, occurring

Yellow Warbler is found throughout much of North America, and the male's sweet, bubbly song is a welcome sign of spring.

Many warbler species change into a duller plumage after breeding season, with some showing a completely different plumage coloring from their breeding condition, while others have a muted version. Think fall warblers are confusing? Not really, if you take the time to study the differences and take note of the varied physical structure of each species. Clockwise from upper left, all immature females: Chestnut-sided Warbler, Hermit Warbler, Common Yellowthroat, Magnolia Warbler.

as a breeder or migrant in all Canadian provinces and United States. Wherever Yellow Warbler calls home, it seeks out wet, brushy habitats, but also early successional-growth and mangrove forests. It is one of the earliest fall migrants, departing as early as late July for wintering grounds from Mexico to South America. Resident populations of a subspecies called Mangrove Warbler occur in the Caribbean, Antilles, Mexico, South America, and the Galapagos Islands. This energetic ray of sunshine always brightens up your day, even more so when you hear its sweet, bubbly song.

CHESTNUT-SIDED WARBLER
Setophaga pensylvanica

A crisp-plumaged, mostly eastern warbler, Chestnut-sided is a locally common breeder in recovering second-growth forests and disturbed areas from southern Canada to the northern United States and south along the Appalachians to Tennessee. In winter, it occurs from southwestern Mexico through Central America, where it is one of the most common warblers. First-year birds are a breathtaking, unique chartreuse green and are regarded by many as more beautiful than the adults.

BLACKPOLL WARBLER
Setophaga striata

Large and long winged, this long-distance champion breeds in boreal forests from Alaska across Canada to northern New England. In fall, this half-ounce bird makes the longest overwater migration of any songbird: after doubling its body weight, it travels nearly 1,800 miles nonstop over the Atlantic, over several days, to its wintering grounds in South America. Males have a crisp plumage with a black cap and white cheek, while

females are grayish green with strongly streaked backs. First-year birds have a yellowish wash below.

BLACK-THROATED BLUE WARBLER
Setophaga caerulescens

The dapper black-and-blue male and grayish green female seem like different species, but their affinity for the shady understory of mixed coniferous and deciduous forests unites them from the Maritimes and Great Lakes region to northern Georgia. Their winter range is mainly the West Indies, but also the southern Yucatán Peninsula. The numbers of this tame warbler of low to mid-elevations increased 163 percent from 1970 through 2014 (Partners in Flight), which accounts for the numerous birds seen in migration.

PALM WARBLER *Setophaga palmarum*

A tail-wagging, ground-hugging specialist, Palm Warbler breeds mainly in Canada's northern boreal forests, where two distinct subspecies occur. The eastern subspecies (*S. p. hypochrysea*), also known as "yellow Palm Warbler", winters in a narrow range of the Southeast, while the western subspecies winters widely from the Southeast to Texas and on the Yucatán Peninsula to the Caribbean. Palm Warbler does not require any special habitats in winter and thrives in disturbed areas and around buildings as well as in natural open areas, where it forages on the ground for insects.

PINE WARBLER *Setophaga pinus*

Having the longest tail of any warbler, this large, big-billed, sometimes drab (immature) warbler with a yellow breast and orbital ring breeds in eastern pine forests from extreme southern Canada to eastern Texas and Florida. Immatures are mostly grayish and often confuse birders who don't see them on a regular basis. This hardy warbler is resident in the lower half of its United States range, where it is rarely seen away from pine forests.

Northern birds join resident Pine Warblers in the southern United States in winter and rarely leave the United States, although some remain in northern areas in winter and survive with the help of seed and suet feeders. Pine Warbler regularly eats a variety of seeds and is one of the earliest warblers to return north in spring. Resident populations occur on some Caribbean islands, including the Bahamas.

YELLOW-RUMPED WARBLER
Setophaga coronata

This active jack-of-all-trades uses a variety of techniques to secure food. These include gleaning, sallying, hovering, foraging high, foraging low (even on the ground), plucking prey from water, even consuming fruits and dried berries in winter. In many northern locations, Yellow-rumped is the only warbler encountered in winter.

Breeding in coniferous and mixed deciduous-coniferous forests from Alaska south to Arizona and east to West Virginia, this abundant warbler floods a variety of habitats in migration and winter. Its winter range is vast, but entirely south of Canada, and continues all the way to Panama. This hardy warbler can survive in cold climates in winter, as it eats a wide assortment of dried berries, including wax myrtle, poison ivy, and junipers. Two distinct subspecies occur: the western Audubon's and the eastern Myrtle. A large resident population occurs along the upper Pacific Coast of the United States.

YELLOW-THROATED WARBLER
Setophaga dominica

A large, distinctive, long-billed eastern warbler with a black mask, strong white eye stripe, and yellow throat and upper breast, Yellow-throated breeds in open pine forests and deciduous woodlands near streams in the eastern United States (central and southern). Its winter range includes the far Southeast and Texas south to Honduras and the Caribbean, where the birds often forage in

palm trees, using their long bills to pry into dead palm fronds for insects, which are also attracted to the sticky fruit. They are resident in the far Southeast and several Bahamian islands.

PRAIRIE WARBLER Setophaga discolor

Small, yellow, and brush loving, this warbler with an animate tail and black streaks down the sides is common in open successional-growth habitats throughout the eastern and south-central United States—not the prairies, despite its name. It typically forages low as it gleans insects from leaves and branches and sometimes hawks insects in the air. A separate resident subspecies occurs in Florida mangroves. Prairie winters mostly in southern Florida and the West Indies, but also coastally in the southern Yucatán and Honduras.

GRACE'S WARBLER Setophaga graciae

This attractive bluish gray warbler with a yellow face, throat, and upper breast breeds in southwestern pine forests, where it is a bird of treetops. One of the least known American warblers, it winters from central Mexico south to Nicaragua, where it is resident in pine forest habitats. It rarely perches in the open, and very few studies exist for this beautiful warbler owing to its remote, tree-top lifestyle.

BLACK-THROATED GRAY WARBLER
Setophaga nigrescens

Notwithstanding its neutral black, white, and gray tones, this common western warbler is eye-catching, partly because of the arrangement of black tones and white stripes on the head and a small yellow spot in front of the eye. It frequents pine and mixed pine-oak forests west of the Rocky Mountains and spends the winters farther south from southern Texas to Mexico, where it settles into open dry woodlands on lower slopes. A fair number winter every year in various southern U.S. locations.

TOWNSEND'S WARBLER
Setophaga townsendi

This western "golden-cheeked" warbler favors old-growth coniferous and mixed forests from Alaska to Oregon, Idaho, and Montana, foraging mostly in the canopy. This hardy species winters along the U.S. Pacific Coast as well as in Mexico and Central America. Its golden face with black cheek, cap, and throat are complemented by yellow underparts with bold, black streaks, creating a striking overall portrait. This is one of the most numerous western warblers, with a world population estimate of about 21 million birds (Partners in Flight).

HERMIT WARBLER
Setophaga occidentalis

Golden headed with a black throat and nape (male), Hermit is a denizen of tall, western coniferous forests of Washington, Oregon, and California. It winters along central California coastal areas, as well as Mexico and Central America, where it joins mixed-species foraging flocks. Since it lives in the tops of some of the tallest trees on the planet, it is often heard more than seen.

GOLDEN-CHEEKED WARBLER
Setophaga chrysoparia

A rare and federally endangered species, this warbler of juniper-oak forests is truly a Texas specialty, since it breeds only in central Texas, mostly on the Edwards Plateau. It is the only bird whose entire population breeds in Texas. Its golden face with black hood and eye line creates a striking image. Its winter range is a very narrow band from southern Mexico to northern Central America, where it occurs in montane pine-oak forests.

BLACK-THROATED GREEN WARBLER
Setophaga virens

The eastern "golden-cheeked" warbler sports a yellow face, black throat, and two bold white wing bars and is a common breeder from northern boreal forests to cypress and

hardwood swamps of the upper Southeast. This large, tame warbler is commonly seen during migration, where it often forages low and close to birders. It is closely related to Golden-cheeked, Townsend's, and Hermit Warblers. Black-throated Green winters from southern Texas to northern South America and from southern Florida through the Caribbean.

CANADA WARBLER
Cardellina canadensis

Uncommon and goggle eyed, this slate-backed warbler with yellow underparts, a bold yellow eye-ring, and a black necklace breeds in the shaded undergrowth of northern mixed conifer and deciduous forests and winters in South America on the east slope of the Andes. It is one of the last warblers to return in spring and one of the first to leave in late summer/fall. Thanks to its striking appearance, it is highly sought after by birders.

WILSON'S WARBLER *Cardellina pusilla*

A small, bright, active yellow warbler with a black cap, Wilson's navigates willow and alder thickets, often near water. It breeds mostly in northern forests and mountains and occurs in all lower 48 United States during migration, or as breeders. Wilson's has about six distinct breeding groups, which segregate on winter territories. Pacific birds are brighter, and Rocky Mountain birds slightly larger. Winter range includes Louisiana south through coastal Texas to Mexico and Central America.

RED-FACED WARBLER
Cardellina rubrifrons

A visually arresting sprite, Red-faced is a colorful bird of Mexican mountains and high-elevation forests of Arizona and New Mexico. Its red head with black cap and earmuffs paints a unique picture in the world of warblers, and its tame demeanor delights birders who enjoy views of this striking war-

bler. It winters from central Mexico, where it is also resident, south to Honduras, where it uses similar montane habitats.

PAINTED REDSTART
Myioborus pictus

A warbler of surpassing beauty, Painted Redstart is a specialty of the borderlands of the Southwest. This animated songbird flashes its wings and tail while foraging, often clinging to the sides of trees as it picks insects from the bark. It occurs mostly in montane riparian and arid woodlands and canyons. Its winter range is central Mexico south to Nicaragua, where resident populations occur. It often joins other warblers in mixed flocks at lower elevations after breeding.

Cardinalidae: Tanagers, Grosbeaks, Cardinals, Buntings, and Dickcissel

The small to medium-sized New World songbirds in this newly constituted amalgam differ in function and form but are genetically linked. The family includes some of North America's most beautiful and best-loved birds, most notably Northern Cardinal and Indigo Bunting. Constituted from species formerly housed within the Emberizidae and Thraupidae, and ranging from Canada to Peru, the 58 family members are most concentrated in Central America, while 14 species spend all or part of their time in North America. The Cardinalidae are distinguished (and united) by their heavy, mostly conical bills, and many males are richly attired in reds or blues, while females are more subdued. All are arboreal species except Dickcissel, and some are forest dwelling while others frequent forest edges or open areas with shrubs. All but Dickcissel build cup-shaped nests in bushes or trees and have diets that include insects, seeds, and fruit. Many are excellent vocalists, and

Although the name "tanager" is still part of these birds' names, they are no longer part of the true tanager family group, but instead part of a newly constituted family group that includes some very different songbirds. From top, all males: Summer, Scarlet, and Hepatic Tanagers.

all North American breeders are migratory except Northern Cardinal and Pyrrhuloxia.

HEPATIC TANAGER *Piranga flava*

This large, fairly common and widespread reddish tanager of montane open pine and pine-oak forests ranges from the tropics to temperate regions. It breeds mostly in the mountains of Arizona, New Mexico, and western Texas and winters mostly in Mexico, where it frequents a variety of habitats from arid lowland scrub to mountains. Hepatic Tanagers also occur as residents from Mexico to South America. Mostly insectivorous, they also eat small fruits, seeds, flowers, and nectar. Males are red and females a dull yellow, and both have dusky cheeks.

SUMMER TANAGER *Piranga rubra*

The strawberry-colored male Summer Tanager is the only completely red bird in North America, and it specializes in catching bees and wasps on the wing while avoiding being stung. The female is a mustard yellow color. This long, heavy-billed forest tanager breeds across much of the southern and central United States, ranging across much of the Southeast west to Texas and California. Eastern birds favor mature oak-pine forests while western breeders prefer riparian and mesquite woodlands, especially cottonwoods. Their winter range is from Mexico to mid–South America, where they utilize a variety of open- and second-growth habitats. During migration and winter, fruit is an important part of their diet, and their song is very pleasing, almost oriole-like.

SCARLET TANAGER *Piranga olivacea*

Arguably one of the world's most striking tanagers, this scarlet red songbird with black

wings and tail (male) is a common forest breeder across much of the eastern United States and southern Canada, but is absent as a breeder in the southern United States. The hoarse, slightly sluggish notes of Scarlet Tanager's song filter through the leaves of mature deciduous (mostly oak) forests during hot summer days. It feeds on insects (mostly moths and caterpillars) that it gleans from leaves. Before summer's end, with young on the wing, the male sheds his brilliant red courting plumage and dons the cryptic yellow-green garb worn by the female and young, though he retains greenish-tinged black wings and tail. During molt, males are a patchwork of green and red. Their winter range is northern and western South America, where they inhabit mature forests and forest edges.

WESTERN TANAGER *Piranga ludoviciana*

The aptly named Western Tanager is one of the most visually arresting songbirds in North America, with the male's orange-red head, bright yellow body, and black wings. The female has dull yellow underparts, a grayish olive head and back, and dark gray wings. They breed in open woodlands, particularly evergreens, all through the West. Virtually the entire population winters from central Mexico south to Costa Rica, where they favor pine and pine-oak forests.

NORTHERN CARDINAL
Cardinalis cardinalis

This hearty, iconic, pertly crested red songbird (male) with black throat and bill border is a resident of brushy understory, forest edges, and riparian woodlands across the eastern United States and extreme southeastern Canada. Its range also extends through Texas to Arizona, and south to northern Guatemala. The female is a soft buffy brown color with a red-tinged crest, wings, and tail. Both sexes have rich, orange bills. Their diet of mostly seeds and fruit is supplemented with insects. Ideally suited for suburban

environments, Cardinals are a favorite visitor to feeding stations featuring sunflower seeds.

PYRRHULOXIA *Cardinalis sinuatus*

This red-trimmed, grayish desert cardinal with a parrotlike bill and sporting a dapper plumage and extra-tall crest is a resident of hot, arid deserts of the Southwest, Texas, and northern Mexico. Pyrrhuloxia is omnivorous and forages on the ground for grass seeds, fruits, and large insects. Where ranges overlap with Northern Cardinal, Pyrrhuloxia usually occurs in drier habitats. It may move to suburban locations in winter, but it is basically nonmigratory.

ROSE-BREASTED GROSBEAK
Pheucticus ludovicianus

A black-headed, black-backed grosbeak with a bright red bib and striking white underparts, this bird's song is just as good as its looks. The triangular, conical bills of both this aptly named species and Black-headed Grosbeak assume gargantuan proportions, and they use them to masticate both animal and vegetative fare. Females and immatures are mostly brownish with streaked, buff chests and bold white eye stripes. Songs resemble those of a hurried American Robin. They breed in a variety of habitats, including moist deciduous and deciduous-coniferous forests, from the Maritimes south along the Appalachians to northern Georgia, and west to northeastern British Columbia and central Nebraska. Their winter range is from Mexico south to northern South America, and the Caribbean islands.

BLACK-HEADED GROSBEAK
Pheucticus melanocephalus

Stocky with a striking orange body, this western breeder occurs in a wide variety of habitats that are usually near water. They range from open forests with tall trees and rich understories to suburban developments with similar habitats. Their breeding range is from central British Columbia east to the

Northern Cardinal (top) and Pyrrhuloxia (center) are medium-sized, crested songbirds with strong seed-cracking bills. Both are residents where they live, and Northern Cardinal is one of North America's most iconic birds. Both shown here are males. Dickcissel (bottom) is a smallish sparrowlike bird that breeds in a nomadic fashion in grassland habitats, where it places its nest on the ground in dense grass. This species seemed to be lumped into this bird family without good reasons, since taxonomists don't seem to know where it belongs at this time.

Dakotas and south to the Mexican highlands, where they join a resident population. Feeding primarily on fruits, they also eat roosting monarch butterflies, targeting less toxic males. They sometimes form small, loose flocks in winter.

BLUE GROSBEAK *Passerina caerulea*

This medium-sized vibrant blue bunting with chestnut wing patches and a silvery bill inhabits brush-studded fields, woodland edges, and riparian woodlands across the lower half and central interior of the United States and northern Mexico, where resident populations extend south to Costa Rica. Their winter range includes the Greater Antilles and Mexico south to central Panama, where they occur in open grassy areas, thorn forests, and roadside vegetation. They often occur with Indigo Buntings during migration, where they adorn lawns and roadsides with striking blue colors.

LAZULI BUNTING *Passerina amoena*

Turquoise blue is the color of the head and upperparts of the males of this pretty little western bunting that is common in a variety of habitats, including brushy hillsides, weedy fields, open scrub, and hedgerows, especially near water. Brown replaces the turquoise color in females, and both have rust-orange upper breasts and white bellies. They breed widely throughout the western United States, with the exception of the Southwest, and their winter range is from southeastern Arizona to western Mexico and the tip of Baja,

where they occupy open grassy areas and forage mostly on fruits and seeds.

INDIGO BUNTING *Passerina cyanea*

Along the Gulf Coast in April, residents eagerly await the arrival of the "blue canaries" that festoon lawns by the scores after their arduous flight across the Gulf of Mexico. This event is a sure sign that summer is returning to the United States. Then the birds surge north, occupying overgrown weedy fields and forest edges bracketing the fields, where they feed on seeds and insects. Females are warm brown overall. They breed in the United States and extreme southern Canada from the Rockies eastward, and winter in Florida and the Caribbean, including the Bahamas, as well as Mexico south to northern South America. In migration, Indigos migrate mostly due south, so eastern birds stay east, and western birds stay west to their wintering territories.

VARIED BUNTING *Passerina versicolor*

You need to have good light to appreciate the richness of the colors—red, burgundy, purple, and blue—of male Varied Bunting. Given the sun-drenched desert regions this bird calls home, it would seem hardly a challenge. The trick is getting this arid, thorn-scrub- and desert-wash-hugging bird to step into the open, which happens during the summer breeding season. Females are deep brown. They breed in border regions from Arizona to Texas and winter mostly in Mexico. Resident populations occur from extreme southeastern Texas through central Mexico.

PAINTED BUNTING *Passerina ciris*

With its rainbow array of colors, male Painted Bunting looks like the kind of bird you might get from the easel of a preschooler with a new box of crayons. Found in brush forest edge and adjacent habitats, they readily visit open platform bird feeders. Uncommon, local, and geographically restricted,

Grosbeaks are medium-large songbirds with massive bills that are well suited for cracking open seeds and nuts. Males sport vibrant and colorful plumages, while females share muted, earth-toned plumages, some of which are streaked below. While the larger grosbeaks are forest species, Blue Grosbeak is a bird of open, brush-studded fields and woodland edges. From top, all males: Black-headed, Blue, and Rose-breasted Grosbeaks.

Smallish songbirds of open spaces with woodland borders, buntings sing sweet songs and share a diet of insects, seeds, and fruit. Males have strikingly colorful plumages, with Painted Bunting one of the most flamboyantly plumaged birds in the world. Females share a muted, earth-toned plumage of brown, gray, and buff shading, except for female Painted Bunting, which has an unusual lime green plumage. From top, all males: Painted, Indigo, and Lazuli Buntings.

they breed in northern Mexico and the south-central and southeastern United States (mostly South Carolina) and winter in Florida, the Bahamas, and Hispaniola, as well as Mexico south to Panama, where they settle into overgrown pastures, scrub habitats, and open forest edges. Females and immatures are a unique lime green with yellow underparts.

DICKCISSEL *Spiza americana*

While its placement among the Cardinalidae remains uncertain, this pretty little grassland bird with a yellow breast, black bib, rusty shoulders, and yellow eye stripe is a widespread, if somewhat nomadic, breeder across most of the American heartland north to the Canadian border and south to southern Texas. Occupying a variety of grassland habitats, especially native prairies and restored grasslands, it is not particularly choosy, but does require a patch of dense grass to place its nest, and sufficient insects to feed young. Its winter range is from Mexico to northern South America, with a core winter range in central Venezuela, where flocks seek out rice and sorghum fields for food, and sugarcane plantations and tall grass for roosting. Females lack the black bib, and immatures resemble female House Sparrows.

Thraupidae: Tanagers

In the aftermath of recent taxonomic purges, this large New World group remains one of the planet's largest families. They are widespread across Central and South America and the Caribbean, but only marginally represented in North America with a single species, Morelet's Seedeater (formerly White-collared Seedeater). While tanagers are generally celebrated for their complex and vivid colors, many of these species are cryptically garbed in black, grays, and yellow-greens.

Morelet's Seedeater is a small, buntinglike bird with a massive bill and was formerly part of a family that included sparrows and buntings. Recent taxonomic changes placed it with the true tanagers, like those that you encounter in the tropics. This species occurs only as a rare resident in cane thickets along the lower Rio Grande in Texas, but in Mexico and Central America it is a very common bird along roadsides and disturbed weedy patches. Pictured here: male (left) and female (right).

Other than being generally small, tanagers share few binding traits aside from their arboreal preferences (especially cloud forests), though some species, like seedeaters, occur in grassy habitats. Diets of most tanagers show a degree of seasonality, with many species consuming both insects and fruit. Some join mixed feeding flocks that follow army ant columns. Four North American species once housed in this family, and still called tanagers, are now ranked among the Cardinalidae (Hepatic, Western, Summer, and Scarlet Tanagers).

MORELET'S SEEDEATER
Sporophila morelleti

This tiny, snub-billed, buntinglike bird occurs from Panama to southern Texas. Favoring savannah, disturbed areas, and brushy habitats, it feeds almost exclusively on seeds. In the United States, it occurs in small groups that inhabit stands of cane flanking the Rio Grande in Texas, where it is localized and uncommon. Eschewing the bright colors of many tanagers, North America's only Thraupidae is olive drab above with a black helmet and white lower eye crescent and buffy below, with two bold wing bars. Females are brownish buff with weak wing bars.

Acknowledgments

Pete Dunne: The task of writing this book would not be complete without acknowledging the support of my agent, Russell Galen; editor Lisa White; and the editorial assistance and support of friends Dorothy Claire and Beth Van Vleck, Rene Buccina, and especially my wonderful partner-in-life, Linda, who figures in everything. Kevin Karlson's artistic eye and Photoshop skills are key to this book's visual appeal.

Kevin Karlson: Special thanks to my wife, Dale Rosselet, for reviewing my revision of the manuscript and adding interesting natural history tidbits to some species accounts. While a majority of the photos in this book are mine, I want to give special thanks to the 17 other talented photographers whose 60 superb photos added to the visual impact of the book, including Robert Fogg, Tom Johnson, Linda Dunne, Brian Small, Greg Lavaty, Erik Bruhnke, Mike Danzenbaker, and 10 others.

Pete and Kevin: Kudos to Cornell University's *All About Birds* website; its invaluable up-to-date information about all aspects of North American avian life is unparalleled. We would also like to commend the many contributors to the *Handbook of the Birds of the World,* whose combined wisdom reflects a great deal of knowledge of the planet's birds. Lastly, we would be remiss not to acknowledge the insights gleaned from the *Sibley Guide to Birds,* a resource that goes beyond the standards of a mere field guide.

Bibliography

These are the resources we consulted in the writing of this book.
Their insights and factual information figure in this writing.

All About Birds, Cornell Lab of Ornithology, wwwallaboutbirds.org.

American Ornithologists' Union. *Checklist of North American Birds.* 7th ed. Washington, DC: American Ornithologists' Union, 1998. *Note:* The *Checklist* and its annual supplements are now maintained by the American Ornithological Society (AOS).

Cornell Lab of Ornithology. *All About Birds* website. wwwallaboutbirds.org.

Del Hoyo, J., et al. *Handbook of the Birds of the World.* Vol. 1–16. Barcelona: Lynx Edicions, 2011.

Dunne, Pete, and Kevin T. Karlson. *Birds of Prey: Hawks, Eagles, Falcons, and Vultures of North America.* Boston: Houghton Mifflin Harcourt, 2017.

———. *Gulls Simplified: A Comparative Approach to Identification.* Princeton, NJ: Princeton University Press, 2019.

Economidy, John. *Hawkwatch Data for Veracruz, Mexico, and Corpus Christi, Texas, 1998–2014.* Salt Lake City, UT: HawkWatch International.

Gill, Frank B. *Ornithology.* 2nd ed. New York: W. H. Freeman and Co., 1995.

Howell, Steve. *Petrels, Albatrosses, and Storm-Petrels of North America: A Photographic Guide.* Princeton, NJ: Princeton University Press, 2012.

International Union for Conservation of Nature (IUCN). "McKay's Bunting, *Plectrophenax hyperboreus.*" *IUCN Red List of Threatened Species.* https://dx.doi.org/10.2305/IUCN.UK.2016-3.RLTS.T22721046A94695922.en.

Kushlan, J. A., et al. *Waterbird Conservation for the Americas: The North American Waterbird Conservation Plan,* version 1. Washington, DC: U.S. Fish and Wildlife Service, 2002.

Lawson, John. *A New Voyage to Carolina.* Originally published 1709. https://www.gutenberg.org/files/1838/1838-h/1838-h.htm.

Morrison, Guy, et al. "Population Estimates of Nearctic Shorebirds." *Waterbirds* 23 (3) (January 2000): 337.

Partners in Flight. Avian Conservation Assessment Database 2017. http://pif.birdconservancy.org/ACAD/.

Sauer, J. R., et al. *The North American Breeding Bird Survey, Results and Analysis 1966–2013.* Laurel, MD: U.S. Geological Survey, Patuxent Wildlife Research Center, 2014. https://www.mbr-pwrc.usgs.gov/bbs/.

Sibley, D. A. *The Sibley Guide to Birds.* 2nd ed. New York: Alfred A. Knopf, 2014.

Svensson, Lars, et al. *Birds of Europe.* Princeton, NJ: Princeton University Press, 1999.

Photography Credits

All photos are by Kevin Karlson except as follows.

Angel Abreu: p. 186

Erik Brunhke: pp. 89 (all), 149 (top and middle), 188

Mike Danzenbaker: pp. 36 (middle), 92 (left), 94 (left and middle), 95 (right)

Linda Dunne: pp. 21 (all), 47 (all), 88

Scott Elowitz: p. 178 (bottom right)

Bob Fogg: pp. 42 (top right), 68 (top and middle), 90 (all), 94 (right), 95 (left)

Sam Fried: p. 33 (bottom right)

Paul Guris: p. 91 (middle)

Ned Harris: p. 119 (top and middle)

Tom Johnson: pp. 15, 33 (bottom middle), 174 (top), 184 (top and middle), 206 (all)

Greg Lavaty: pp. 33 (top middle), 91 (top and bottom), 184 (bottom), 203 (bottom)

Chas W. McRae: p. 191

Greg Prelich: pp. 134 (bottom right), 174 (bottom)

Sue Puder: p. 190 (bottom), 205 (bottom)

Don Riepe: pp. 68 (bottom)

Brian Small: pp. 35 (bottom), 160 (top right), 173 (top right), 189, 210 (bottom right)

Lloyd Spitalnik: pp. 42 (bottom left), 71 (right), 92 (middle)

Jim Zipp: pp. 122 (bottom right), 203 (top), 226

Index

Page numbers in *italics* refer to text graphics.